DUELING DRAGONS

A Bipolar Journey from the Darkness into the Light

Dr. Indigo Debra Triplett

CAREERS IN TRANSITION

Dueling Dragons: A Bipolar Journey from the Darkness into the Light

Copyright © 2015 Careers In Transition, Inc.

Published by:
Careers In Transition, Inc.
3300 Buckeye Road, Ste. 601
Atlanta, Georgia 30341
770.414.1026
indigo@indigo-insights.org
www.indigo-insights.org

Cover and Interior Design by Words of Passion

ISBN: 978-0-9843491-9-7

Contents

Dedications and Appreciations

I dedicate this book to my sons: Russell, who allowed me to tell my story based on his impact and love. Austin, whom I love dearly and appreciate more than words can ever express. When I was at the end of my rope, he tied a knot and helped me hold on for dear life. Many kisses and hugs to Hunter who continues to be a light that helps me find my way based on his resilience. I believe we choose to come here as spirits to experience a physical life, and we even choose our parents. I thank them for choosing me and helping me to become a better person and better parent.

This book is also dedicated to my big brother, Kevin Triplett. I love that guy. He was there for me during my conscious darkest days. I say the conscious darkest days because I was fully aware of my mental condition and attempting to manage it, which was far more difficult than being unaware. He always answered my calls and listened to me during my ups and downs. He encouraged me, pumped me up, and accepted me. I'm so grateful and thankful for our relationship. He encouraged me to become public about my condition and to find my passion in healing and helping.

Lastly, and as importantly, I want to thank Sheila Belcher, Tammy Davis, Cynthia Hayes, and Lisa Rozzelle who never gave up on me as a leader and employer. They had a front row seat to my madness and never walked out of the show. Thank you so much for being with me, loving me, and dedicating your career to my company and leadership.

About the Author

Dr. Indigo Triplett is the Founder of Indigo Insights Foundation, a 501(c)3 nonprofit that provides mental healing by nourishing the spirits and minds of people who are challenged on life's journey. She is also author of the book series *Playing by the Unwritten Rules*. She is one of the most intuitive and insightful souls  that you may ever meet. Her life's journey has been a remarkable display of perseverance, resilience, and intrigue as she broke through barriers for herself and lifted others to a higher level of success along the way.

She is best known for her many accomplishments as a business woman. She started her business Careers In Transition, Inc. as a solopreneur in her basement in 1995. She crafted her trade and moved onto the entrepreneurial platform, and after many years of building an impressive clientele in the federal government, she became a small business owner with offices in Georgia and DC. She led her company to being recognized by Inc. Magazine as one of the Top 500 Fastest Growing Companies in America in 2012 and 2013, and then she landed on the Inc. list again in 2014. You can read about Dr. Indigo in *Ebony Magazine*, *The New York Times*, *Huffington Post*, and *Inc. Magazine*, to name a few places that took an interest in her story of being a successful business woman. She has a weekly mental health column in *Inc. Magazine* online edition at www.inc.com.

However, the story that few are privy to is the story of her life journey from the darkness into the light. Dr. Indigo was self-admitted into a treatment center after her world spiraled out of control as she was working on her PhD, raising a family, managing her multimillion dollar business, and speaking around the world, and all the while feeling as if she was going insane. She was diagnosed with Bipolar Disorder II, and she can attest that she was a textbook case for the disorder with bizarre behaviors that she shares with audiences and in this book.

By doing the work, she was able to pull herself from the abyss with the help of mental health professionals, spiritual advisors, the support of her family, and understanding and collaborative employees. She formed Indigo Insights to help people with mental health challenges learn to embrace their mental condition and thrive. She speaks, coaches, and teaches courses about mental health challenges from a holistic and personal viewpoint. She turned a mess into a message.

Dr. Indigo has received many awards and recognitions for her life's work in Human Resources, and she has now devoted her life to humankind. It is not just a calling, but rather a ministry for her as she shares with others practical tools and techniques that allow her to manage her condition with great success. She weaves humor with a poignant look at reality for people who live with dis-ease, people who live with those with dis-ease, and those who work with people with dis-ease. She says that she had to lose nearly everything to truly find herself, and now she serves as a success GPS for others. She helps people to find tranquility, serenity, and balance when everything seems chaotic and uncertain.

She served in the U.S. Marine Corps before earning her Associates Degree in Psychology and Journalism, a Bachelor of Arts in Radio and Television with a Minor in Psychology, a Master of Arts in Human Resources Development with an emphasis in Counseling, and a PhD in Values Driven Leadership. Visit www.indigotriplett.com and www.indigo-insights.org to learn more about Dr. Indigo.

Foreword

Having worked in the field of mental health treatment for many years, I have found times to rejoice and times to feel sad and even discouraged. A particularly bitter pill to take is the client who comes to treatment, learns all the right words to parrot back to the therapist, but does not indorse recovery. In this book, Dr. Indigo presents a vivid newsreel of her journey into and within recovery. In that journey she offers descriptions of the experience of slaying some dragons, making peace with others, and never running to hide from them. Dr. Indigo's willingness to be open and candid in exposing herself is characteristic of one in recovery.

The disorder identified as Bipolar Disorder is skillfully dissected with recognition given to both the negative as well as positive consequences of having the disorder. Speaking out publicly to identify ways the disorder had been helpful may be an important step taken in opening the door of shame and guilt which has blocked many sufferers from seeking treatment. Perhaps the fear of openly accepting Mental Illness as a treatable disease is rooted much more deeply in the human consciousness. We humans tend to fear that which we do not understand. That fear is then managed often with denial, avoidance of acceptance, and the creation of fictitious cause/effect relationships. Indigo offers the reader a clear view of her battle with and means of attempting to cope with the reality of having the disorder.

There is nothing to be feared about mood swings. We experience negative consequences only from the behaviors of one exhibiting the various mood states. The ebb and flow among states is a common fact of life on this planet. Individuals, cultures, and countries are all in flux. The goal then, as Dr. Indigo so brilliantly shows the reader, is to accept, honor the swings, and manage the behaviors. If I were still teaching, this book would be on the required reading list for my students. Thank you, Dr. Indigo, for this important contribution to the field of Mental Illness Treatment.

V.P. Gilbert, MSW, LISAC

Sierra Tucson

Introduction

This book was truly a labor of love. I pulled an entire chapter from my dissertation *Leading out of the darkness into the light: My story of building a business as a leader with bipolar disorder* to use as the foundation of this book. I thought it would take a week or two to merely add additional information and further elaborate on what I had already written, but writing this book took much longer than I had anticipated because it was very heavy. In an effort to be authentic and transparent, I combed through my personal journals to give accurate and real accounts of experiences and situations. I would go page by page pulling out information to include in this book. I would turn to a page and see distorted writings as if I were crying out in pain that life wasn't worth living and that I wished I had the courage to end it all. Then I would turn to other pages that described bizarre behaviors that at the time seemed rational, and within days I would have writings that described results and accomplishments.

There were pages of sadness, hope, joy, fear, and pain, so there was a lot of heavy lifting to pull that information from my journals and transfer that information to this book. I was reliving the pain and the wonderful memories that I had forgotten in an effort to bring to you, the reader, a candidly honest look at what it is like to live with bipolar disorder. This book gives a full range of mental illness from unawareness to diagnosis to denial to acceptance. Some days I would have to simply write a few pages and lie down and rest my mind to defrag and recalibrate and then return to writing a few days later. So the book took much longer to write than I could have ever imagined because I had to write in small dosages. That's all that I could handle. And you may have to do the same to absorb what I am sharing with you.

I had to ask myself over and over what is the purpose of this book. I am writing to inspire, inform, educate, heal, and encourage. I am exploring the benefits as well as the setbacks associated with mental illness to discover options and alternatives to mental wellness. But the real question is why are you reading this book? What do you want to receive as a result of reading about my life's journey? Even though I give information on how to manage a well-balanced mind that is afflicted with mental illness, there is a thread of information that I hope creates a space for you to become more authentic about your own mental health challenges. This book is for both the people who have mental health challenges and those who share a space with them as a coworker, family member, friend, etc. I want you to read this book and become a voice for the voiceless and an advocate for mental health awareness and recovery. I want this book to inform and inspire through a compelling story of denial to awareness, hate to love, and much more. And, my greatest desire will be achieved if those of you with a mental illness learn to embrace your condition, but not identify with your diagnosis. I acknowledge and accept that I have the disorder that causes much dis-ease, but I am much more than the disorder. It doesn't define me. I have bipolar disorder, but I am not bipolar. However, I have to accept my diagnosis to embrace all of me, which is being beautifully human.

I feel deeply honored that the spirit chose me to tell my story and that I'm courageous enough to step from the cloak of darkness into the light in an effort to pull so many people with mental health challenges from their own abyss. In fact, this book isn't just for those of us with mental health challenges, but also for those of us who work with people who have a mental illness and we all work with someone who has a mental illness (trust me). This book is also written for colleagues, family, and friends of people who have a mental health challenge. I'm making my mess my message and my triumphs my truths to share with you. If you can find one answer to the many questions that you have about that loved one or yourself, then this book has served its purpose.

I ask that you read this book with love and without judgment. God knows that I have judged myself enough, and that doing so will only cause you to miss the real meaning behind it all. Instead, read as if you are searching for meaning to something that has been perplexing and allow yourself to be free to discover things about yourself, as well.

Chapter 1

Baseline Understanding

My journey has not been a journey of tranquility. I've experienced much pain balanced with some joy; but, overall, I have been surrounded by darkness, as far back as I can remember. Similar to many entrepreneurs, I have lived through my business. I identify myself through my business and vice versa. It is seamless where I begin and where it ends. This was how my business was birthed, as an extension of me. So when I am in darkness, so is my business. This story is about my journey as a small business owner leading a company with bipolar disorder, and how I may not be cured, but I have been healed.

Before going any further, I believe it is important to share with you that many of the names of people who have traveled on my path to recovery have been changed, and all the names of companies and clients have been altered. Also, I want to give you the description of bipolar disorder. I don't want to assume that you know what bipolar disorder is or is not. A huge misstep in my life was that I didn't know what bipolar disorder was. Maybe a description will assist you in understanding my journey and possibly what you are experiencing personally or as a family member to someone who is afflicted. But first allow me to share with you the loose definition of mental illness: *A **mental illness** is a medical condition that disrupts a person's thinking, feeling, mood, ability to relate to others, and daily functioning.*

According to the National Institute of Mental Health (www.nimh.gov), bipolar disorder, also known as manic-depressive illness, is a brain disorder that causes unusual shifts in mood, energy, activity levels, and the ability to carry out daily tasks. Symptoms of bipolar disorder can be severe. They are different from the normal ups and downs that everyone goes through from time to time. Bipolar disorder symptoms can result in damaged relationships, poor job or school performance, and even suicide. But bipolar disorder can be treated, and people with this illness can lead full and productive lives.

The previous definitions are a baseline understanding of bipolar disorder. I truly believe that this book should be a supplement to additional readings and to an actual diagnosis from a mental health professional, if you believe that you may have the disorder or that someone you know may be suffering from bipolar disorder. I'm neither a psychiatrist, counselor, nor therapist working in the mental health field. I'm a mental wellness advocate, transformational coach, business leader, and someone in recovery. I don't espouse to be the expert here in terms of diagnosing anyone, but I feel it necessary to give you a foundation in which to understand what I am about to share with you. If you want a more in-depth description of bipolar disorder, I highly recommend the Desk Reference to the Diagnostic Criteria from DSM-5 (2013) for a diagnosis. You will read things such as inflated self-esteem or grandiosity; decreased need for sleep (e.g., feels rested after only three hours of sleep); more talkative than usual or pressure to keep talking; flight of ideas or subjective experience that thoughts are racing; distractibility (i.e., attention too easily drawn to unimportant or irrelevant external stimuli); increase in goal-directed activity (either socially, at work or school, or sexually) or psychomotor agitation; and excessive involvement in activities that have a high potential for painful consequences (e.g., engaging in unrestrained buying sprees, sexual indiscretions, or foolish business investments).

The above-mentioned points are merely the tip of the iceberg for a hypomanic episode, as you will learn as you read through this book. Then there is the depression side of the disorder that includes markedly diminished interest or pleasure in all, or almost all, activities most of the day, nearly every day; significant weight loss when not dieting or weight gain (e.g., a change of more than 5% of body weight in a month), or decrease or increase in appetite nearly every day, fatigue or loss of energy nearly every day; feeling of worthlessness or excessive or inappropriate guilt (which may be delusional) nearly every day; diminished ability to think or concentrate, or indecisiveness, nearly every day; and recurrent thoughts of death (not just fear of dying), recurrent suicidal ideation without a specific plan, a suicide attempt, or a specific plan for committing suicide. These are but a few things that are present when someone has bipolar disorder and is experiencing depression. These and additional symptoms can last hours to days to years depending on the severity and person. In my case, I experience hypomania and depression and sometimes a mixed episode, which is to experience both at the same time.

Keep the above description in mind as you read through this book, and refer to it occasionally to put things in perspective as I share my journey with you and provide recommendations towards the end of the book. If you feel that you need more information, just hang tight. I will be giving you additional symptoms and characteristics throughout the book.

Chapter 2

Formative Years

I had no clue that I would ever own a business. I'm a first generational success. A first generational success is one who attains a position, status, and responsibilities that far exceed that of your parents. First generational success is something I coined in my second book that I will talk about a little later. My parents worked in factories in the Midwest; thus, they were blue-collar workers. They provided what I felt was an upper middle-class lifestyle based on significant earnings. As an African-American growing up in a predominantly white environment, I had everything that I wanted and needed. In fact, I believed that I had the best of everything. But looking back best was relative. It simply seemed like the best for the environment in which I lived, such as a house with an inground pool, three cars, one of which was for the teens, and no need to want for anything. We traveled as a family, and I dressed in the latest name brands, even before name brands were popular. I lived a wonderful life growing up in Aurora, Illinois which is now considered a suburb of Chicago. However, in the 60s it was a distant little country town that afforded me the opportunity to live life to the fullest.

My journey into darkness started at an early age. Everything was so normal to me except the occasional abuse from my mother that included the severe whippings with extension cords, hits with Fuller brushes, or verbal abuse complete with cursing and yelling. My mother had a way of having me get on my knees, lay my head sideways on the bed, and she would then sit on my head with my butt between her legs. This allowed her to whip me with either a belt or extension cord without the distraction of my running, jumping, or moving. I often had welts and cut skin that I would hide with a makeup concealer in an effort to avoid being shamed at school. But I think that the deepest scars came from being called a whore, heifer, stupid, and so forth. That whittled down my self-esteem. I thought her meanness came from working in a factory on the third shift for many years at Caterpillar, a huge tractor earthmoving company. My mother worked in an environment where it was predominately white men. She encountered a lot of racism and sexism in a very hostile environment back in the 60s to early 70s. I have my ideas on why she was so kind and generous at one point and then cruel and bullying at other times, but I'm not a psychiatrist nor do I feel comfortable making any kind of judgment about a woman who worked very hard to provide the lifestyle that afforded me to become who I am today.

But her abuse impacted me greatly as a child, and even with therapy as an adult I struggled with reconciling in my mind how easy it was for her to drag me down the hallway and throw me in a closet where I would sit for hours just peeking through the crack between the folding doors. I would watch the dust particles in the air drift about. In fear of making a sound, I would simply daydream and see a much bigger world than the limited view that I had peering out of the dark closet. I was able to exercise my creativity without knowing such; I learned to be alone in the dark and to see beyond a narrow stream of light and the confines of my immediate surroundings. Naturally, I was a free spirit that sometimes was imprisoned in darkness both mentally and from the closet. Sometimes as a child, I felt my safest in the closet.

My journey into darkness started at an early age. According to Ronald R. Fieve, MD, professor of clinical psychiatry, Columbia Presbyterian Medical Center, and author of the book *Bipolar II (pg. 82)*, environmental stressors also play a role in triggering bipolar episodes in those who are genetically predisposed. Being placed in a closet for hours at a time created its very own type of darkness. I learned to be in darkness both mentally and physically and began to think that it was normal. Dr. Fieve goes on to say that children growing up in bipolar families often live with a parent who lacks control of moods or emotions. Some children may live with constant verbal or even physical abuse if their bipolar parent is not taking medication for the illness or is trying to self-medicate the mood swings with alcohol or drugs. My mother loved me deeply but she often could not control her emotions or anger. Thus, I learned at an early age to do the same. My behaviors were attributed to both nurturing and nature. I was a product of my environment and a predisposition to mental health challenges took away my options to be well and whole, as a child and young adult. But as an adult I had the power and responsibility to choose, which you will come to understand as you continue to read.

Life, ironically, seemed normal aside from the constant trouble that I got into at school. I was a fighter. My mother made sure of that. Her words were, "You either fight someone who hits you, or you will have to fight me." I saw my mother fight my father and she was no one to tangle with, so I fought the kids in school whenever I felt attacked or wronged. I often did not initiate a fight. But I found myself in situations wherein I was either defending myself or sticking up for someone whom I felt was being picked on. I never backed down from anyone, and I had a strong sense of fairness and justice. But such kept me in the principal office and in afterschool detention. And my mouth often got me in to trouble; I would say whatever I thought. That was unheard of during a time when children were to be seen and not heard. I had this strange gift of knowing things without evidence and I would often share what came to me, which would often embarrass or make adults uncomfortable. I was said to be an old soul with the ability to know about things that were often secret. Today it is called insightful and intuitive.

Looking back, I possessed wisdom as a child, but I was physically aggressive. There was a significant memory from elementary school that indicated that something could have been wrong with me as a child. I was sitting at my desk, and I reached over to my best friend's desk and pushed all her papers off her desk for no apparent reason. I laughed aloud as she picked up her things and looked at me. Once everything was back on her desk, I again swiped everything off her desk. She asked me to stop as she picked up the papers and tried to go back to working on an assignment. I laughed and did it again. She reached over and hit me on my arm and began picking up her papers, pencils, etc. I instantly became enraged and began hitting her uncontrollably. The teacher pulled me off her and rushed me to the principal's office. They asked me a flurry of questions, and I did not have the answers to any of them. Initially, I felt confused and still a little angry. In particular, they wanted to know why I attacked my "best" friend. I didn't know, and I became very saddened that I had hurt her. The school wanted to place me in a different school for juvenile delinquents, but my parents wouldn't hear of it. So I was placed in a special education class. As a child, I didn't mind so much being in this class because we, the few students in this often dark room, were given candy. But I knew something didn't add up with my being there because some of the children looked intellectually challenged. Interestingly, while having to go there a couple of hours out of the day, I would also be escorted to upper classes because my reading and comprehension were well above grade level. I was hostile but incredibly smart. I believe that I was sent to the special education class because of my behavior and not my ability to learn. Maybe the school simply did not know what to do with me. That only lasted a short period of time, and then I was able to rejoin my class.

As I grew up and moved into junior high, and then high school, I knew that I was different. I saw the world differently, and I was talented and smart. I had a quick mind and a quick temper to match it. However, when I was not in trouble I was leading. In high school, I started a dance troop and began the production of a talent show. I also founded the first Black Student Affairs organization at a predominately white school. This took a lot of negotiating and an entrepreneurial spirit to pull off in the 70s. The only problem was that once I launched the club, I needed to fill several officer roles. I opened the nomination to everyone based on my desire to be inclusive. I even placed the presidency on the table, which I was advised not to do, but I wanted to be "fair." Who would ever have thought that Mike, a basketball player and very popular guy, would run for the presidency considering he never attended any meetings or showed interest in the club? But he did. On the day of the elections, Mike paraded the entire basketball team into the room where we met and they each cast their votes. I lost the president's seat by two or three votes. What a disappointment. I was so infuriated and disgusted that I left the club. Many students wanted me to stay and lead informally because the organization needed a true leader, but I was not inclined to be in someone else's shadow. I carried that anger and hurt feeling with me well into adulthood. And I believe it often fueled my need to cover my butt when things could be left up to chance.

I had to find my own spiritual truth as a young adult. My mother was a non-practicing Christian and attended Baptist churches infrequently, and my father was a practicing atheist who always argued about philosophical and religious ideation. I led many students to Christ on the steps of one of the main hallways of my high school. I was a devout Christian and often struggled with the darker side of me. But these played into my duality of sorts. At one point, I was partying and having a great time, and then I would switch up and witness to others and become a spiritual leader. This was me. I moved between many people and various interests in high school. I was not the most adept pupil nor did I really care for school. It was merely a social center for me, and I stayed in and out of trouble for one thing or another. But I had a deep connection with the spirit, and I was always in search of the truth and meaning of life.

My friends would often say that I was crazy. I never understood why people called me crazy, but I would feel offended. I was humorous and pulled many funny antics, but I hated being called crazy even in jest. I often heard, "Girl, you're so crazy," as I made people laugh. But people would soon stop laughing and see my actions as truly crazy when I had my first public crazy display in my mid-teens. I was at a party with a few friends, and I looked across the room and saw my boyfriend with another girl. I acted as if it didn't faze me as friends kept asking me whether I saw them or not. Then they left the party together, but not without him acknowledging that he saw me. I was furious. How dare he leave with this girl when he was my first true love?

That following week I called him and tried to talk about what I saw over the weekend. He became curt so I dropped it. I can't remember if I asked him at that point or later that week to come over and hang out, but the invitation was offered. He came to my house and I had a few other friends join us for swimming and fun. I found that he was smug, as if he could treat me any kind of way since I "forgave" him for being with someone else when I felt that we had a monogamous relationship. I excused myself from the group and went inside the house. I went to my parent's room where my mom kept a gun. I loaded two bullets and left the third chamber empty and loaded two more bullets with the next chamber empty. I then rejoined the group and suggested that we all take a walk to the park, which was down the street from my house. My friends wanted to stay at the house and swim, but I was very persuasive so they agreed to walk to the park which was two blocks away.

During the walk, I whispered to my girlfriends that something was going to occur but not to worry about anything because I had everything under control. We entered the huge park with baseball fields, basketball courts, and a playground where kids and teens were playing. As we walked towards the basketball court, I asked my boyfriend why he betrayed and hurt me. He looked at me with anger and shouted that he wasn't going to talk about that shit. I stopped and walked close to him and pulled out the gun, and told him that he was, in fact, going to talk about that shit. I began cursing and yelling at him about hurting me, and I shot two bullets in the air. I then pointed the gun at him and began yelling at him and threatening him. I then pointed the gun away and clicked off that round and another shot. By this time he was terrified, and I relished his fear. After a few more minutes of taunting him, I heard sirens. I was in a controlled frenzy as one of my friends yelled that we had to go because the police were coming. I gave a few more threats as I pointed the gun at him and I quickly tucked the gun away and we ran as he stood there completely frozen and terrified.

Once we were clear of the park and police, we arrived at my home. My friends left and I went to the backyard and dived into the pool and swam like nothing happened. My mother came to the edge of the pool, and said that someone called and said that I had shot at my boyfriend. Initially I denied it and claimed that I was home swimming all afternoon. However, I was not one to lie, no matter the consequences, so after a few minutes, I went inside and told my mother the whole story. My mom was shocked, but didn't seem angry because she, too, was violent. This brings up my concern that many people seek support from family members who often suffer from the same mental illness with the inability to truly give appropriate support. Unfortunately, most family members are not prepared or in a position to give help, which can have dire consequences, especially if family members don't see a behavior as needing attention.

FORMATIVE YEARS

The following week my parents had me seen by a psychiatrist. He asked me a few questions and I don't remember much else. I shared with the doctor that I had no intention of killing or harming my first love, but rather I wanted to scare him. It was an aggressive and reckless act that made me feel justified for how he treated and made me feel.

Nothing came of my visits, so I thought. While conducting research for my dissertation as an adult, I learned that my parents knew that something was wrong with me. When talking to my father he shared with me that the psychiatrist told him and my mother that I had a mental illness and there was nothing that could be done because it was hereditary. This was not shared with me, and I went through school and life oblivious to my mental illness. I only saw that psychiatrist once (or maybe twice) and moved on with my life without any knowledge that I was given a life sentence of mental illness. Probably during that time period the only options were to institutionalize or prescribe dangerous medications neither of my parents would have consented to, thank God. I'm actually appreciative that I didn't know that I was "mentally ill" at that time in my life because that would have greatly impacted me. I don't think that I would have become who I am and may have become debilitated based on identifying myself as ill. However, Dr. Fieve stated in *Bipolar II* (pg. 76) "that admittedly, most patients I see spend years living with 'mood misery' as they wonder what is happening in their minds but are too afraid to talk to a professional to seek a diagnosis and treatment."

I knew that I was different and that I often felt sad, but I had nowhere to go or anyone to talk to which was very difficult and a lonely existence. I fantasized about suicide as a teen quite often, but

I thought everyone considered suicide as a way to get away from their parents. I really thought that what I was experiencing was normal. I would dream up and think about these elaborate suicidal scenarios. Many of my suicidal thoughts and wishes were a way to punish and escape from my mother. I would always imagine killing myself in such a way that would include writing a letter to my mother expressing my disdain for how she treated me and then I would be ever so certain to kill myself in such a way that she would find my body. However, I never went through with my thoughts. I either never had the courage because I was afraid that she would kill me if I lived through it, or I believed that I would miss out on something if I were to check out too early based on an internal optimism that I carried. As I said earlier, I am thankful that I was not aware of what my father told me. I think it would have greatly altered my life and possibly caused me to become worse. So, I attended high school like everyone else, and carried on with what seemed like a normal existence.

According to Dr. Nassir Ghaemi, a professor of psychiatry at Tufts University School of Medicine and director of the Mood Disorders Program at Tufts Medical Center in Boston, in his book titled *A First-Rate Madness Uncovering the Links Between Leadership and Mental Illness in Times of Crisis* (pg. 8), manic depressive illness starts in young adulthood or earlier, and the symptoms come and go (they're episodic, not constant). And they generally follow a specific pattern (for example, a depressive phase often immediately follows a manic episode). Unfortunately, I struggled with highs and lows through my teenage years, and I was often hiding that I was miserable. Many thought that I had the perfect life with a financially secure, intact family, but I was wearing two masks as I attempted to appear happy, all the while thinking that I was different, but yet what I was experiencing was normal. I couldn't have been further from the truth as the sun is to the moon.

In my senior year, I was voted best dressed by the student body. That was my claim to fame. Not most likely to succeed, not most athletic (although I was very athletic), and nothing studious. I was best dressed, and that is something that I still boast about because I was the best of something. As I prepared to graduate, I had to meet with my high school counselor who asked me, "What do you plan to do upon graduating?" In a matter-of-fact way, I stated, "Go to college." I figured if that was where my friends were going, I would go to college as well, keeping in mind that I did not take any college entry exams nor did I even consider where I would go. I just figured that I was going to college. However, my counselor remarked, while looking over the rims of her glasses, "No, you aren't college material." There was no indignation or "how can this be" thoughts that entered my mind. I shrugged and said, "Okay." I left her office and told my best friend that I was not going to college, and we went down to the Armed Forces recruitment station. I just knew that I would not work in any factory, even if college was not an option for me. I then developed a fear that I was not college material that I carried with me for years. I simply did not feel worthy or smart enough.

I took a test for the Air Force and scored fairly high. They were interested in placing me in some type of administrative position. I was not sure that an admin position was enough excitement for me. So I went over to the Army and began asking them questions, and then I walked next door to the Navy and chatted with them for a moment, and then I walked into the Marine Corps recruiting office. Comparing apples to apples, they each were the same; however, the Marine Corps stood out for me. The recruiter was dressed in a uniform that was to die for (literally). Everything on the uniform was symbolic and that impressed me, and the Marines looked physically impeccable. It became obvious that if I was best dressed according to the school newspaper, and the Marine Corps was best dressed amongst the military branches, then the choice was clear. I would join the Marines. They were best dressed and I was best dressed, which was enough for me. What more could a girl want?

I knew that I did not want to be in an administrative type position, so the recruiter asked what I would want to do as a career. I expressed that I would want to be in radio and/or television. It was explained to me that I could go into the Corps as a field radio operator. The recruiter glorified the job and told me about the position in such a way that I believed my dreams had come true. I believed that the word "field" meant a type of industry like the field of medicine, the field of technology. Little did I know that in the Corps, the field actually meant the field where there were snakes, bugs, and all sorts of critters. Being outside in the elements, in the woods or anywhere there was a field, was not my idea of fun. I was actually lied to, which was a common practice during that time period. I was told what I wanted to hear and I was so excited about the Marine Corps that upon enlisting I convinced two friends to join the service. However, I was tricked and did not discover the mistake until I was actually in a military school to learn how to work those damn radios that I had to carry on my back. I wasn't on a radio show or station, I wore a radio on my back to communicate with other radio operators in the #$&* field. I was being taught to call in airstrikes, communicate with other platoons, and perform other war type communications. I absolutely hated that job. In fact, I did not like the Marine Corps, to be really truthful. You couldn't pay me a million dollars to do it again; however, you could not pay me a million dollars to not have done it.

The Corps was a difficult environment for me. I was often sexually harassed by both men and women. I was a young woman still in her teens with a high level of naiveté. I could not wrap my head around the many abusive things that occurred. When I was fondled by a woman while leaving a shower stall, I reacted by yelling and threatening the woman, and then I reported the incident. But I was reprimanded for conduct unbecoming of a Marine. This is only one of many situations I found myself in as a vibrant, outgoing young adult in the Corps. I did not conform and I stood out like a sore thumb. I was miserable with the abusive treatment and sexual harassment that I received from both men and women. I became pregnant and married within a year of being there. In all honesty, I don't know if it was my way of escaping the military, but I was discharged from active duty because I had a severely difficult pregnancy. I had what was termed as Hyperemesis Gravidarum. Some theorize that it is a psychosomatic disorder while others believe it is a chemical imbalance. The disorder caused me to throw up violently for the first seven months of pregnancy. I stayed in the hospital on IVs to be fed because I couldn't eat. It was a miserable existence, but I was free of the Marine Corps and its constant sexual harassment and abusive treatment.

After having my child, I divorced my first husband and rejoined the Reserves to complete my obligation to Uncle Sam. As a woman of honor and justice, I felt that it was my obligation to complete my service time, but under a different set of circumstances. I was a Reservist with limited exposure to the Corps, and I was placed in Public Affairs based on my college courses, which I loved. As time went on, I continued to live what I thought was a normal life. I served my time in the Marine Corps Reserve and went on to receive an Associate of Applied Arts, Bachelor of Arts, and Master of Arts, all with a minor in psychology. Each degree was difficult because I had my high school counselor's message playing in my head like a reel-to-reel tape. Even though the work was relatively easy, I was so afraid that people would find out that I wasn't college material. It wasn't until a woman by the name of Shirley Borel, at Waubonsee Community College, took an interest in me that I began to blossom. She was my journalism instructor and she was the only person in my life who believed in me and accepted me fully, other than a grandmother who had died from leukemia when I was 23 years old. What was interesting about Shirley was that she was an older white woman who was compassionate about veterans because of her political views surrounding Vietnam. She loved me unconditionally, but I wasn't taught that love transcended color. I remember telling my mother that Shirley thought that I was smart and I could earn a scholarship. My mother said, "She only told you that because you are gullible." Boy, that was like getting two flat tires. I could hear the proverbial air escaping my tires (self-esteem) making the sssssss sound. My mother deflated me. But Shirley didn't give up on me. In fact, she continued to pump me up and fill those tires that allowed me to drive to success. She helped me to get the President Academic Achievement Award, which was the highest scholarship and recognition anyone could receive at Waubonsee Community College. And I was the first African American to receive that award, thanks to Shirley. Many years later when I became a success, I started a scholarship in her name that I continue to this day. A year after someone was awarded the scholarship in Shirley's name, Shirley died in a multi-car pileup. She was the only person who died. The Community Foundation that manages my scholarship called me at work to deliver the bad news. I got up, closed my office door when I heard the news, and wept like a baby.

As I finished my Bachelor's degree, I remarried and started my career in higher education. According to Dr. Fieve in his book *Bipolar II* (pg. 131), when you combine ability and higher education with hypomania, you often have the combination for tremendous accomplishment and great achievement. I was fortunate enough to have a career in higher education that allowed me to express my creativity, develop career programs, and work in recruitment and placement offices. I held many jobs in a variety of colleges and universities. Those were the best places for me to thrive.

Chapter 3

Pushed Not Pulled into Entrepreneurship

Many years passed, and this was the beginning of my journey into entrepreneurship in 1995. I was a relatively young business woman at 31 years old with a lot to give and much to learn. I was working for a school where my job was the Director of Student Placement. I was wined and dined from another job to join that school. What attracted me to that job was a salary that finally supported my ego. I had an office that was supposedly designed by the same interior designer that designed a famous singer's condo, and I had an incredible expense account to entertain hiring professionals who represented large corporations. This was the ideal job for me. It was everything that I had worked for up to that point. I was responsible for turning a defunct career placement department around and helping students find employment upon graduating. This was a culmination of several jobs that I had held over the years. I was a masterful sales person and could talk anyone into hiring our students. I quickly developed relationships wherein the school rapidly became a go-to source for graduating students. This took working long hours and creating standard operating procedures that I researched, developed, and wrote.

Everything seemed fine for the first couple of weeks, but things declined rapidly. I was giving more than a hundred percent and I expected the same from my employees. Often they complained that I worked them too hard. Thus, I was told by my boss that I needed to learn how to "soft-pedal." But the real issue came to light that I was the first African American to be hired or rather hold a management position in that organization. I encountered extreme racism. I was constantly told that my peers felt that I stepped on their toes and that they were uncomfortable with me. As a few employees confided in me, my peers felt that I made them look bad because I was working like a mad woman and doing things that they had been unable to do in their departments. I was there only three months and had built a program to manage placement, created a system for students to conduct job searches, and completely pissed off my peers and employees. I could not understand why half of the people were angry by the success of the programs that I created and the other half were cheering me on. I found out by one of my peers that my boss had shopped around my resume prior to hiring me and asked everyone if they would have a problem with me being hired because I was black. I worked even harder to prove my worth as the heat of racism turned up each week.

There was an incident wherein I was called "Buckwheat" after a meeting by a peer. I was told the meeting would happen at a certain time, but then the time was changed while I was off campus. When I came back from lunch, having been with a client, all the managers were in the conference room. I hurried in after seeing a sign that indicated the time change. The time of the all-hands meeting was changed while I was gone to lunch and no one told me. I slipped into a chair, with all eyes on me, to hear the remainder of the meeting. My boss concluded and asked my coworker to share with me what I had missed since I was late. I was so embarrassed because I was late, which was unlike me. And I was annoyed because it was not my fault that I was late. But I could not very well argue with my boss who had actually changed the time. My peer shared with me what was discussed, and when she finished, she said, "Got it, Buckwheat?" I was shocked and embarrassed to be called such a name considering the connotation. I was the only African-American at this company aside from a cleaning lady. I had no one to talk to about how I felt. So this ate at me for a while. I finally mustered up enough nerves and went to my peer and shared with her how such a name was derogatory and offensive. After explaining myself to her, she said, flustered, "I hate when people are overly sensitive." I knew then that I was fighting a losing battle.

It became painfully clear that they were trying to push me out. The harder they tried to push me out, the more I dug in and worked harder to prove that I was on board and the right person for the job. I started working even longer hours, designing more programs, and so forth. I had on a dry erase board in my office as a reminder to me *I'm dancing as fast as I can*. I needed to remind myself often that I was giving all that I had in an effort to keep my sanity. I was doing everything to salvage my job because the writing was on the wall and I really wanted that position. As fate would have it, I had to leave suddenly for my grandfather's funeral for a few days, and when I returned my office was packed up and I was asked to go to the conference room. Assembled in the conference room were several people ranging from a peer to my boss's boss. It was explained that my services would no longer be needed. They took turns expressing how I was not a good fit and gave examples of why "the witch must be burned." All I could do was look at one of the senior vice presidents and ask, "So does this mean we won't be having lunch next week to discuss how I can improve?" He awkwardly said, "Yes, we won't be having lunch." They asked me to leave immediately and return after work hours to pick up my boxes. I complied. I left looking like a million bucks with my head held high as I walked to my car in the garage. But when I got to my car I cried uncontrollably. I could not understand what I'd done wrong and, more importantly, why they did not like me or value what I offered. I'd done everything that they asked of me and more.

At this point in my life, I felt normal and was pleased overall with my career, except for this recent occurrence. However, I was displaying hyperthymia. According to Nassir Ghaemi (pg. 155), the features of hyperthymia include high energy, elevated libido, workaholism, sense of humor, risk-taking, extraversion, sociability, and marked ambition. I worked incredible hours, including weekends, and I felt that I was being treated unfairly. I was able to establish relationships quickly and I was very ambitious. As I was being terminated, I cracked a joke. It was not something that I had planned to say, but humor was my way of dealing with a very difficult moment. I was able to remain composed, but depression would soon be my dark passenger.

PUSHED NOT PULLED INTO ENTREPRENEURSHIP

As I left the building, my mind was drawing a blank, so I began to drive. I found myself driving off the property and heading for the company that I had just left a few months earlier. I was driving back to my old job where I created and designed programs and made a huge impact. Surely, they would want me back. Upon my arrival, I immediately went to HR to see my old boss. I shared with her what had happened as tears ran down my cheek. She grabbed some tissue for me to dry my eyes and then grabbed her purse. "Let me treat you to lunch," she said. I was not hungry for food but some compassion. I needed true consoling because it felt as if my world had stopped spinning.

We walked down the block to a local eatery, and we talked about the job and the place that fired me. When we got a table and continued our discussion she explained that they wanted what I had to offer but they did not want me. She went on to say that my being black was always an issue that they probably thought they could overlook if the work was good. But unfortunately, my strong presence was too much. She also explained that I started there with long hair and slowly took on a more ethnic look, which more than likely made them uncomfortable. What she was saying was all making sense, but I was still hurting.

Midway through our meal I asked, "Can I have my job back?" I knew that the position was still vacant. I was their career mobility representative in a position that was newly created.

Looking at me with compassion, she said, "No. I do not believe that this is what you want."

Through tear-filled eyes I said, "Yes, I really want my job back."

Placing her hand on top of mine she said, "There was a reason that you left and that reason hasn't changed. You are bigger than the job and you should be doing much more."

I did not care at that point. I just needed and wanted a job. I felt like a failure and even though going back was not my ideal situation, I needed something to identify with. I did not wake up thinking that I would find myself back in an environment that paled in comparison to my most recent employer, but I did not care. I needed a job. To my surprise she refused to rehire me, so we finished our meal and started walking back to her office. We entered her office and I picked up my briefcase to leave. As we started to say our goodbyes, she said, "Here is an application." She reached into her drawer and handed me an application. "Go home, fill it out, and bring it back. If you are serious, I will hire you back." She crossed her arms with a smile and stood there as I left her office. I went home that afternoon feeling completely violated and dejected, but I still had a sense of hope because I could go back to my previous job.

I was at home feeling confused and rejected. I was sitting with the application on the floor between my feet. Tears were dropping on the paper like raindrops before a major storm. I sat there and stared at the application, hating the position that I was in despite all of my hard work. Then I heard a voice. It was so very distinct. The voice said, "Ye of little faith. I brought you out and now you want to go back." It was God speaking to me. I did not want to go back. I hated that place but felt that I had no options. My old boss was right. I left there for a reason. I contemplated going back, but I started to think about what I heard. I felt a burst of energy come across me, so I got off my butt to go downstairs to my basement. In my basement, I started thinking about all the programs that I created over the last few years. I started thinking about the relationships I had forged, and I focused on the many successes I had at the various colleges to include my most recent employer. I was a maverick that made a huge difference everywhere I went. I started to think that if I could do so much for students, then I could do the same for myself. I began looking at business cards in my rolodex and calling on people to let them know that I was corporately detached and seeking a job.

I was energized, but after several weeks, I could not find a job, especially something that would pay me what I believed I was worth. So, I started looking at contract opportunities and my company was born. I placed a folding table in my unfinished basement and bought some of the most basic items such as a file cabinet, telephone, and so forth to be self-sufficient. The space was so bare that the insulation and wiring were exposed with one light bulb in the ceiling. It was not an ideal place to work, but it was a start. I would work for myself.

Reflecting on this time in my life, I now realize that I experienced a hypomanic episode during my time at that company. I was experiencing a period of extremely high optimism and energy, which allowed me to produce programs and establish relationships so quickly. There was blatant racism that occurred, but I also have to take some accountability for my termination. I was manic most of the time. I was exuberant about the job and worked crazy hours. At the time, I chalked up the need to work those hours to the job. I could not see that I was burning people out including myself. I should have spent the first few months getting to know the organization instead of burning it down to build it back up. No one, especially my staff, was able to keep up with me. I was like the Tasmanian Devil. I was bursting with ideas that I implemented and they worked. Instead of them embracing my whirlwind methodology, I was terminated.

Dueling Dragons

According to Kay Redfield Jamison, a professor of psychiatry at the Johns Hopkins University School of Medicine, in her book *Touched with Fire: Manic-Depressive Illness and the Artistic Temperament* (pg. 3), most people find the thought that a destructive, often psychotic, and frequently lethal disease such as manic-depressive illness might convey certain advantages (such as heightened imaginative powers, intensified emotional responses, and increased energy) counterintuitive. I accomplished a lot for that organization, but my presence was, in fact, too strong. But, hey, I could take that condition and apply it to my own business.

I was not pulled into being an entrepreneur; I was pushed into owning my own company. I never wanted to be in a position whereby someone else controlled my career or livelihood, so being terminated worked out for me. However, I sank into a deep depression at that time. When I came out of my depression I worked hard at securing new opportunities. According to Nassir Ghaemi in his book *A First-Rate Madness Uncovering the Links between Leadership and Mental Illness in Times of Crisis* (pg. 28), when not manic or depressed, those with bipolar disorder are normal, just like everyone else, but they retain an awareness that makes their perception just different enough to be unusually creative. I was able to make things happen rather quickly from networking to meeting with a variety of people selling my knowledge, skills, and abilities. I was very creative in finding opportunities and being in the right place at the right time.

Killing it at Career Nation

The first business opportunity that I obtained was a contract position with Career Nation, a premier international outplacement company. I was trained to help people transition out of companies where they were terminated. I brought my own experience of losing a job to the table. I was empathetic beyond the norm and my ability to place students, that I garnered from several previous jobs, was instrumental in helping employees from large corporations transition from their current jobs into the job market. I recall how ecstatic I was to join Career Nation's impressive team of consultants, although I had to attend a weeklong course to actually be contracted. To become an actual consultant you had to complete their course and deliver an audition session. I was blessed to attend the one-week course, and now it was time for my presentation.

I will never forget that day. I woke up earlier than usual and there was a terrible storm. The storm cast darkness across the city and the sky poured down buckets of rain. As I made my way over the top of the Perimeter on the expressway in Atlanta, I could see time flying off the clock. I'd left early, but traffic was at a halt. I literally began to feel the pressure of being late. For God's sake, this could not be happening to me because I am never late, I thought to myself. It was so engrained in me about being early and on time from my military days that I could not fathom being late for an audition. I had prepared all week for that audition, and by looking at the clock I could tell that I was now 30 minutes late. The traffic kept creeping and now I was nearly an hour late as I turned into the parking lot. I found a space, parked my car, grabbed my briefcase, and ran for the ivory tower building.

DUELING DRAGONS

I entered the building that I had visited for the past week, but this time I was soaked and wet from the storm. The entire team had gone upstairs to begin the audition phase of the hiring process. I stepped off the elevator and turned the doorknob to the room where all of my competition and the instructor sat. As I entered, a peer was setting up for her presentation. I immediately went over to the instructor and apologized profusely. "Frank, I am sooo sorry that I am late. I swear; I am never late," I said with tears nearly welling up in my eyes. This was the most important thing that I had encountered in my career and I did not want to ruin my chances of joining the organization. Career Nation was a leader in the outplacement arena and I so badly wanted to be a part of that organization. Frank said with the most caring and gentle voice, "Do not worry about it. We're just starting." I did not know how much to believe of his statement. I took an empty seat and thought about whether he was being polite to avoid a scene or if, in fact, it was okay. I knew that I had to let the entire morning of being late and embarrassed leave my mind because my turn to present would be soon. One of my peers arranged the front of the class to accommodate her presentation and she then began her performance. I listened intently for the first few minutes because she was the competition and I wanted to hear what she had to say, but there was a deep sickening feeling that I could not shake because I was late. I could not help obsessing over how I sat in the car for over an hour and that I was late. Now, it was my turn to present. I cannot remember what all I said, but I know that I streamed together information from Career Nation's workbooks and my experience of being fired to create a presentation that brought tears to some of my peers' eyes. "It was difficult being fired from my last job," I shared with the cohort. "It has to be difficult for anyone to lose their job." This was my shining moment as I explained what a person truly experiences from the loss of a job and possibly their identity. I turned to Frank and he nodded with approval. I took my seat when I finished, feeling relieved that I'd done an excellent job, but I was still angry with myself for being late. Everyone in the cohort completed their presentations and we thanked Frank for his time and fine facilitation of the weeklong course. The day ended, and as I was leaving, I went to Frank and again apologized in hopes that I was not secretly eliminated from the pool of candidates who would be selected.

At that time, Frank shared with me that he had already selected me, not based on my performance, but based on my overall ability to grasp the material and add value to it through my personal experiences. "Are you serious? I'm selected?" I asked while hugging him.

"Yes. Did you have any doubt?" he asked surprisingly.

I slumped over a little and said, "I just knew that coming in late was a deal breaker."

"But I expected some people to be late with the weather and bad traffic. So do not worry about it," he said with a smile and a handshake.

I reached out my hand and thanked him for everything and left the room, got on the elevator, and headed back to my car. Quickly, I became one of the top consultants for the organization. Both the company and I received letters from companies and individuals thanking me for helping people to transition into new jobs and careers. Working for Career Nation was awesome. I was doing what I loved and helping people. I was able to be me fully as I touched and changed lives. I was growing by leaps and bounds professionally. I felt so alive working in the outplacement arena.

After doing that for over a year, I realized that I was truly on to something. I could do this for myself, I thought. Reflecting on this period of my life, I can truly say that I was upbeat and positive. Even though I was fired from a very good job, I was able to bounce back. I found that I was very resilient in my ability to win a spot on the Career Nation's team. I think what carried me through was that I was able to heal by helping others who were faced with being terminated. In his book *A First-Rate Madness Uncovering the Links between Leadership and Mental Illness in Times of Crisis* (pg. 18), Nassir Ghaemi says, "I don't claim that depression invariably leads to realism, nor that mania always enhances creativity, nor that depression on every occasion increases empathy, nor that hyperthymia inevitably promotes resilience. Rather, I argue that, on the whole, more often than not, those mental illnesses enhance or promote those qualities more frequently than is the case in the absence of those mental illnesses." I have found that having bipolar disorder can cause a high degree of compassion and empathy. Also, this new position was solely based on crisis situations. Every time I taught a class or coached someone who had been terminated, that presented a crisis situation and an opportunity to lead that person out of it. Working in the outplacement space allowed me to be empathetic coupled with resiliency. I healed from being fired from the school and I helped others to transition in their lives.

Despite my success with Career Nation, the idea of striking out on my own became more of a calling. I had become a master at outplacement services. I did not plan on starting a company that would grow into what it is today. I merely wanted to have more control over my time and destiny. The process of starting my own business was simple only because I did not know what I was doing. I selected a name for my company that would describe what I did very well. I came up with Careers In Transition, which landed well on me. I went to a local printer and had some cards made up and began pitching myself to organizations. I continued to work with Career Nation, but I also began attempting to secure my own clients.

I networked my way to developing a course as a subcontractor for someone who was an independent contractor. This entailed writing the course and creating a workbook that included a trainer's and participant's manual. I worked night and day on that project. I really felt that my eyes were bleeding from staring at the computer screen for hours upon hours. This was when I had my first disappointment in my company. I worked on that project for weeks, cramming in over 12 hours a day to create materials. When I finished the work, I proudly turned in all the course materials that I created to the woman who hired me. The woman who secured my services received all the materials and did not pay me the balance that she owed me. Unfortunately, I was so green at doing contract work that I did not require or ask for a contract. I trusted her word based on her relationship with a pastor who referred her to me. I cannot remember the many excuses that she gave me for not paying me, but I felt hurt and angry. I felt at a loss, so I called the government agency that would ultimately receive the materials and told them that I was never paid for the work from that project. It was explained to me that if I had had a contract with her that was attached to a specific contract then they could have withheld payment on that contract, but I had nothing in writing. I was very angry that I had been used and did not get paid for all of that hard work. This was the first lesson that I learned—have a contract.

As I reflect on this scenario, I can see that I did the same thing that I did with all my jobs. I worked tirelessly to produce a new and creative product. I displayed signs of hypomania, but more importantly, I exhibited the creativity that is associated with bipolar disorder. This was my first opportunity to create something independent of a structured work environment. I produced some of my best work and felt the internal pressure to create something that would exceed the client's expectation. I literally worked around the clock to pull it off. I was thrown into a hypomanic state by not sleeping. It meant everything to me to produce a training program that would top everything that I had done up to that point. I was still feeling the sting of being let go from my previous employer. Thus, I needed to succeed and I became obsessed with developing and creating a training program with curriculum. According to Kay Redfield Jamison in her book *Touched with Fire: Manic-Depressive Illness and the Artistic Temperament* (pg. 103), profound changes in mood, thinking, personality, and behavior can occur during all phases of manic-depressive illness. Even during normal states many individuals with the illness, or who have a cyclothymic temperament, will experience striking fluctuation in the intensity of their perceptions and feelings. All these changes have potentially important effects on personality and thought, but perhaps most relevant to the discussion of artistic creativity are those changes that occur during the milder manic, or hypomanic states.

Dr. Fieve said in his book *Bipolar II* (pg. 23), "Most hypomanic men and women are very self-motivated and have what I call the entrepreneurial personality. In fact, a high percentage of the entrepreneurs I've studied have Bipolar II disorder, which may explain their attraction to entrepreneurship in the first place. They have a strong inner drive or stimulus that motivates them to work harder, be more productive, achieve more, and also snap back quickly if life's interruptions or business setbacks block their paths." I was truly an entrepreneur. I was creating something from nothing and enjoying the freedom of creating and working autonomously. I had truly found the ideal environment for myself: entrepreneurship. At that time, though, the more appropriate title would have been solopreneur.

Upon real examination, what is very telling is that I did not have a contract nor did I attempt to have one. This would be considered a risky business venture that is attributed to bipolar disorder. Often people who are bipolar will rush into situations too quickly without giving them complete consideration. I am sure that I was more concerned about doing the work than getting a contract and conducting business. That was a costly lesson. But it did not deter me from wanting to be an independent contractor and having a business. Kay Redfield Jamison in her book *Touched with Fire: Manic-Depressive Illness and the Artistic Temperament* (pg. 54), along with Psychologist William Joe and clinical psychiatrist and scholar Emil Kraepelin, both writing early in the twentieth century, emphasized the positive features associated with certain kinds of madness and speculated about how these features might, in some instances, combine with other talents to produce an extraordinarily creative or accomplished person. This was the beginning of something huge and great for me that would pay off for years to come. However, I was still unaware that I had a mental illness of any kind that was actually fueling my success.

Flying high with my first real client: Free to innovate and create

I kept trudging along. I used every avenue from newspapers and membership portals to attending various professional associations. I was still working from my basement, and I would use every and any opportunity to be around people. What worked to my advantage was that I was an extrovert and networking was second nature for me. I became very well known in the Human Resource's circle around Atlanta. In 1995, I earned my first real client, a federal government agency known here as Managed Results. They needed a contractor who could develop training programs and create curriculum. For the first time in history, the federal government was experiencing a possible downsizing. The contractor would provide outplacement services. This position required writing standard operating procedures, creating workbooks, and delivering transitional assistance workshops. This was a dream come true again. I could and have done all of that which the contract called for. I submitted my resume and within time I was invited in for an interview with Pam, a contractor, and Tom, the director of the Career Center. I went in and wowed them both. I showed them the very same course that I created and developed but did not get paid for several months earlier. They were astonished by the quality and detail of the workbook so much so that I won their business. I won my first government contract. I was officially a government contractor, which was huge for me.

Bodies in my path: The relational cost of volatility

I worked tirelessly on projects. Initially, I offered sessions to help employees prepare for a possible downsize. This was unique and new to the client, so I led them through what was a difficult time of change. After a few months, the budget was approved, which meant that layoffs would not happen. This changed my deliverables. I was then responsible for establishing internal relationships and developing training courses that ranged from conflict resolution to diversity.

It did not take me any time in establishing myself in the organization. Because I was a contractor, I had a high level of autonomy. I found that I worked best in environments where I was free to create and design at my own pace on projects that I saw were beneficial. I absolutely loved being on that contract. After conducting performance consulting with decision makers, I discovered that they needed more than just training. They needed something that would be ongoing training and direction from highly successful people. Thus, I created a mentoring program that was customized and launched across the entire country. I delivered the workshops that I developed and designed. I selected a full-time employee as a co-facilitator and we traveled around the country rolling out the program. It was a huge success. I was on a constant high. People would comment on my ability to be upbeat all the time. I was gregarious and animated. My workshops were result-oriented fun-filled days of introspection that caused the client to want more and more of what I had to offer. The program received so much recognition that it received a national award.

Everything was wonderful; however, my peer, Pam, became jealous and resentful, and attempted to have me keep her in the loop, and even suggested that I could not work on certain projects without her authorization. This was the beginning of the end. I blew up at her trying to control me and things went downhill from there.

"Hello, Debra (my former name), one of your clients is in the office needing a form that you completed for her," Pam explained over the phone.

I was on my day off and my computer was locked. "That's on my computer, and that is locked," I said without giving any thought to the request. "I'll be in tomorrow. Can she come back?" I asked while recalling that I had finished the form that the client needed.

"She needs her boss to sign it today. What is your password?" Pam prompted me.

I had no plans on going in and it was a harmless form, I thought. I was really uncomfortable sharing my password, but I could not deny a client what she needed, so I gave Pam the password. I hung up and continued to do whatever I was doing before I was interrupted, and that conversation became a distant memory.

Weeks later, I was talking to another employee who shared with me that he wanted me to work on a project but needed to get permission from my boss, Pam. "Pam's not the boss of me!" I said with a confused look on my face. Yes, Pam was a part of the team that hired me and was the full-time contractor, but she was not my boss by any means. What the hell did he mean that Pam would need to okay something for me? "What are you talking about?" I asked Jerry.

"Well, it's my understanding that the Career Center is now under Pam," Jerry explained.

"I do not think so. Pam is my peer," I said with a smirk because I knew that Jerry must have been misinformed.

"Debra, you had to know that she was promoted to be your supervisor." Jerry looked at me as if I was joking.

"No. I never heard anything about Pam being anything besides another consultant under contract like me," I said, now looking a little worried because it seemed that the joke was on me.

Jerry got up and left my office and returned with a memo. "Here, Debra. This is the memo that we all received, including you," Jerry said as he handed me the memo.

I read the memo that actually had my name as recipient and was copied to a variety of managers in the organization. The memo stated that Tom had designated Pam as the manager of the Career Center upon his retirement, and that all employees and contractors would work on assignments based on her discretion. Now it was starting to make sense why some of my internal clients deferred to her for things.

She was my boss? This was unsettling because I did not want or need a boss. Pam was my peer. I was pretty sure that her alleged promotion was fraudulent.

I called up to Washington to find out if they authorized such an arrangement. They did not know what I was talking about and requested to see the memo. I faxed the memo to Karen, in DC, who was the Director over everything. She called me in a matter of minutes. She was confused that I did not know about the proposed change since it was sent directly to me. I then looked at the date on the memo and compared it to my schedule. "Damn it, Karen, I was off that day and Pam called me for my password. She must have sent it to me and then deleted it off my system!" I exclaimed like a private eye catching a cheating husband.

Pam and Tom had devised this plan to control me, is what ran through my head. Pam was the original contractor and would be over the prime projects, but I had managed to develop some pretty good relationships and products that allowed me to travel and interact with decision makers around the organization that minimized Pam's exposure. Pam felt that she should have been the person who traveled and had the interesting projects because she had been there longer. I became the "go-to" person and that did not sit well with her. Now, we had the issue of what was next.

"Well, let me look into this, Debra, and we'll call you back. This has never happened before," Karen said with concern in her voice.

In the meanwhile, I went to Jerry and explained what I believed happened and returned to my office.

"What is this?" Pam shouted as she entered my office. She had in her hands a receipt from the fax that indicated that something was faxed to headquarters. "You aren't allowed to speak with headquarters before passing it by me," Pam said with total disdain.

"Well, wouldn't you like to know? I found out about Tom and your little plan." I said smugly.

"What plan?" Pam shouted as she closed the door.

"The plan to have you as the manager when legally you are a contractor and cannot be over this center. And do not think that I do not know that you went on to my computer and sent an email to me that you erased," I said looking down at my desk.

She saw my eyes glance at the email and she lunged to grab it off my desk. I was much quicker. I grabbed the paper and she attempted to take it from me. Unfortunately for Pam, she was a rather short woman and could not reach the paper that I held high in the air. She kept trying to take it from me. I had scratches on my hands where she kept trying to snatch the paper. I just laughed as she became more and more frantic and upset. The commotion that we made attracted people to my office. When she saw that she was attracting an audience, she straightened her clothes and left not only my office but the building.

Later that day, I heard from Karen. "We are flying down next week to sort this out," she said with authority and irritation.

When they arrived, they spoke to people about the situation and what had transpired the day of the fax fiasco. The DC leadership met with Pam and me separately. What was decided was that Pam's contract would not be renewed and she basically lost her full-time gig and that ended within a few weeks of that meeting. I still had time left on my contract, but when the contract ended, it was not renewed, as well. I did not feel that this was fair, but I was able to work independent of the Career Center and I began working with clients with whom I had established relationships throughout the organization. In essence, I continued to work in the agency, but not under a steady contract. This was a disappointing and dark time in my life because I felt attacked by Pam, and I lost my contract. I really enjoyed the autonomy that I had initially. It allowed me to express myself through my work and I created a mentoring program that helped the organization win a national award. However, everything I built by way of that contract was burned to the ground to include that of my peer who lost her livelihood.

Looking back on this situation, it was clear that I had bipolar disorder even though I was unaware of such. According to Kay Redfield Jamison in her book *Touched with Fire: Manic-Depressive*

Illness and the Artistic Temperament (pg. 13), other common features of hypomania and mania include spending excessive amounts of money, impulsive involvements in questionable endeavors, reckless driving, extreme impatience, intense and impulsive romantic or sexual liaisons, and volatility. I had turned the workplace into a volatile place when I became irate about the changes that occurred. I cost myself and a peer our jobs. I was able to create an award-winning national program, but I left bodies in my path. My hypomania served me well in being able to design and create a variety of programs that made a huge impact, but the irritability and anger associated with bipolar disorder cost me. According to Kay Redfield Jamison in her book *Touched with Fire: Manic-Depressive Illness and the Artistic Temperament* (pg. 14), in its milder variants, the increased energy, expansiveness, risk taking, and fluency of thought associated with hypomania can result in highly productive periods. I was flying high and carried a part of the organization with me; however, that high became too high and destructive.

Chapter 4

The Personal Turning Point

I had been practicing spirituality for several years, and after that incident I decided to rename myself. I went through so much heartache and pain without doing some of the things that I would have done as a teen, such as fight and physically hurt Pam whom I had worked with on the last contract. I no longer felt like I was Debra. Debra would have reacted and responded entirely differently to Pam when she kept trying to snatch the memo out of my hand. Then she went on a crusade to destroy relationships that I had with other departments to no avail, which would have caused me to be volatile. It was all that I could do to stay grounded and not fight back. I felt that I had truly evolved as a person. I was practicing love and light, so I selected the name Indigo for many reasons. In a spiritual context it means intuitive and insightful. It was a name that I believed could direct my actions and keep me centered on being a good person despite what happened around or to me. But the truth of the matter was that I simply didn't want to be me anymore. I thought that by getting rid of the name I associated with a lot of negative thoughts and memories, and then by taking on a spiritual name, I could become more of who and what I wanted to be.

So I hired an attorney to legally change my name. I went to the courthouse one evening after work and had my name changed from Debra to Indigo. This wasn't such a difficult task and it seemed quite normal. Many years ago while living in Beaufort, South Carolina, I came across a plantation called the Indigo Plantation in the near vicinity. That name resonated with me. I researched the name and found out that it was a plant that produced the color indigo. Slaves used to process the indigo plant with their hands to extract the color blue. The dye was then sent to the old country and used by royalty and aristocrats. That is how we have the color royal blue.

But what I found most compelling was that these slaves would die with bluish green arms and hands, which reminded me that I need to stay grounded. I am always reminded of my connection to my ancestors and their sacrifices. I vowed to name my daughter Indigo based on the connectedness with earth and spirituality associated with the color/name. Two sons later, I realized that I was not going to have a daughter, so I adopted the name for myself. I took on the name Indigo spiritually and mentally.

However, looking back over the fax fiasco I was experiencing another hypomanic episode. I did not become depressed over the situation but rather more intense. Kay Redfield Jamison, in her book *Touched with Fire: Manic-Depressive Illness and the Artistic Temperament* (pg. 105), states that many of the changes in mood, thinking, and perception that characterize the mildly manic states— restlessness, ebullience, expansiveness, irritability, grandiosity, quickened and more finely tuned senses, intensity of emotional experiences, diversity of thought, and rapidity of associational process—are highly characteristic of creative thought as well. I had never met anyone who had changed her name and my family was quite upset. But I felt a need to become new and I thought such would happen through a name change. I was beginning to become more aware and intuitive in many ways. I had always been able to have a read on people and see people for who they really were, but that gift had seemed to heighten over the last few years. My gift of knowing definitely revealed itself when I was consulting in the outplacement space. I was able to help people see what was often hidden, and my new name really resonated with my spirit. However, having a new name with the same mental condition wasn't going to save me from myself.

I was now without a job again, although I still did consulting work for Career Nation and I taught at Blue University. Oddly enough, I did quite well anywhere where I was not supervised. My saving grace was that while I was at the federal agency Managed Results, I had access to other government agencies. I would use my lunch hour to go door-to-door to meet with other HR departments' training officers. After two years of working with clients, I learned that business cards weren't enough. I needed to have a full and legitimate company.

Connecting on a higher level of success

In 1997, I registered my company with the Georgia Secretary of State. I was a 33-year-old African-American woman entrepreneur with no idea how difficult owning and operating a business was going to be. Becoming incorporated gave me a license to hunt for contracts as a small business versus an independent contractor, which made things a little easier.

I also designed my company's logo which was an owl. The many attributes that an owl possessed seemed to align with me and my new name. I was wise, could see in the dark, and have a nearly 360 degree view of things within an organization. My company's logo was very telling of me and my company which were seamless. I would shop around to potential clients the many projects and courses that I designed. Within time I won the U.S. Protection Council as my second client. I began conducting a variety of training sessions for them. I became very close with decision-makers within that organization and everything was great. I was allowed to offer them innovative sessions and I created customized workshops based on my performance consulting. I was always on a high with my client, but there was always a bit of sadness. I never felt that I was where or as far as I should have been in my career. I had an excellent product, but growth was God awful slow. But over the years, I kept adding more high profile clients.

Even though I had behavioral problems at the last two work engagements, I was unaware that anything was mentally wrong with me. I continued working for years without mental stability and my company steadily grew at a turtle's pace because I would acquire a new client but struggled with maintaining the relationship. At this point, I worked steadily with the U.S. Chambers Council and U.S. Protection Council. Then there was the occasional speaking engagement on careers and job search topics, but nothing seemed to be clicking.

THE PERSONAL TURNING POINT

I thought that relationships with peers would close the gap and help me grow. This prompted me to establish a relationship with Mark, who had an established HR company and was also the president of a professional training association. He was well-known in the city and in the industry. I believed that I could learn a lot from him. Over time, he became my mentor. I would visit his office frequently. "Mark, you have so many things on your shelf," I said impressively as I looked at the items he collected from clients, conferences, and things like that. It just showed that he had been around and I admired it for some strange reason. In my office located in the basement of my home, I did not have anything that would prove that I was even alive, let alone a business owner with clients.

"These are things that I have gotten while speaking at conferences and working with clients. You'll have your own someday," he said encouragingly.

But I did not feel like that would ever happen. It was taking forever to grow my business. Then Mark won a contract with a clandestine organization in DC. During one of my many visits to his office he shared some good news with me.

"Indigo, I have a contract that I think you would be ideal for," Mark said with a smile on his face.

"Great. What is the contract?" I asked very excitedly. This would be my first opportunity to work with Mark and I had complete admiration and respect for him.

"It is with the Directorate Council Center (DCC). And it is a mentoring program," he answered. He remembered that I created a national mentoring program for Managed Results. He needed me to customize a program for his client.

"Will we partner on this?" I asked.

"No, I already have a partner. I will subcontract this work to you," he explained.

"But that doesn't give me any name recognition or past performance," I complained.

"I know, but it gives you more experience and some exposure," he assured me.

I was grateful for the opportunity but I wanted to be a part of the actual contract. So we agreed that everything would be copyrighted in my company's name. We entered a contractual agreement and I began working on the project. I spent many hours producing the materials. When I presented the workbooks and train-the-trainer materials he was ecstatic. My materials exceeded his expectations. As we sat and chatted, he said, "I need for you to deliver the sessions." He knew that this would be a dream come true for me. I accepted the offer gladly and within a couple of weeks we were on our way to the DCC, in DC. We arrived as a team at the DCC to present my mentoring program that included a training session. This was a big day for me, although I felt a little drained. The night before I was sick to my stomach with flu-like symptoms because I often got very ill when I got excited, and this was cause for excitement. The day went off without a hitch and Mark was very pleased with the results. This moved our relationship up a notch. As time went by we became very close, and I began to trust him, which was something I had to work at based on past disappointments and an underlining paranoia that I carried into every relationship.

I was continuing to work on growing my business and generating contracts. Everything was coming together. One day I was sitting at a breakfast meeting with peers who represented a professional human resources association. We were meeting because they wanted me to serve on a committee to help develop and launch a mentoring program. Just before the breakfast came, I remember having to excuse myself, and I went to the bathroom because I wasn't feeling well. As soon as I entered a stall, I began throwing up. I often got sick when excited, but working on a committee did not excite me in the least. After vomiting everything up, I took care of myself and went back to the table to finish our discussion. Later that evening, I was walking through the parking lot of a shopping center with my husband, Curtis. "Curtis, I feel really really sick. I do not know what's wrong. I feel like I have to throw up," I said as I held back the urge to bend over and let it all out.

"What do you think is wrong?" he said looking concerned.

"I do not know. But I feel awful," I said while walking very slowly into the grocery store, hoping not to throw up. "What can I take for nausea?" I asked the pharmacist behind the counter. He gave me a bottle of medicine for nausea, and something told me to get a pregnancy test, too. I can't remember why that crossed my mind, but I had that same feeling when I was pregnant years earlier. I purchased the items, and began drinking the nausea medicine as I walked back to the car.

That evening when I got home, I took the pregnancy test. Before I had a chance to finish peeing on the wand a positive sign glowed like a neon light. I was PREGNANT! This was not something I'd tried to do or wanted to be. I showed Curtis the results and we just sat there dumbfounded. Having another child was not a bad thing in the least, just not planned. Moments later, I quickly became panicky because I had Hyperemesis gravidarum with my last two pregnancies and had to stay in bed for the entire time because I vomited night and day until I become dehydrated and usually needed hospitalization. This was the sole reason that I was separated from the military. It was a horrible way to live, especially while my body was changing from being pregnant. I was terrified. Curtis tried to console me by saying, "Maybe this time things will be different with the new technology and medicines." But nothing could console me. I just knew that I was headed for a nightmarish experience.

I made a doctor's appointment and sure enough I was pregnant and undoubtedly I had Hyperemesis gravidarum again. I spent the next few days attempting to get all my affairs in order, as if I were dying. I called Mark to let him know that I would be out of commission for the next several months, and to let him know that I would refer my clients to him. The next seven months I was totally out of commission with many hospital visits, pumped with a variety of drugs, and living what felt like near death experiences day in and day out. One of the things that had to happen was that I had to stay in a dark and quiet room. Any kind of stimulation would cause me to throw up, and once I started, there was no end in sight. I could only eat crackers, ice, and some baby food, which always came back up. Things got so bad and so intense after I lost all of my weight that Curtis sat on the side of my bed and said that he would agree to my getting an abortion. "We'll tell the family that you lost the baby," he said, while trying to comfort me.

We made an appointment with the abortion clinic and it would have been a matter of days and then I would be free from that horrible condition. It is hard to explain what it was like to expel everything until it felt like the lining of your stomach was being pulled out with each violent vomiting. I wished that I would die and each day and night I would lie there with no relief. But in two days I would have an abortion and could have my body and life back. However, I was so sick that I ended up in the hospital the day before my abortion appointment. The hospital kept me for a few days and the abortion clinic would not take me because I was too sick. Every time I attempted to get an abortion I was too sick for the procedure to be conducted. I was miserable and I felt dead, as if a demon possessed my body and I was trapped inside to endure the pain and suffering. This went on until the seventh month and then things started to get better. I was on all types of drugs from nausea pills to sedatives. It was the absolute worst time of my life. I did not think once about my company or career. All I could think about was living from day to day. I would lie in a dark room serving as a human incubator. Finally, I gave birth to my third son. By this time, Curtis was doing well enough in his career that I could be a stay-at-home mom. So I took off nearly two years to be with my sons, especially since I'd just lost nearly a year of being mom to them because of my illness. I'm wondering if my mental medical condition had any bearing on that physical medical condition.

Building a business

I was 35 years old and feeling a tug-of-war between career and family. Two years later, I decided to return to my practice. I was resilient in my coming back. I could have sought to get a job, but I returned to my practice in hopes of growing my business. This time it was like starting from the beginning because I had no contracts or business prospects whatsoever, but I did have my business cards and an uncanny ability to network. I started attending networking functions and became immersed in my career again. I picked up a few small contracts here and there, but it was a slow process.

Reflecting on this phase of my life and my company is bitter-sweet. It was a year or two later, and I had settled back into my business. Unlike my initial experience in owning a business, this time it was different. I wanted to own a business and not just be an entrepreneur (solopreneur). I really wanted to be a success and grow my business. My husband would criticize my failing efforts and nag me about getting a job. I became depressed at my inability to bounce back to where I'd left off. After my husband noticed that I was becoming more and more difficult to be around, he urged me to visit a psychiatrist. But I ignored him. It wasn't until we started having severe behavioral problems with one of my sons that we decided to seek help, but for him. He was diagnosed as having bipolar disorder, and the psychiatrist turned to me and shared that the condition was hereditary. The psychiatrist asked me a series of questions and then diagnosed me as having bipolar disorder, too. That could not be! I wasn't crazy. I refused to accept that diagnosis; however, I felt pretty crummy, so I was willing to take whatever he prescribed in hopes to feel better. He placed me on Depakote, which made me very lethargic. We tried numerous medicines over the next several months. The one that I fell in love with was Effexor. I recall that I never felt sharper. I was able to work on assignments without stopping. I never felt better. Then one day I realized that if I was taking medicine I must have been crazy because only crazy people take meds. I decided that I wasn't crazy; therefore, I would not take medicine. And I also decided that I was not bipolar. I went into complete denial. The stigma of having a mental illness was far greater than the need to be well. I never even bothered to read or learn anything about bipolar disorder. I knew that depression was a part of the condition because of the phrase manic depressive. But

I had no knowledge about the disorder or what awaited me. Unfortunately, I did nothing to understand the disorder or accept the diagnosis, which had dire consequences in the years to follow.

Finding stability to grow my practice

My company was growing, and there was an opportunity to work on yet another national project. The U.S. Department of Creativity was trying to fill a position for a Management and Leadership Specialist in the Atlanta office. I wanted the role and responsibility of that position, but I did not want a job. I had come to realize that I did not fare well in jobs. I was still teaching as an Adjunct Faculty member at Blue University, I occasionally conducted classes for Career Nation, and I had my own clients. I was able to sustain those relationships because they were contractual. I called my peer, Dorothy, who was looking to fill that position in her Career Center because the opportunity was so appealing. We met over coffee across the street from her building and we discussed the particulars of the job. I expressed that I did not want a job, but I was very interested in the position. "Is there any way that you can make this a contract?" I pleaded. "If it were a contract, I would be all in. You know that I can do this job for you," I said trying to convince her that she should outsource that position.

"I wish that I could, but I can't. But I assure you that you would be able to continue to do whatever you are doing as long as you get your work done," she said, attempting to assure me that the job would be like a contract. In my mind I needed to feel as if I did not work for anyone. I needed the freedom and autonomy that kept me out of trouble. But there was one problem. I knew that I had difficulties in a structured environment. Therefore, I needed something to help me assimilate. I went through the formal interview process and was hired on a term appointment.

I contacted the psychiatrist who diagnosed me with bipolar disorder and asked him if there was anything that he could prescribe to help me stay balanced. I still did not accept that I was bipolar, but I knew that most employment situations would end horribly for me. I started taking a medication, and the first few weeks were awesome. What should have taken a year to accomplish I was able to do in three months. But it came at a cost. I stopped taking my medicine because I was gaining a tremendous amount of weight. Within time, I started to hate my boss because I felt that she was controlling me. Dorothy would insist that I run everything through her and that all correspondence would appear to come from her. I could abide by those terms, but the crap hit the fan when she shared with me that the regulations were clear that I was not supposed to have a company that provided the same service as the center because it was a conflict of interest. I reminded her that we discussed that before I came onboard. I was really resentful that though I was able to exceed her expectations and I did whatever she asked of me, she wanted to control my outside affairs too.

That was the straw that broke the camel's back. I became so frustrated that I met with her boss to complain. Fortunately, everyone loved the work that I was producing, but unfortunately, Dorothy became irate that I went around her. I did not care. By that time I was jokingly telling people that I was envisioning placing poison in my coffee that she made a point to drink every morning. I spent many nights murder plotting. According to an internet definition, murder plotting is an inactive thought of ending a life. Of course, I had no intentions of doing anything, but I was miserable working under her leadership. I started losing sleep and feeling trapped. I felt that I was able to get so much more done, but she started to get in my way.

Instead of addressing the matter with Dorothy as a rational adult or rather professional, I went to her boss's boss in DC to complain about her "inability" to manage. Now, don't get me wrong. Many people complained about her management style and lack of leadership, but I took it to a whole new level. I really thought that I could work around her. In a matter of months from the time I started, she asked me to resign. I obliged and contacted headquarters to let them know that I was available for any work that they may have wanted to contract out. Within two months, I was signed to a contract with headquarters to do a series of programs. I actually made more money over a couple of months working on an assignment in DC than I did as an employee in Atlanta. I was grateful for the opportunity and I worked very hard.

Interestingly, before I was fired from the position, I received a letter from Dorothy's boss's boss praising me for my work and the remarkable speed in which I was able to stand up a full-scale management and leadership program within three months when they anticipated it taking at least a year to do. As for Dorothy, we had bad blood between us. But a year later, during the holidays, I had a tradition of reconciling that brought us back together. I gave her a call to apologize for how I left the organization and for complaining about her. She broke down and through her tears she said, "I have known you a long time, and whatever I did to make you complain was partly my fault. I'm so glad that you called, and I'm sorry for how I treated you." That really made me feel good because I felt bad for how things had ended, but I also felt that I was pushed into a corner at that time. I completed my contracts with the headquarters and I moved on.

Reflecting on this period of my career, I can see that having medicine without any type of therapy was not effective. And I never bothered to learn about the nuances of bipolar disorder since I was in denial. I knew that the doctor said that I had bipolar disorder, but that meant nothing to me. I am not sure whether I was taking the right strength or kind of medicine since I did not have a psychiatrist regulate my medication. I just took something that would keep me even-keeled, but that obviously did not work, since I only took the medicine for a few weeks. I was very disruptive even though my work performance and productivity were astonishing. I often felt that nothing really should have mattered if I was getting the work done.

It is common knowledge that many people with bipolar disorder have a difficult time functioning in a structured work environment. I was no different. I really regretted that I damaged the relationship with Dorothy, my peer as a consultant, who became my boss on a job. If I could have been left alone to complete my work, I would have succeeded, but that is not the real work world. According to Dr. Fieve in his book *Bipolar II* (pg. 12), bipolar disorder is a complex genetic disorder characterized by dramatic or unusual mood swings between major depression and extreme elation, accompanied by disturbances in thinking, distortions or perception, and impairment in social functioning. The mood swings of bipolar disorder can range from very mild to extreme and can come on gradually or suddenly within minutes to hours.

The Personal Turning Point

My perception of being controlled became overwhelming and I acted irrationally. The real problem was that I stopped taking my medication, which is a classic problem for people with bipolar disorder. And I failed myself and everyone around me by choosing to be ignorant of my disorder. I lived life as if I was normal. After all, I believed I had had a normal life since I was a child. I took medication because I knew that I would become edgy, but I was suffering from something more than edginess. According to Dr. Fieve in his book *Bipolar II* (pg. 28), many patients stop treatment altogether, oftentimes within weeks after taking the medication, which can result in the mood soaring too high or falling too low, accompanied by suicidal ideation. Maybe if I had stayed on the medication prescribed by the psychiatrist I could have avoided a lot of the pain and discontent that I caused.

I continued to work hard at establishing relationships. I had formed a healthy relationship with Edward of the Browning Group, a small- to medium-size career and leadership development company. I aspired to be like Edward. As with many relationships, I maintained them at a distance. I started to become known for my government relationships and Edward wanted to get into that game.

I got a call from Edward one day. He wanted to meet over breakfast where he shared with me that he had heard some really good things about me and my company. He was interested in our collaborating. He offered me an opportunity to join his team but I knew that would not be in my best interest. I shared with Edward the benefits of owning a minority-owned company. I gave him a write-up on how the government had initiatives to conduct business with minority-owned companies.

After discussing what such a company would look like, Edward recommended that I meet with his leadership team. I went to Edward's office to meet with him and three of his company's executives several weeks later. He then offered to start a new company with me as the president after buying my company. This was huge, especially since my company was not worth much. This was an opportunity to be a part of something larger than what I was able to build. There were many opportunities for minority-owned companies at that time, and Edward was a white man who could not touch those set-asides. Through a joint relationship we could compete for government contracts together. He had the success and track record in growing his company, but he wanted to be able to compete for set-asides. I was all game, even when he proposed that I partner with another African-American gentleman who worked for him.

Things were moving rapidly. Edward arranged for me to meet Joe, who would be my partner in the new company. When Joe and I shook hands there was an instant bad feeling. I did not like Joe and he did not like me. We were led to a room where I guess Edward and his team thought we would consummate the deal.

"Indigo, can we start our meeting by saying a prayer? I will lead the prayer," Joe said as he prepared to bow his head.

"I do not pray before meetings. I'm sorry. I prefer to get right to business," I said and looked at him without blinking. That ruffled his feathers, and as he regained composure we talked about what percentage of ownership he would have and what percentage I would have in the new company. But that unraveled before it could be written on paper. "Joe, you have never owned a business. Do you really believe that half ownership is fair? I'm bringing products. What are you bringing?" I asked. He was flustered. He could not give me a rationale and tried to rely on what Edward and his team had shared with him, which was his senior experience in the industry. After a few minutes more of talking, we realized that we needed a mediator. We left the room and I went to Edward's office.

"We need to talk," I said as I stood in the doorway.

"Come in, Indigo. What's going on?" he asked, based on the frustration he saw on my face.

I explained that Joe and I could not agree on anything so Edward proposed that we all meet together. He assembled his team and Joe into a conference room. Before anyone could say anything, Joe blurted out, "I can't work with her. She's a heathen." I just sat there and looked at him as if he had two heads. Joe was so emotionally charged that he left the room. Everyone at the table was shocked and decided that we would continue to move forward, except with someone else. They attempted to partner me with another guy a week or two later, and that fell through as well. I was always the youngest person in the room, but I held my own and negotiated fair terms.

After a month of things not coming together, I asked whether I had to have a male partner or a partner at all. After all, I'd had my business as a sole proprietor for years. They expressed that a partner was their preference. Who was I to argue when it was their money to oversee this project and endeavor? I saw this as an opportunity to join something bigger than I had, and it was a chance to really start generating revenue. I started to think about people who could partner with me. I got it, I thought to myself. I made a phone call to an old friend and associate. "Hey, Mark. This is Indigo," I said with excitement. "How are things?" he asked. We exchanged small talk and I then jumped right into business. I felt proud that I could bring something to him since I considered him to be my mentor. I explained to him that the Browning Group wanted to start a new company that would be primarily minority-owned. Because of the Browning Group's size and reputation he was instantly interested. I further explained that I was tasked with finding a partner. I explained to him that they attempted to partner me with guys that they knew, but nothing had worked. Mark's biggest question was how much would something like this be worth. I did not have that answer or the answers to many of the questions he was shooting off. Unfortunately, I was not asking the right questions or getting enough information to make an informed decision. I slowed him down and proposed that we meet with the Browning Group to discuss this further, together. I honestly felt that leaving my company to join a group would be advantageous on so many levels. I was still relatively young and naïve, but I felt a sense of security by having Mark alongside me.

I wrote up the structure of the new company and wrote a quasi-business plan that I shared with everyone. Everyone was all in and ecstatic. About a week later, Mark and I met with the Browning Group. They loved Mark, and he really shined. This was great; I had found a partner they liked. They proposed that they would buy both of our companies, and we would form the new company. That meeting ended and Mark and I met the next day. It was time for us to decide what percentage we would both own in the new company. "I believe it should be a split with me getting 26 percent and you receiving 25 percent. We have to own at least 51 percent," I said with a smile. Mark's eyebrows furled as he said, "I was thinking a 30 to 21 split with me as the President." I was shocked. I did not feel that it was fair for him to get as much as I did when I brought him to the table. Besides that, he would make more money in the sale of his company, which then leveled the playing field for both of us. But he believed that since he was senior to me, had owned a company much longer than me, and offered more to the mix, that he should get more. When we could not come to an agreement, we went back to the Browning Group to let them know we were at an impasse.

While sitting at the table to discuss the next steps and how to move forward, Mark said out of nowhere, "I'm not sure that I'll be able to work with Indigo in a partnership. We have worked well on projects together, but a partnership may not work." I was flabbergasted. He started seeing dollar signs over our relationship. He then talked about the possibility of one person having 51 percent which would make a minority ownership still viable. What the hell, I thought to myself. He just worked towards cutting me out of the deal. What happened to our long-term friendship, trust, and integrity? He was my mentor, for goodness sake!

The Browning Group team asked if they could speak to me in private. I just knew that they were going to share their utter shock and disdain about Mark's suggestion. But instead, they agreed that Mark may be right that I was too difficult to work with. Edward mentioned how each attempt to partner me did not work, and that such an arrangement would not be in their best interest. I was so hurt. Just like that my deal was off the table and they decided to go with Mark.

I was leaving to walk to the parking lot when Mark stopped me to talk. "Indigo, this was not personal. This was about business. We were both going to lose this deal and so I tried to save it," he said, as if I could not see that he betrayed me.

"Mark, I brought you to the table," I said angrily.

"Indigo, can't you see? They kept picking men and older men at that. They wanted someone with whom they could have a peer-to-peer relationship. It was never going to work because you are too unseasoned, and, quite frankly, a woman," he said righteously.

I had never been so angry in my life. I walked off. I did not speak to Mark again, and I found out later that the deal that they were attempting to structure fell apart. What Mark did not know was that the Browning Group wanted to make sure that the company was minority-owned, and that no one person had the majority of shares besides Edward. Edward would have 49 percent ownership which meant he needed two people to split the 51 percent. I found this out much later, but I was still hurt by how I was discarded by Edward and betrayed by Mark.

I shared this story because it was another example of how I was actually reckless and there was betrayal. This time it came from two men whom I trusted and admired. In leading a company, there was always so much competition to worry about. People really did only think of themselves and became opportunistic when they thought for a second that they could get ahead and have it all. I did not trust easily which is why I brought an associate to the table. What I now realize is that someone with bipolar disorder takes unnecessary risks. I should have had things placed in a contract with the Browning Group before attempting to negotiate anything with a third party. I should have had a non-compete contract with Mark before taking him to the table. At that time in my life, I was very young and the guys were very seasoned. I was in my early 30s while they were in their fifties. I had a lot to learn. Mark was right about them wanting to have a peer-to-peer relationship. There were many things that I could have done differently. This shows how my journey was often

66

difficult as I attempted to grow the company through a variety of avenues.

The Browning Group stayed in touch with me, but nothing ever came of that relationship. I harbored true resentment about how they initially attempted to partner me with strangers and then had me bring someone to the table that they walked away with. I wish that they could have been honest with me from the beginning. If we would have been working from a standpoint of transparency, the deal could have possibly worked.

I had been off the medication for nearly a year. I was diagnosed as bipolar and still in denial, but I hated taking those damn drugs. I had been able to control my anger to some extent and my depression seemed regulated, as well. I was learning to accept disappointment, pace my emotions, and move on without storing the negative feelings. So I thought.

According to Kay Redfield Jamison in her book *Touched with Fire: Manic-Depressive Illness and the Artistic Temperament* (pg. 13), hypomanic or manic individuals usually have an inflated self-esteem, as well as a certainty of conviction about the correctness and importance of their ideas. This grandiosity can contribute to poor judgment, which, in turn, often results in chaotic patterns of personal and professional relationships. I felt that I was the central and key figure to the deal, which demonstrated grandiosity. As I met with potential partners, I thought that I brought more than everyone else; therefore, I was quintessential to a new company. It was my idea and I felt that I was correct in whatever I had to say on the matter. I missed a lot of signs along the way, and then I managed to destroy two relationships at one time. This situation fed into my paranoia which later developed into a fear whereby I always thought that people were out to get me or take advantage of me.

I continued working as a solopreneur, feeling that I had to protect myself at every turn. I eventually moved from my basement into a teeny-tiny office space that accommodated three people. I was not trying to hire an employee because I really did not have the revenue. But, as luck would have it, I called a peer at Blue University to help me with a spreadsheet and a problem. He was not in his office to help me, so I explained the purpose of my call to a work study student named Laura. I remember that Laura took an interest in my problem when I discussed it with her. She took my message, and she even gave me the solution to my problem and asked me to send my spreadsheet to her. I was shocked that she was able to help and more grateful that she did, in fact, help. I was used to helping others, but for someone to show me an act of kindness was refreshing.

Laura and I talked off and on for a couple of weeks and she shared with me that she was losing her job because the program she was working in was ending. Talk about perfect timing! I could afford her work study rate and she began working with me. The first few weeks were great, but over time I became agitated with her because she was, in effect, a student and I wanted more than she could offer. I needed a professional to help me, but I felt that I could not afford to hire someone with professional experience. I really struggled with trust issues and I was often paranoid. My greatest fear was that someone would copy or steal the many course materials and workbook designs that I had created. Because she was a Blue University student she knew technology far better than I and that kept me awake at night and paranoid.

Looking back, it was a matter of time before she would be fired. I was very detail oriented and self-reliant, but I began delegating things to Laura. I was working on a slide presentation to accompany a workbook as part of a session that I was delivering to a client. I realized that the colors were off and could not be seen, so I asked Laura to make the corrections for me before my next presentation. I arrived at my client site early, as usual, to set up the room for my workshop. I scrolled through the presentation and noticed that many of the pertinent corrections were not done; thus, my slide presentation was not really useable. At the time, I was not as technically savvy as Laura, so I was stuck with what she gave me.

"Laura, did you make those corrections that I asked of you?" I asked her when I called the office. I knew the answer, but I wanted to hear what she had to say.

"Yes, I did," she said with confidence.

"No, you did not!" I yelled. I explained to her that I was looking at the presentation and that some important parts were left out and corrections were not made. I was irate, to say the least, because I liked for everything to be perfect. I was a perfectionist who prided herself on giving clients only the best.

"I assure you that I did make the changes," she stated as I hung up to get ready for my class.

All day I obsessed over the inaccuracies and the fact that she lied by saying that she made the corrections. When I arrived at the office that evening, she placed a copy of the presentation on my desk which showed that the corrections were made. I was annoyed. This was exactly what I needed, but she sent me to a client site with something that wasn't usable. I was certain that she had not made the changes. I went into my office and I could tell that she had been on my computer where the course materials were stored. I accused her of going on my computer and changing the document. She denied being on my computer, but I was confident that I was right. The next day upon her arrival to work, I fired Laura.

This would be the beginning of a long line of employees who would come and go. My paranoia got the best of me. Even though I still contend that she changed the document, I'm not too sure that firing her was fair. I was still feeling wounded after what happened at Managed Results with Pam who went on my computer and deleted something years ago. I guess that I just could not let go of being tricked by Pam to the extent that anything that looked like an effort to mislead me would be met with negative consequences.

According to Kay Redfield Jamison in her book *Touched with Fire: Manic-Depressive Illness and the Artistic Temperament* (pg. 13), during hypomania and mania, mood is generally elevated and expansive (or, not infrequently, paranoid and irritable); activity and energy levels are greatly increased; the need for sleep is decreased; speech is often rapid, excitable, and intrusive; and thinking is fast, moving quickly from topic to topic. I was working at a rabbit's pace in nearly everything that I did; however, there was a profound sense of paranoia. I became suspicious of everyone. This certainly caused my company to grow at a much slower rate than I anticipated. It would take me days to make a decision for fear of trusting people and circumstances.

My ticket to DC to expand my practice

Around 2000, I received a phone call from a past client at the U.S. Protection Council. I had developed and conducted a workshop for a client named Helen years ago when she worked in Atlanta. Helen had been promoted to a Senior Executive Service position and was now working in Washington, DC. She wanted me to deliver the same program in DC that I delivered to her employees in Atlanta years ago.

I completed that task and my name spread like a wildfire and I began working in other parts of the U.S. Protection Council in DC. Eventually I started working in different agencies in DC. For several years everything was coming together and my business was growing. I was networking, creating programs, and taking advantage of limitless opportunities. However, things came to a halt when I was working on a new project with Helen's group. I was tasked with creating a mentoring program for her branch. I worked really hard on customizing the program and on working with a team that consisted of attorneys, experts, etc. As I was completing the project, I requested that the team review everything so that I could make any and all final changes to the course work before going to print. After a week of trying to make sure everything was fine and working closely with the team, I had the materials printed and shipped to the client site. I then sent a consultant to DC to deliver the session.

To my surprise, I found out that the client changed a few pages in our book. I did not mind the changes. What was upsetting for me was that each page that they inserted in our customized and copyrighted book was subpar. The workbook did not reflect the level of professionalism or polished look that I was accustomed to delivering. Some of the changed pages were actually embarrassing. I blew up at the team and complained about what I felt was a disrespectful act and I said that their act was copyright infringement. Well, telling attorneys that they broke the law will certainly get their attention.

This created such a backlash that I was unable to do work with Helen's group again. I basically got into trouble for wanting to give them the best product. Or rather, I got into trouble for overreacting. I guess the way that I handled it was very disruptive.

This is yet another example of how I lost a client because I became agitated and retaliated. The fighter in me would be awakened when I felt that I or my company was being treated unfairly. As happy-go-lucky and accommodating as I could be in working with clients, I could become hostile and volatile in resolving issues. According to Dr. Ronald Fieve in his book *Bipolar II* (pg. 58), when a Bipolar II patient experiences hypomania, it is not always a pleasurable high, particularly when behaviors include being hot-tempered or argumentative. For every two steps that I took forward, it would seem that I would take a step back. My behavior drastically altered my growth and success in the U.S. Protection Council. Dr. Fieve (pg. 128) goes on to say that impulsivity, or the failure to resist an internal drive or stimulus, drives many Bipolar II patients into risky behaviors, and many often regret the action after it is over. I was like a train wreck. I could not stop myself and no one was able to talk me out of approaching my client in a hostile manner. I felt that I was protecting my company's interest, but my perception was skewed.

I continued to do some work in different parts of the agency, but not nearly to the same extent. Reflecting on this situation brings back painful memories. According to Dr. Fieve in his book *Bipolar II* (pg. 141), many hypomanics are outspoken and often irritable to the point of being downright rude or abusive. They can also screw all of it up impulsively by dropping the ball or being discourteous to the wrong person.

The Personal Turning Point

I stepped on one too many toes that time. It was one thing to fall out of grace with peers, but losing a client because of my erratic behavior was a whole new level of crazy. After this incident my name was basically blackballed as someone who was difficult to work with within that agency. This was unfortunate considering that was one incident out of many positive experiences within the agency. I had worked in many parts of the agency conducting a plethora of services, and this one incident changed all that. In fact, I almost lost a dear friend who was also my client as a result of working many years at that agency. She called me on my cell phone to share her disappointment with me. That was probably the most difficult part of losing the client, in general. I had let them down in terms of their expectations of me. I hated that I often could not control myself and would destroy relationships. Unfortunately, I was not on any medication, and having bipolar disorder was the furthest thing from my mind. It was as if I was never diagnosed as bipolar, even though my behavior revealed otherwise. Dr. Jamison states, in her book *Touched with Fire: Manic-Depressive Illness and the Artistic Temperament* (pg. 16), that manic-depressive illness, often seasonal, is recurrent by nature; left untreated, individuals with this disease can expect to experience many, and generally worsening, episodes of depression and mania. It seemed that each incident was a greater disappointment and more severe than the last; however, I was not on medication nor did I feel that I needed help. As far as I was concerned, I was an eccentric and quirky entrepreneur. It was everyone around me that was the problem. I focused more on what I was able to produce and achieve versus how I engaged people when I was either hypomanic or depressed.

Self-medicating to keep up with myself

Fortunately, I had several small contracts that sustained my company. I completed the U.S. Protection Council project and chalked up that experience as yet another lesson learned. I was finally bringing in enough money to hire staff. I then hired several months later another employee whom I liked a lot. Kathryn was my first real office manager. We would travel together quite a bit and she made it okay to have liquor in our drawer back in the office. We would go to lunch and have drinks to the extent that we would come back from lunch and I would need to take a nap. I was still working very hard, but I was self-medicating with alcohol. That should have been a red flag, but it felt natural. Work like a mad man and take a swig of vodka. I did not have a drinking problem at all, because I would never get drunk or drink to excess, but I found that I wanted to drink to take the edge off, occasionally.

As Dr. Fieve explains in his book *Bipolar II* (pg. 111), other experts contend that the risky behaviors are related to the patient trying to self-medicate his or her various moods, realizing that sex, alcohol, or recreational drugs, and even high-risk financial acts, can fan the fire of hypomania or numb the lows of depression. I should have realized that something was wrong with our drinking while on the clock, but I was what the doctor said that I was: bipolar. I was drinking to deal with the lows of the company and my mood swings. In hindsight, I never saw my drinking as a problem, but rather a relief from my often hectic day. According to Nassir Ghaemi in his book *A First-Rate Madness: Uncovering the Links Between Leadership and Mental Illness in Times of Crisis* (pg. 63), people with bipolar disorder often abuse alcohol. When they're depressed, anxious, and restless, alcohol soothes them; when they're manic and they can't control their impulses, alcohol serves them—along with sex and spending—as an appetite to be indulged. I found myself drinking, not only at work, but when I would get home I would make myself a martini to prepare dinner and then have a glass of wine to help me fall asleep at bedtime. I never ever believed that I abused alcohol, but then again maybe I did.

Many years ago, I even found myself asking people such as my kids, husband, and employees for their leftover prescription pills. I was very open about my desire to take the pills as a way of relaxing. Oddly enough, I refused to take medicine for headaches and things like that but I would want to indulge in prescription drugs occasionally. I had no idea where that desire came from since I didn't get high as a practice. I would take these pills along with a drink to relax my mind that often raced like a car in the Indianapolis 500. I often felt bad about how I treated my employees, especially Kathryn, whom I really loved and cared about. I needed something to feel better, especially on the weekends after I worked long hours during the week. I wouldn't take these pills often, just every now and then. According to Dr. Fieve in his book *Bipolar II* (pg. 128), when a person is hypomanic and wants to go even "higher," he may turn to stimulants, painkillers such as Oxycontin (oxycodone HCL) or Vicodin (hydrocodone-acetaminophen), cocaine, diet pills, or caffeine. But that came to an end many years later when I got terribly sick while I was alone in a hotel room and vowed to never do it again. The room was spinning, I was nauseous, my heart was beating rapidly, and I couldn't stop sweating. This broke me of that habit. But over the years, it never occurred to me that I was mixing drugs and alcohol to self-medicate. As far as I was concerned, I did not do illegal drugs such as marijuana, cocaine, or things like that. I simply took a painkiller with wine or something chic like a martini. I now know that I was being characteristic of someone suffering from bipolar disorder.

An employee as a security blanket

As much as I loved Kathryn and had fun with her, unfortunately, she would make rookie mistakes which would infuriate me. I found myself becoming very irritated with her within time. She was great from five to nine, but not so much nine to five. I did not want to fire her because we had fun, but her performance was not giving me what I needed. She would make me laugh when things went wrong. But that was not enough . . . I needed someone who could help me grow the company. I really liked Kathryn and I wanted her employment to work. She often helped protect me from the other employees. I was, in fact, crazy and she worked around it. I was very moody and she was able to either clean up my mess or talk me down from blowing up with clients. Then there would be days she would simply run interference by not transferring calls, etc. Kathryn helped to insulate me, which was helpful and invaluable. She was unable to help me with some of my clients at whom I would lash out when I experienced episodes. Unfortunately, what I would learn years later is that my bipolar disorder is accompanied by rage. She shielded me from the outside world and often absorbed my abuse, but she couldn't keep me from entering the dark cave and the darkness that often surrounded me.

I really needed to believe that I was not bipolar because of the stigma, but the reality of it slapped me squarely in the face one day without warning. I wanted to surprise my husband one Saturday afternoon. I had always been a prankster, so when I heard his car pull into the garage as I was watching television in our bedroom, I quickly grabbed a tray from where I had finished lunch, slid it under the bed, turned off the TV, and I crawled under the bed to hide. I planned to wait for him to come into the room then jump out and yell, "Surprise." I was known to do the same thing around the office by hiding under my desk or behind doors and jumping out. For some strange reason, I loved startling people and seeing everyone laugh. Well, on this day I was the one who got startled. I heard Curtis climb the stairs as he was talking on his cell phone with his cousin. He sat on the bed under which I was hiding. "Ann, I'm tired. She is crazy," he said to his cousin. There was a brief bit of silence, and he said, "She's bipolar and I do not know how much more I can take." There was another pause of silence as Ann spoke. "I told my mom, but no one else knows," he said.

I felt my heart sink. Here was the man whom I trusted, and he betrayed me by telling his cousin that I was crazy. If you tell anyone then you told everyone was what I thought. I was certain that his entire family knew and thought that I was crazy. When he hung up from his conversation, he changed clothes and went downstairs. I slid from under the bed and made my way to the kitchen. I was "fit to be tied." I waited a few days and then I confronted him. He denied telling anyone that I was bipolar, but I had my own proof, and I just let him think that he got away with a lie instead of telling him that I was under the bed eavesdropping on his conversation. I moved to the guest bedroom to sleep after I confronted him. That was the beginning of a marriage that was headed for divorce, which is a common occurrence with people who have bipolar disorder.

According to Dr. Fieve in his book *Bipolar II* (pg. 13), "most patients initially ignore treatment and experience a second episode of hypomania or fall into a major depression, which is often more intense and occurs sooner than the second one did, and may result in a spouse leaving or family members turning away from the person altogether. As life progresses and episodes recur without stabilization, the prognosis for unmanaged mood swings is not nearly so good as the first episode. That is why education, early diagnosis, and effective treatment of the Bipolar II patient with medications that stabilize mood prevent the worsening of the illness that would otherwise occur." I did nothing to change my condition but rather sulked at the thought that my husband had revealed my diagnosis. I could not accept that I was bipolar and I certainly did not want anyone reminding me that such was in fact true. However, things were worsening over the years. I really should have learned what bipolar meant and what impact it would and could have on my life. But all I knew was that it was a mental illness and I would not be a crazy person no matter what anyone said.

Chapter 5

Moving from an Entrepreneur to a Small Business Owner

In 2004, the pages on my business were turning and I turned 40. For the first time I felt like an adult. I was now at a point where I could start hiring more employees. This was great; however, I could not afford top talent. I often had to hire people who did not meet the qualifications of the job, but were affordable. This is when the proverbial revolving door was installed at my company. I found that having more than one person around me at all times was very taxing. I hired two more employees and business was going pretty well. Kathryn was instrumental in keeping balance in the office. As her performance improved, she became my go-to person. When I would be in a negative mood she would run interference with the other employees. I found that the employees would go to Kathryn to complain about me. I was hard on them and would expect them to work at the same level that I worked. Often when I would coach or counsel the employees they would be in actual tears. I could not understand why they were crying all the time. But I continued to be very demanding and, unfortunately, engaging them without filters. Filters are something that people who are experiencing a shift in their moods seem to lack. We can and often do say things that simply come to our minds without taking into account how we may affect others. In fact, I studied Emotional Intelligence (EQ), and I understand the benefits of connecting with people: however, when I was either manic or depressed, I communicated with no EQ because my filters were down. So this, coupled with a dogged mentality to produce results, was a combustible combination.

In hindsight, I can see that I wanted my employees to be like entrepreneurs. I wanted them to work as hard as I did and to see things that I saw effortlessly. I could see a solution ten steps ahead of the employees and I would become frustrated that they did not see what I saw. I found myself belittling them for being normal. Having bipolar disorder gave me an edge in how I saw things. I learned along the way that people with bipolar disorder can usually think ten steps ahead of people. It's a crazy ability that often leads to frustration. I find myself sharing information that others cannot see or understand, and the more I try to get them to see it the more I start feeling as if they lack insight. Years later, I recall my primary psychiatrist sharing with me how quick of a thinker and insightful a person who is bipolar can be, and that answered a lot of concerns and questions, but far too late in the game. If an employee seemed slow in his ability to pick up on things or to produce at the crazy rate that I was able to produce, I would fire him. Finally, Kathryn started coaching employees on how to survive me. For the most part, I was caring and giving, but when my mood changed as quickly as the temperature on a summer evening, I was very harsh and hard on the employees. Kathryn remained vigilant and would try to help the other employees, but I would get rid of them within a matter of weeks or months, all the while attempting to push them to excellence through tough love and sometimes abuse, depending on my mood.

Wanting out of this world

Over time, I simply burned myself out. I wanted success so badly that I was working everyday with little to no sleep. In fact, I had a pull-out couch placed in my office for the nights when it did not make sense to go home only to come back in the wee hours of the morning. One Sunday, like all other Sundays, I went to work earlier that morning, but when I went home I crawled into bed. I had been watching television most of the day and relaxing. I had been in and out of sleep. I kept thinking about suicide by taking an overdose of sleeping pills and ending it all. I had suicidal ideations dating back to my teenage years. But the only problem, in my mind, was religion and social beliefs. I was afraid of being punished if I checked out of this world on my own. But that seemed so damn unfair to me. Why should it matter? I would think to myself. I just wanted out.

For the first time in a long time, I was not mad, sad, or anything. I was just tired of trying. I really felt like I could go home, wherever home was, and leave this life of struggle behind me. I just knew that I no longer wanted to be a part of this world. I wished that I could do it. I wished that I had the courage. I just did not see the sense in living. Maybe this would pass, I thought to myself, and was what I wrote in my journal.

According to Dr. Fieve in his book *Bipolar II* (pg. 28), bipolarity has one of the highest suicide rates of all mental illnesses—an extraordinary 10 to 20 percent of unmedicated bipolar patients, as estimated by the National Institute of Mental Health. Again, I did not attribute my suicidal ideation to bipolar disorder even though that is a significant characteristic of having bipolar disorder. I just knew that I was tired of working so hard and feeling so depressed even when things were going well. I was tired of hiring employees that did not work out. It was becoming too difficult for me to understand. I just wanted out.

Nassir Ghaemi makes an interesting point in his book *A First-Rate Madness: Uncovering the Links between Leadership and Mental Illness in Times of Crisis* (pg. 13), that in the worst-case scenario, the depressed person takes her life, the manic ruins hers. In manic-depressive illness, one suffers from both tragic risks. I was both suicidal and ruining my life. But I was unable to come to terms with having bipolar disorder, especially since I really did not know what it meant.

Putting to paper what I've learned

In 2006, I was 42 years old with an old spirit and wisdom beyond my years. I still did not see me as the problem; the problem was due to the employees that I hired. I decided to write a book. Even though I was at the center of all of the previous dismissals in my life, I could truly see that there was a significant problem with the workforce. I had a keen insight into what many employees lacked based on my HR consulting experience. My company had become a source of inspiration for my book. After I came out of my deep depression, I took a week off to go to an island and just write.

It literally took me a week to write *Playing by the Unwritten Rules: Moving from the Middle to the Top*. Being hypomanic, I worked into the wee hours of the morning and all day and night. The words poured out of me. I wrote about things that I learned along the way and then I focused on all the things that employees did incorrectly. This was easy to do. I had now spent a couple of years observing employees in my company and at several client sites. Things that I thought that they should know, but did not, fascinated me. I wrote the book in a week, but it took several months of editing for the book to be completed. I shopped the book to past and current clients. The book sold extremely well because decision makers could identify with the topics. The very things that I wrote about were often taboo for them to discuss with their employees. My clients had a tool that could speak on their behalf without repercussions. My book sales ranged from one to 1,000 books per order. Agencies bought my book by the thousands and I was asked to speak about and design workshops around the book.

Eventually, Kathryn resigned for a better paying job and we remained friends. Even today we are close. We now laugh about my past antics. I asked her once if she knew that something was wrong with me, and she explained that she not only knew that something was mentally wrong with me, but that she loved me because she saw the good in me despite my mood changes. Interestingly, many of the people who had been fired remained in touch with me. I did not just fire employees without cause or some level of empathy. I would pinpoint their problems and reveal to them areas of weakness that they were unaware of. This was probably unfair because I had more of an advantage by my being their boss. I was bipolar and not on medication, which also gave me keen insight. I saw things that the average person would miss. When I dismissed employees they were hurt but they had new insight on what to improve upon. Often, I had employees say that they learned a lot from me during their short time with me. This was due to me always being in the performance consulting mode. I would analyze, diagnose, and recommend change.

However, terminating employees quickly was only the half of it. I also found that my leadership skills were terrible. I would treat employees the way that I was treated in the Marine Corps. I wanted them to be the best of the best from dress to execution. I was yelled at in the Corps, which I now realize was an old school way of leading. The command and control method was all that I knew. I was young in the military and when I got out, many of my managers were laissez-faire. I did not have access to a lot of "leaders." This caused me to overmanage employees. I found myself attempting to break them down to build them up, which is what makes the Marine Corps so effective. This was what I learned in the Corps. However, no one joined my organization to enlist into my madness. Ironically, hardly anyone ever wanted to leave, because when things were good the company was a great place to work. I would treat employees with love and genuine concern as if they were the most important part of the company. But when I was moody I would become irate with them and that included yelling, cursing, and throwing fits. How could this be such a duality? I had a Jekyll and Hyde persona that drew people close to me but I pushed them away as they got too close. As Dr. Fieve states in his book *Bipolar II* (pg. 25), the Bipolar II Jekyll and Hyde transformations can be painful and totally disruptive to everyone. No one in my world was unaffected. I impacted everyone either positively or negatively. There was no neutral place to stand in my world.

I had forgotten all about the bipolar diagnoses. I just saw myself as someone who was managing a company and trying to grow a business. I had moments and periods of true elation and I felt invincible. However, I never saw myself as a leader or as someone who was leading a company. I thought of myself as a quirky entrepreneur and I was attempting to hire people who could support me. As Dr. Fieve states in his book *Bipolar II* (pg. 18), hypomania is a far more productive, active period that is usually associated with highly successful individuals—those who are highly ambitious overachievers and entrepreneurs. I truly regarded myself as an entrepreneur more so than a leader. Through my research I discovered that many small businesses fail because of a lack of leadership. I theorize that what often happens is that entrepreneurs and people with mental disorders do not fare very well in a structured environment or corporate America, so they strike out on their own. Unfortunately, they leave before they reach a leadership track, which means an organization has not invested in them by taking them through leadership development. This comes back to haunt them when they have to lead in their own company. The very thing that they ran away from catches up with them. They start to notice the games that are played in organizations—company politics and the less desirable duty of being responsible for others. This usually causes them to fail miserably in many ways.

I started to speak at conferences and at venues for my clients who held special events. I would speak on topics from my book with so much passion and zeal that people started to take notice. I traveled around the country speaking in small- to medium-size venues. My presentation was unique in that I would sometimes employ antics such as faking a faint and bringing members of the audience on stage for a variety of demonstrations. I was very animated and colorful in my word choice in the stories that I would tell. I was loved by the masses. The book sold at an incredible rate, and I loved what I did as a speaker. My presentations were more of a performance. This opened up opportunities for my company to provide products and services as add-on contracts to my speaking engagements.

An interesting relationship developed between my speaking engagements and my company's training and development products and services. One would often create opportunities for the other. I believe my having bipolar disorder allowed for me to present in such a creative way that I was more like an actress than a speaker. I came alive when I was on the stage. It was as if I was taken over by another life force that allowed me to see things differently and share with the audience uninhibited stories. I introduced my clients and readers to a new way of looking at things. I talked about a problem that many people did not know existed. This allowed me to become an expert in performance consulting.

According to Nassir Ghaemi his book *A First-Rate Madness: Uncovering the Links between Leadership and Mental Illness in Times of Crisis* (pg. 38), for leaders in any realm, creativity is not just about solving old problems with new solutions; it's about finding new problems to solve. Mania enhances both aspects of creativity: the divergence of thought allows one to identify new problems, and the intense energy keeps one going until the problems are solved. My book and many of the projects that I was starting to work on were original and creative. They exposed people to problems that they did not know even existed, but I gave solutions to these problems. I became known for bringing into the forefront that which often mystified a decision maker. My hypomania served me well with my clients. But I bounced between hypomania and depression regularly over several years. According to Ronald Fieve in his book *Bipolar II* (pg. 52), many patients with Bipolar I and Bipolar II experience major depression where they are in a depressed mood most of the day, for weeks, or months at a time. I found myself in deep depressions that seemed unending. I only found relief when I was on stage presenting. That is where I would be on automatic pilot.

Years came and went and I was still running through employees, not feeling or seeing that anything was wrong. I'm not talking about hundreds of employees, but one or two here and there over the course of several months. I was in darkness, but I felt like I was in the light when I would perform, so I did not realize anything was wrong. It was not until a few years ago when an employee who saw me speak to a group was hired to work for the company. Everything was fine the first two months or so, but I became increasingly irritated with him, as I had with other employees. The routine was almost cyclical. I would hire, become annoyed, and fire within a three-month time frame. This employee was talking to one of the other employees and he expressed that I was nothing like what I projected when I addressed an audience.

It was a true duality. When I dealt with an audience I was alive, happy, and insightful, but back at the office I was brooding, irritable, and constantly upset. I never felt that anyone could give me what I needed, especially at the pace that I needed it. He was eventually fired, but he did not go away quietly into the night. He filed a claim against the company with the Department of Labor. They investigated, but nothing came of it. However, that was a wake-up call to be careful with employees who could and would file grievances and lawsuits. I often gave a small severance pay or something to make amends even when a termination was completely justified. And, in my opinion, all the terminations were justified. But this guy was lazy and would not work the hours that he was scheduled. Fortunately, I was able to document his insubordination, which helped prove my case. But I then realized that I could not keep hiring and firing without consequences. That frightened me because I now had to be concerned with the Department of Labor monitoring me, which felt like control to me.

Unfortunately, knowing and doing are two different things. I knew that I had to be careful how I treated employees, but having bipolar disorder doesn't allow you to always control your emotions or do what your mind says is the right thing to do. I would still hire employees and sometimes treat them less than favorably. According to Dr. Ronald Fieve in his book *Bipolar II* (pg. 135), most hypomanics do not like anything or anyone to be slow, from their cabdrivers to their administrative assistants to the waiters at their favorite restaurants. They are genetically wired to move fast, think fast, and talk fast, and in so doing, they sometimes irritate those around them. Hypomanics want results, and they want them now.

I simply wanted from my employees what they were reasonably unable to deliver. I wanted them to be like me when I was hypomanic. No one could live up to my expectations. And looking back, this has been the case since working in a structured environment and being fired from the school just prior to starting my own business. I would work through the days "never" taking a lunch break except to meet with clients. In general, I worked throughout the day only drinking coffee. I did everything fast from talking to walking, and the average person simply could not keep up with my pace. My daily work schedule was 6:45 a.m. to 6:45 p.m. and a few hours over the weekend. Not to mention the nights or rather mornings I would arrive at 3 or 4 a.m. because I couldn't sleep. I lived, breathed, and ate my company, and I resented that my employees would not and could not do the same. So I would become abusive towards those who worked outside my perception of high performance and skewed reality.

I received a couple of calls and letters from the Department of Labor because I worsened in my behavior and employees that were being fired complained. By this time, I had in place two people. I had other employees but I fired most of them in one day. It seemed that two employees were all that my temperament could seem to handle, but their employment did not come without bittersweet tears. I still have with me an employee by the name of Frances who was with me during the time Kathryn worked with me. She learned a lot over the past few years in how to deal with me.

Over the years, I have had so many office managers that I cannot remember their names or faces. But one stands out as I think about her. I was now making enough money to place an advertisement in the local paper to recruit possible candidates and pay a competitive rate. Frances was good at what she did, but she was no office manager. That was when we interviewed Sabrina, who was an excellent candidate. Sabrina worked in higher education and she was a lay minister for her church. She was someone who could be trusted. She had the kindest smile and she really took pride in her work. I finally had someone who could take care of the company's finances and do the things that I did not care to do. I was more interested in getting the business and doing the work rather than focusing on the operational tasks. I was constantly traveling somewhere (mostly DC) every week for the past five months or so. I was tired and getting worn down. Business was good, and I hired a great right-hand person when I hired Sabrina, but as with everyone else, I did not trust her initially. And, as usual, I would hire other people but within a matter of a month or two it would be back to Frances and Sabrina in our small office.

As we began to grow, I was able to expand into the office space adjoining my office. This gave us more room and subconsciously that gave me the ability to hire a third person who could last. So we interviewed people for a position that would allow that person to do many different things in the small business. But it never worked. The honeymoon phase would be blissful, but soon after someone's arrival I would become distant and irritable. But Sabrina made it through the honeymoon phase and I began to trust her completely. After a year or so, things began to unravel as Sabrina returned to college to finish her degree and she could never work weekends because she was a minister. This became an issue when she was unable to accompany me to out-of-town conferences or speaking engagements. It just seemed that she had become more defiant in not working the hours needed and this was just when I was starting to see things turn around in my company. I needed Sabrina and Frances to pick up their pace.

In 2009, I was 45 years old, still finding my way, but leading many through my presentations, seminars, and workshops. Around this time I also completed my second book *Playing by the Unwritten Rules: From a Job Defense to a Career Offense.* This book took a few weeks to complete and it was much more extensive than the first book. As indicated by Kay Redfield Jamison in her book *Touched with Fire: Manic-Depressive Illness and the Artistic Temperament* (pg. 105), two aspects of thinking, in particular, are pronounced in both creative and hypomanic thought: fluency, rapidity, and flexibility of thought on the one hand, and the ability to combine ideas or categories of thought in order to form new and original connections on the other. My book took an analogy of sports and equated that with the workplace. It was a very unique and creative concept that took off in the federal government like a brush fire. I was starting to speak on the book and even gain media attention. I can now attribute my success in this area to having bipolar disorder, but at the time, I was just doing my job and sharing with the masses what I thought was insightful.

I became more and more demanding with Sabrina and Frances. There were other employees, but they were truly in the background. One day I was cleaning the bathroom and I picked up a soap dispenser that I discovered was broken and glued back together. What was troubling about this was that my office was designed with a personal touch in every room. My office looked more like an upscale condo than an office. There were tasteful pictures, a lot of art work, and contemporary pieces around the office. I had always felt that if you had to be somewhere most of your time, that place should be aesthetically pleasing. When I saw that the glass soap dispenser, which was really nice, had been broken, I asked Frances and Sabrina if they knew how the soap dispenser got broken. They both denied knowing anything about the dispenser. But when I pressed the issue, Sabrina confessed to breaking the dispenser.

"I did not tell you because I did not want you to get upset," she remarked as if that was a reasonable excuse to hide something from me.

"But I have the right to get upset if something of mine is broken," I said with intensity and added, "You do not have the right to choose what I can and cannot be emotional about." I was so upset that I went to my office, slammed the door, and cried. I did not want them to see how upset I was over the dispenser because it was more than just the dispenser to me. I felt that if someone was willing to hide a soap dispenser, for God's sake, what else would they hide from me?

I obsessed over the soap dispenser and started wondering what else could be going on right under my nose. I grabbed my purse and briefcase and left for the day. On my way home, I called nearly everyone in my support circle to get their opinions on how I was feeling. Very often, I did not understand my feelings or know what was or was not a real emotion, so I often bounced ideas off people. Everyone, except one person, thought that I was overreacting. "Indigo," they would say, "It's a soap dispenser. Let it go." But I could not; I felt betrayed and fooled again. As usual, I obsessed over the act of Sabrina hiding the broken dispenser for the next few days. It was yet another betrayal in my opinion.

Several months passed by, and I was still conducting one- to two-day workshops, but we were on the brink of getting a contract that would allow us to conduct week-long sessions at a substantial profit. I started writing more and more proposals for substantial contracts. I came across a Request for Proposal with the Department of Correctness. This proposal had a due date for the Tuesday after Martin Luther King's birthday. I remember that time period vividly because this was an opportunity for us to possibly win a contract that would move us several steps beyond where we were residing. I told Frances and Sabrina that they needed to work that weekend and plan to work that Monday although they planned on taking the holiday off. They moaned and groaned, but I was insistent. I just knew that we had a good chance of winning that contract. It was a gut feeling that I had and I was often right when it came to my intuition. They explained to me that they had plans to travel. They tried to appeal to my more empathetic side, but to no avail. I pretty much threatened them that it was either come to work and help me get the proposal out of the door or they would be terminated. Frances showed up, but Sabrina did not. She did not answer her phone on Monday, either. So I had to call a family member to come in and support us.

When I arrived the next day, I called Sabrina into my office. She showed up as if nothing happened. I was prepared to reprimand her, but she tendered her resignation. I was surprised to say the least, but she explained, "I have other plans that would get in the way of what you are trying to accomplish here. I'm preaching more on Sundays at my church and I simply need to be able to concentrate on that and school." I accepted her resignation and asked, "Would you be interested in contract work until I could fill your position or as a long-term option?" She seemed to like the idea, but she never came back once she left the office.

I needed to move on and replace Sabrina. I did not seem fazed by these events. As mentioned by Kay Redfield Jamison in her book *Touched with Fire: Manic-Depressive Illness and the Artistic Temperament* (pg. 18), the depressive, or melancholic, states are characterized by a morbidity and flatness of mood along with a slowing down of virtually all aspects of human thought, feeling, and behavior that are most personally meaningful. Either I didn't care or I was too tired to care. So I called a fellow business woman who owned a temp company. She sent over an accountant to take care of my monthly reconciling. After a few days of the accountant being in my books she came to my office and knocked on the open door.

"Excuse me, Indigo," she said as she walked into my office. "You have a problem," she said holding a ledger.

Now what? I thought to myself.

"It seems that Sabrina had been stealing from you," she said with certainty.

I could not believe it. I asked, "Stealing what? She would show me everything and I kept the check book."

"She was obviously showing you one spreadsheet that had the taxes, but when she would submit things to the IRS she would back out the taxes and pocket that money for herself."

It was a complicated embezzlement scheme that she explained to me. I could not understand how Sabrina did it or that she would do it. Yes, she broke the soap dispenser and hid it, but embezzlement was a bird of different feather! I hired a temporary office manager to replace Sabrina and to work with the accountant. She confirmed the same thing. I was hoping that the accountant was wrong and was simply trying to make a name for herself, but Sabrina did, in fact, embezzle from the company. Interestingly, I felt that something was being kept secret and wrong when I discovered the soap dish months earlier. My intuition said to me at that time that the hiding of a broken item went beyond a soap dish and that this was a wake-up call to watch Sabrina. I should have listened to myself. I kept saying to myself and others that if she would hide a stupid soap dish what else was she hiding, and everyone told me to let it go. Now here I was in trouble with the IRS, and I had to get my actual CPA involved who was able to sort out how Sabrina actually embezzled. He contacted the IRS, but it was too late. We ended up owing thousands of dollars in back taxes, fines, and penalties. This was a horrible and stressful time for the company and me. Through it all, Sabrina had the nerve to apply for unemployment.

Several weeks passed and I hired a full-time permanent office manager named London. London was responsible for dealing with the books to get them straight based on input from the temporary office manager and accountant. She was also responsible for making sure Sabrina did not see a penny from unemployment. London had a rough first month. It was incredible that she even survived. I had little to no trust in people, any more, which made it very difficult for us to work together. It seemed that whenever I would let down my guard, I would get burned. London was efficient and knew how to save me money and tap into resources that no one else did up to that point. She was a godsend. Then she had to go down to the Department of Labor to defend our position against Sabrina. To London's surprise, Sabrina approached her at the hearing and said, "No one lasts at that company. It is just a matter of time before she fires you, too." That ruffled London's feathers, but she stayed focused and won the case.

Now, the next step in closing the chapter to Sabrina was in effect. London met with IRS agents who came to our office to investigate Sabrina who, ironically, did something dishonest somewhere else. We never got the whole story because the investigator was not at liberty to say, but a case was being built against her by the IRS. That whole ordeal really took me aback. Just when I started trusting again, I was betrayed, and this time from someone whom I loved. There was nothing that I would not do for Sabrina. I could only believe that maybe things were so bad in terms of my mood that she felt justified in taking from me. I could not begin to understand how someone steals from their employer, especially in a way that created a lot of harm. But I survived that crisis and moved cautiously forward with the team I had in place.

According to Nassir Ghaemi in his book *A First-Rate Madness: Uncovering the Links between Leadership and Mental Illness in Times of Crisis* (pg. 4), depression makes leaders more realistic and empathetic, and mania makes them more creative and resilient. Depression can occur by itself, and can provide some of these benefits. When it occurs along with mania—bipolar disorder—even more leadership skills can ensue. This was truly a test of leadership. I had to slow down and become methodical in my thinking and logical in my reasoning. I believe that I was able to remain calm and collected during this time of crisis based on my having bipolar disorder.

Just when I was ready to throw in the towel

I was still battling with depression so much so that I started taking medication again. It was easy to admit that I was depressed to my primary doctor, but that did not get to the real heart of the matter. Interestingly, I was taking antidepressant pills and I could see a definite improvement in how I responded and reacted to things, but there was still darkness all around me. I was crying and constantly sad, even wishing I were dead. According to Nassir Ghaemi in his book *A First-Rate Madness: Uncovering the Links between Leadership and Mental Illness in Times of Crisis* (pg. 12), suicidal thoughts occur in about half of clinical depressive episodes. I was experiencing a true depressive episode with no idea that it was attributed to bipolar disorder. I continue to emphasize this fact to drill in the dangers of denial and ignorance. Ghaemi (pg. 11) further states that for some depressives, suicide can seem like the only way out of this morass; about 10 percent take their own lives.

No matter how hard I tried, nothing was coming together. I was pretty bored because my company had lost a lot of business earlier that year and I was not working with my clients nearly as much as I wanted to. I was seriously considering getting a job, which would have been career suicide. I had been interviewing for jobs and I was looking at working for a company and then subcontracting any work that my company would have won from that point forward to consultants I had relationships with. I had London, Frances, and another employee working for me and things seemed really bleak. Everything was getting on my nerves. I did not want to be bothered with my company anymore. Work had become difficult based on some governmental budgetary problems.

"What's this, Indigo?" asked Frances as she walked into my office holding a document.

"It is my resume," I said as I held out my hand to retrieve the document.

"I know it's your resume. Are we bidding on a contract that I do not know about?" she demanded as if she deserved an answer.

I clasped my hands and placed them on my desk as I leaned in to answer her. "Have a seat," I said as I gestured for her to sit down. She sat in a chair in front of my desk with a puzzled look on her face. "I'm looking for a job," I admitted. "I can't keep doing this. It is way too difficult and we're barely making ends meet," I said hopelessly. She just sat there dumbfounded. "But you do not have to worry. Wherever I go, I plan to hire both you and London. That's a promise," I added. We sat and talked about it for a moment, and I shared with her that one of my federal clients had an opening within his department. I shared that I was seriously considering taking the job. "The only problem with this job is that it is a grade 13 and I left the government as a 13 once before. I need to be at least a 14 or 15 based on what I have accomplished here in this business," I said with confidence.

"Well, I will support you in any way that I can," she guaranteed me.

"I know that I can count on you," I said with a smile.

I actually stopped pursuing that job because I really felt that I needed a higher grade for the peer-to-peer relationships that I had already established as a business owner consulting to the government. My ego wouldn't let me take or rather consider the job. But we all know that it would have been disastrous at that time in my life anyway.

Reflecting on this period of my life and in my company, I am so glad that I did not pursue the job any further than a couple of meetings and discussions. It felt and smelled like the same U.S. Department of Creativity situation. Gabe was my actual client over at the U.S. Practice Agency and he was now in Human Resources with this position. He assured me that he could bring me in at the lower grade but not the higher grade I desired. The higher grade would have sealed the deal for me. However, I had no intentions on giving up my company. My plan was that I would work all day on my government job and spend two hours a day after work continuing to build my business. This could have been accomplished, or maybe they were ideas of grandiosity based on having bipolar disorder. I saw myself easily working a 40-plus-hour job and still running a business. After all, I was working 65 hours on average in my company already.

These were dark and long days for me, but I survived. According to Nassir Ghaemi in his book *A First-Rate Madness: Uncovering the Links between Leadership and Mental Illness in Times of Crisis* (pg. 118-119), mental illnesses like manic depression may especially promote resilience because people experience episodes that come and go. Manic depression is recurrent by nature; the episodes go away, but they always come back. People also know that they will go through those episodes again, and so they may learn to develop coping styles, ways to recognize the episodes when they begin, or to help control them. People with manic depression often become resilient. I continued to work very hard even though things were not coming together and I never gave up. Resiliency based on my mental illness kept me in business and helped me to not become an employee again, not that being an employee is a bad thing. I just know it doesn't fit my temperament.

Success finds its way to our door

Just as it seemed that things were getting worse, we won that contract for which I made the employees forgo Martin Luther King holiday. This contract allowed us to design and deliver one-week management programs for the Department of Correctness. That contract was worth over six figures, which was huge for us considering up to that point we were delivering a consistent stream of $5,000 sessions. But to do a one-week session in different parts of the country was huge. We celebrated and that allowed us to form a tight-knit family between the four us. I would continue to introduce new players on our team, but, as always, that would end as soon as it begun. Even though I had little to no success in hiring and retaining employees, I continued to grow.

My next big contract was another substantial contract with a military branch. I wrote a proposal for a diversity program for one-star generals. I was invited to an interview after my proposal was selected by the contracting officer. I took in some of our existing books and showed our materials, which always won us the contract. Our materials were unique and polished. I spent a lot of time creating our training materials and it often paid off. I was very creative from the layout design to the picture selection on each page. Unlike a lot of workbooks, my workbooks were engaging, filled with researched information, and they were graphically appealing. After presenting to a team of decision makers, I got a call a week or two later to let me know that my company was selected to acquire the contract. I hung up the phone and called London and Frances to my office to let them know that we won the military contract. We were so excited; we were finally getting substantial and meaningful contracts.

The military liaison contacted me to set up our first meeting. I went to Washington, DC and met with their team. I made a great impression and it appeared that this would be a great opportunity that could lead to additional work. Upon finishing the meeting and taking copious notes, I gathered my things and waited for an escort. As I was leaving, one of the diversity project team members pulled me to the side and congratulated me. But there was something different about this congratulation. It almost seemed like a *good luck with that* gesture. But I was too optimistic to care or take heed.

Moving from an Entrepreneur to a Small Business Owner

Weeks went by and I worked night and day on customizing a program. There were standing meetings with the diversity project team, and it seemed like everything I proposed they would shoot down. Finally, I just did more listening to them argue amongst themselves and then waited for them to give me my marching orders. Weeks passed and that contract consumed me.

"Indigo, you have a call on the line," said London.

I picked up the phone and it was Colonel Smith.

He asked, "Indigo, do you have a minute to talk?"

"Yes. Certainly," I said with vigor.

"We are here going over some materials that you sent to us, and we're a little concerned," he said and paused.

I got up from my seat and closed the door. "Oh, why are you concerned?" I asked. I knew that this was going to be yet another adversarial conversation. Before he could finish, several people on the conference call started talking about a variety of different things. My head was spinning from the flurry of complaints. "Could you share with me some of the specific things that you would like to see changed?" I asked with a half-smile over the phone. They started to focus on everything from the team that I had selected down to the length of the class. It started to feel like I was just being bullied. After what felt like an hour of complaints, I promised to get them some revised materials and work on the areas that concerned them. When we hung up I had to lie on the floor in my office. My heart was racing and my stomach was wrenching with pain. I felt as though I was having a heart attack, but my stomach had its own storm that had me doubled over on my office floor.

As the day grew closer for me to present our finished product to their team, they requested things that were seemingly impossible to do. But I never saw a challenge or problem that could not be resolved. They requested that we have as our instructors vibrant and upbeat facilitators who retired as senior officers from the military with a background in diversity. Upbeat and vibrant usually does not accompany retired senior officers. Everyone that we encountered, when I cast our net for that request, was in their mid to late 60s and some even in their 70s. And that age group was not a part of the diversity movement. Many of them came with an EEO background, but not necessarily diversity. However, if this was what the client ordered then I would meet their request.

As the diversity project team and I continued to meet and I continued to work on the product, the day for my team to present grew closer. As the day for presenting was right around the corner, the military team became more anxious, even abusive. They would change their minds on a lot of things and appeared indecisive. Even though I was giving them mostly everything that they requested, they kept badgering me. Finally, I called Colonel Smith, one of the main decision makers on the team. We chatted for a few minutes before I asked him a very direct and candid question. I asked, "Colonel Smith, do you have a child?"

He answered hesitantly, "Yes."

I said, "Let's say that your child is little Timmy and you take little Timmy to the amusement park where there is a pony. You place Timmy on the pony. What you see amazes you and makes you feel sympathy for the pony. You see that little Timmy is on top of that pony just kicking and riding, kicking and riding. What little Timmy did not understand was that the pony was tied to a stake in the ground. That poor pony could only go so fast and so far, but little

Moving from an Entrepreneur to a Small Business Owner

Timmy kept kicking the damn pony and riding it as hard and fast as he thought he could ride the pony."

There was silence on the other end of the phone.

"Sir, I'm that pony and you all are kicking and riding me, but there is only so much that you will allow me to do. But if you let me do what you have asked, I promise I will deliver," I said with so much exhaustion in my voice that it could be felt through the phone line.

"Fair enough, Indigo. You just have to be able to deliver. There's a lot on the line with this," he said cautiously.

In preparation for the next week, I flew to DC to work with my facilitation team. When I walked into the room there were three seasoned veterans. On paper they were exactly what the military asked of me, but in person I did not see the vibrant and upbeat style, but then again maybe for their age they were vibrant. Maybe it was a matter of perspective. I went over the materials with them and conducted a mini train-the-trainer session since this was a combination of their materials and my company's materials. They appeared ready and now we had to present to the military team.

The next week, I arrived at the agency early to set up the room. The military required that we all stay near the campus even though all the guys lived in the DC area. After being escorted to the room, I started unpacking all of our supplies. What had set us apart from other vendors were not only our marquee workbooks, but the little giveaway trinkets, interesting exercises, and the overall feel of our classroom set up. I transformed the room along with help from my assistant. The room was colorful and lively, creating an ideal environment for learning.

The military invited a cross section of people to participate in the mock workshop before we presented to actual one-star generals. I also flew in one of my co-creators of the materials, but she could not present because she was not a retired military officer. The room filled up with civilian and military personnel. Music played softly in the background as we attempted to seduce all of their senses from sight to sound. The session was about to begin and my team was introduced. People marveled at the materials, which was a good sign, and the facilitators started off with a bang, but within the hour things started sliding downhill like a snowball on a ski slope. These polished and professional men became grumpy old men out of nowhere. One facilitator actually became argumentative about only God knows what. That was when I jumped up and took over. The audience seemed more like protagonists as opposed to participants. I put on my facilitator hat and waved to my co-creator, Cynthia, to accompany me. We were able to get things back on track and the presentation was wonderful.

At the first break, I pulled the guys off to the side, and asked, "What happened? What made you go off script?" They could not give any real answer aside from their emotions getting in the way. "Emotions. You do not get to have emotions when a contract is on the line," I said heatedly.

They apologized profusely and I recommended that Cynthia close out the session, since it was only a half-day of training. They agreed and sat to the side to provide insight from a military officer perspective when needed. Cynthia and I made it through that session and, to my surprise, many people came up to congratulate and commend us on our presentation. However, the client was not happy.

We began putting things up and bidding everyone farewell as Colonel Smith walked over to me. "We need to see you in our office once you are finished here," he said without an expression.

Moving from an Entrepreneur to a
Small Business Owner

I thanked each of the presenters and said goodbye to everyone as I departed to get my whipping from the military team. I entered the brigadier general's office.

"Indigo, this did not work for us," said the Brigadier General.

"I gave you everything that you asked for and, as you can see, what you wanted does not exist," I said in my defense. Then someone on the team rallied in my defense, and agreed that what they wanted in terms of facilitators was unreasonable. So they made a concession.

"You can redeliver your program with your own facilitators, but I was not very impressed with the material either," said the brigadier general as she continued to look at me hopelessly. "We are under the gun, so I need to see what you have this upcoming Monday."

It was already Friday. This would mean getting new facilitators and new material over the weekend. There was no way I could get new facilitators for a customized program. This was a crisis situation that I had never encountered. As the meeting finished up the brigadier general offered me a ride to my hotel. How bad could this be if she was willing to give me a ride? I thought to myself.

We pulled up to the hotel and as I was getting out she reached for my arm and said, "Indigo, I need for you to make this work. There are many people who want this to fail because they want me to fail." She then went on to explain how the good ole boy club was out to get her. I never felt that the good ole boys were out to get me, but I could understand how she felt. That was called paranoid and I lived with that feeling on more days than not. I empathized with her, and I could not risk losing this contract or looking like a failure.

As soon as I got to my room, I called my office and asked them to call Cynthia and Rose who were both diversity experts that presented diversity from an Appreciative Inquiry standpoint. Cynthia was headed for Las Vegas and Rose was in the Chicago area. I entered into a contract with both of them to fly to DC on Sunday and work with me on fine tuning the program and presenting it on Monday.

I will never ever forget that phone call. My team back at the office was worried. We had never experienced a client not liking our work. In fact, we never experienced failure. They started to sound defeated on the phone.

"Look guys, this is not a failure. It's an opportunity for us to grow," I said as I gave them a real pep talk. I needed them to keep their heads. I instructed them on what flights to book for the consultants, how much to compensate, and where to send additional materials that I could start combing through. However, when I got off the phone I sat on my hotel bed and sobbed like a baby. All the hard work and time that I'd put into this project for it to fall flat on its face was a hard pill to swallow.

The next day I got up extra early and worked on the workbook until the midnight hours. Then on that Sunday my two consultants arrived with their materials. We combined our materials and practiced our presentation until 2 a.m. in the morning. The workbook was completed and it was the best that I had ever created with the help of my two consultants! The Appreciative Inquiry piece was so profound and original that I was even impressed. This was sure to knock the combat boots off the brigadier general.

The next morning, with little to no sleep all weekend, I waited in the lobby for my team. We caught a cab to the site where the training would be conducted. We were greeted by Colonel Smith, who seemed a bit nervous but in good spirits. We were escorted to a small conference room where we set up for the workshop. As we were setting up, I was told that we only had two hours to present what was three hours of materials. So I asked my team "What should we omit?" I wanted to make sure we gave the most impactful part of our presentation. They started looking over the materials and pulled out what was not essential and could be discarded due to time constraints.

People started trickling in, but this group was different than the last class attendees. There were no true decision makers, just the colonel and the brigadier general. We started our session and thanked everyone for attending. I allowed the facilitators to work their magic. The audience was pleased and wowed. Finally, we got it right!

When the two consultants finished up, the brigadier general asked the group for their feedback and thoughts. Everyone expressed how they liked various parts of the session. It was a huge success, but the brigadier general seemed annoyed. She got up and left the room looking very anxious. By this time we were done and people started to leave the room, and we packed our boxes to catch our flights. I complimented Cynthia and Rose for an exceptional job, and we sat and chatted for a moment. The door opened and I was asked to join the brigadier general in her office.

"Indigo, this did not work for me. It was not diversity and I do not think that this is going to work for our conference," the brigadier general said to me with a look of disappointment.

I was shocked and at a loss for words. Tears started to well up in my eyes as I asked her to be more specific on how we can improve.

"There's nothing you can do. I just do not think that this is a good fit," she said as she reached for a business card on her desk. "However, I have already called a company that does this and they are willing to work with you on this contract," she said as she handed me the business card of another consulting firm.

I took the card and stated that I would give them a call.

"I think you'll be pleased with what they can do and you may learn a lot about diversity by sitting in on their program," she added.

I was crushed. I did not cry but I was sure that they saw a tear pool in my eye. Everyone in the room just looked solemn as I left to let my team know that there would be changes.

Upon getting in touch with this other company, I found they were already prepared to swoop in and deliver what we supposedly were unable to do. However, the military team liked our materials and asked that we be responsible for producing all the three-ring binder materials. Our materials were top shelf, and we managed the contract but did not deliver the workshops.

Finally, the day of the conference arrived. Our materials made a huge splash, but the delivery of the workshop not so much. I flew in both Cynthia and Rose to be part of the conference. Unfortunately, Rose was rushed to the hospital from the airplane the night before the conference, but Cynthia was in attendance. And boy was she mad. She knew that we had an award-winning session, but as she smugly said, "I need to see what I can learn from these diversity people." I felt her pain. After all, she wrote a book on diversity that was forwarded by someone considered to be a leading authority on diversity. My company managed the diversity conference, and we sat in on each course. It was a joke!

"Indigo, this is some horseshit if I've ever seen horseshit," Cynthia said in a loud voice, not caring who heard her.

"Yeah, you are right. The stuff that they are talking about is outdated and biased," I added to her insults.

Moving from an Entrepreneur to a Small Business Owner

A few hours later Colonel Smith asked me to step outside with him. "Indigo, I need to be honest with you because I am a Christian and feel that what has happened is wrong." I became very curious about what he was in the process of telling me. "Your presentation was incredible and everyone gave positive feedback, but unfortunately, the brigadier general wanted this other company to win the contract and they did not; your company did. She thought that you would fail based on the size of your company. You overcame every hurdle placed in your way. This was wrong. And I'm truly sorry."

I just stood there in shock. I felt really relieved that I did not fail, but I felt hurt by what the brigadier general had put me and my company through. I wished that she could have just been forthcoming. We went back into the building and I did not let on that I knew the real scoop. We finished off the conference and everything went relatively well, although the attendees were not impressed with the delivery by the facilitators. I could see that we were the better company, but we'd been caught up in office politics.

We closed out that contract. Ironically, the brigadier general was forced to retire within that year and she invited me to attend her retirement ceremony. I hated that woman and never wanted to see her again, but my team convinced me that part of playing the game was to attend the ceremony, which I did. The colonel and I stayed in touch and he retired soon after the brigadier general, as well.

I share this story to reveal the games that I had to deal with as a business owner. You always hope that your clients are honest and possess integrity, but when you start dealing with larger contracts it seems that the games intensify because people have their own players that they want to use. My team, especially Rose and Cynthia, felt vindicated. As Winston Churchill, who also was bipolar, said,

"Never, ever give up." I possess an incredible amount of tenacity. While others would have given up on the first supposed failure, I dug in deeper to make sure we were a success. I find that having bipolar disorder gave me a drive that was uncanny, even though at the time I did not acknowledge that I was bipolar. As Nassir Ghaemi states in his book *A First-Rate Madness: Uncovering the Links between Leadership and Mental Illness in Times of Crisis* (pg. 3), when our world is in tumult, mentally ill leaders function best. This entire contract and ordeal was an example of how bipolar disorder serves a leader very well when there is a crisis situation. The entire project kept me in crisis mode. Dr. Ghaemi (pg. 10) goes on to discuss that first and most important, mental illness doesn't mean that one is simply insane, out of touch with reality, or psychotic. The most common mental disorders usually have nothing to do with thinking at all, but rather abnormal moods: depression and mania. I knew that something was wrong and that the way my company was being treated by the client was grossly unfair. My mind was sharp and I was able to outthink people at every turn. I had tenacity and resiliency to take whatever was thrown at me, but it definitely took a toll on me and my employees.

Back to the drawing board with success under our belt

My business continued to grow. I was traveling back and forth between Atlanta and DC weekly. I would take the 7 a.m. flight up to DC on Tuesday and the 7 p.m. flight back to Atlanta on Thursday. While in DC I would have back-to-back meetings at a variety of agencies each day. This travel would have killed many, but I was so energized that

Moving from an Entrepreneur to a Small Business Owner

I did not pay attention to the wear and tear that it was causing me mentally and physically. According to Dr. Ronald Fieve in his book *Bipolar II* (pg. 128), there are also those Bipolar II individuals who are compulsive about traveling and must be on the go constantly. I traveled around the country to no end. If I wasn't flying to DC for meetings, I was traveling around the country attending conferences and speaking at venues. When in DC I had meetings from the time I landed until I left. Most of my time was spent developing relationships. My clients and potential clients loved me. For an hour and a half meeting, I would ask more personal questions of them than business inquiries. I would show a genuine interest in their family, love life, and all sorts of personal things that they would divulge to me. I would provide career coaching as part of our discussion to add value to the relationship. This built the many relationships that led to contracts, and these personal conversations allowed me to leverage those relationships. Clients were often surprised at how I was able to remember our conversations in detail and recall facts. I saw this as being part of my job. I often developed very intimate and personal relationships, which were authentic. This allowed me to grow my business through small contracts.

We continued to amass one- and two-day workshops that kept us busy, but my efforts did not bring about substantial contracts as of yet. I found pleasure in having close relationships with my clients. I was always on a high whenever I was meeting with them to either maintain or build those relationships. I had an insane schedule that drove me. In essence, I would go to DC to win the business, and then I would go back to Atlanta to create and develop the work. I would spend hours and days working on workbooks and preparing presentations. I thoroughly enjoyed the creativity that was involved in customizing each session. Then I would deliver many of the sessions. I would weave a lot of humor and antics into each session. Often courses were filled to capacity as I developed a reputation around the many agencies. I would walk through the hallways after an event and people would leave their workspace to greet me and share how much I had changed their lives. I was truly making a difference in both the various agencies and with people from all walks of life. I absolutely loved what I did and I embraced the love that I received while working with clients.

However, back in the office it was truly strained when I returned. I would often come back exhausted. I found myself not taking a break or doing anything to rest or maintain any sense of balance. I would come back from the trips and arrive at the office early to catch up on things that I missed due to being out of the office for a few days. It was a crazy schedule that I kept for years. I was living a manic life most of the time. I was like a pop star when on the road, but when I returned to the office I was simply worn out and tired, which reflected in how I treated my employees.

Near a professional and personal breakthrough

Because of my moodiness I could not retain talent, no matter how hard I tried. I simply did not lead an effective company. I was able to attract the employees based on my work in the community, my presentations, and reputation, but once they were onboard it was a matter of months and sometimes weeks before I would fire or push them away. This went on for several more years and I realized that I needed help in either hiring the right people or being patient long enough to see them grow into the job. However, being a small business owner of a struggling firm did not allow for hiring a coach or a consultant to help, so I continued to make mistakes. This all started to wear on me. I was going through tremendous change. I had never been more unhappy with my career. I felt like a failure when I looked at how little my company had made. We were in the hole financially, and I hated being tied down. I worked 12 hours every day except Sunday, when I only worked four hours or so. I found myself in DC all the time marketing for small contracts that did not add up to enough to maintain a small business. I felt that much of my time was spent solely on chasing contracts. It was yielding some returns, so that was good. But I was getting burned out. I enjoyed the speaking aspect of my business and meeting with clients, but that became very daunting too.

A turn in the economy presents a turn in my business

In 2009, I was 45 years old with an incredible amount of responsibility on my plate. Things were tough all over for everyone, especially for people who had corporate contracts. The economy had taken a nose dive. People had lost their savings and retirements. The mortgage industry was all but gone. My husband Curtis's company was flatlining. Money was running low in my business, but we were holding on because my primary client base was the federal government. As I closed out the year, I reflected on that year. It was such a roller coaster. The country's finances fell out and I was truly looking for a job again. A trusted employee had embezzled money from my company through tax fraud. I picked up the largest contract ever for my company, and I was never truly happy.

DUELING DRAGONS

I had been mentally balanced for some time now. My company was growing slowly, but I was seeing more and more potential clients. I actually rented a studio apartment in DC even though we were not making a lot of money to afford it. In my opinion, it was more cost-effective than renting a hotel room a couple days each week. I was now spending a lot of time at my studio apartment in DC. It was the perfect place for me. I felt as if I had some place to run away to and escape. I justified living there by stating that I could spend more time seeing clients and generating business. I often find that people with bipolar disorder need a place of refuge—a place to disappear and heal.

Fall of 2010 I was still traveling to DC Tuesday mornings and going back to Atlanta on Thursday. I all but lived in DC except from Friday to Monday. I found another very nice studio in the Metro DC area, and everything was starting to look up for me again. Things were coming together. I had been elected as Woman of the Year by a prominent business association and I started receiving invitations to join organizations, received awards and recognitions, and had magazines writing about me. But I often still felt a great sense of sadness. I could not put my finger on it. I had everything going for me—a nice studio in the DC area with a nice view of the Capitol, a loving family, and a successful career—but I was still sad, although depressed would be the more accurate definition. I spent time meeting with people with whom I could collaborate on my second book, and I would go to dinner with clients, and I was at my best in networking. I eventually snapped out of my funk, but I wished that I could have managed my feelings of depression better. I had everything to be happy about but I would get very sad for no apparent reason. Slowly I came out of my depression but it took several months. I did not win the Woman of the Year title, but I became a finalist. I would joke with people and say that such was fine because I did not want to carry around such a heavy title. But seriously, it was assumed that I did not get the actual award because the person who submitted my application did not include anything about my community service. What many people did not know about me, including my employees, was that I gave thousands and thousands of dollars to scholarships and foundations. I would usually keep that information tucked away because I felt that it would be bragging to let anyone know. Keeping the philanthropic side of me a secret would cost since it appeared that I had no community service under my belt. That was when I became more public about my giving and about myself, in general.

The game changer

The year 2010 was my company's breakout year. From all of my networking in DC and past work with a client that now worked within another agency, we were approached by the Department of Dependability about a multimillion dollar contract. We partnered with an organization to win that contract and that placed us on the path to Inc. 500|5000. I remember sitting at my desk when I got a call from Ms. Tina with the Department of Dependability.

"Indigo, Ms. Tina is on the line for you," said London.

"Hello, Ms. Tina. How are you?" I asked as we exchanged pleasantries.

"I'm fine," she said. Without a pause, she explained that they were considering me for a contract, but she had to verify that I had substantial enough contracts to demonstrate my ability to hold that contract.

"Well, we have had several six-figure contracts that ran simultaneously, and our past performance is superb. I can send you some letters of recommendations," I said anxiously.

"That won't be necessary. We have already spoken to a couple of your clients," she said warmly.

We continued to talk and I assured her that if we won that contract we would exceed their expectations.

"I'm sure you will," she chuckled. After that she told me that someone would be in touch with me and wished me a good day.

I hung up the phone. I just knew that the phone call was about a proposal that we submitted a few weeks prior. That proposal was for a contract to conduct training. I was excited because this would be a new client and a nice size contract. I ran to a central part of the office and yelled, "Guess who that was?" I continued, "It was the Department of Dependability and we're being considered for a contract. It should be worth six figures, and I think we have a great chance of getting it."

Towards the end of the week I got another phone call, asking if I could come to DC because a proposed partner for the Department of Dependability project wanted to meet with me. The next week the proposed partner and I were in DC discussing the contract. What they were discussing did not sound like the contract that we bid on; this was something much bigger and grander in scope. It wasn't for training, but rather a multimillion dollar contract to provide educational services for officers. Unlike the proposal that I had submitted, this was something that we were selected to bid on based on our 8(a) status and my relationships with quite a few people. Our name was tossed in the hat along with several other companies, and my company was selected to bid on a sole source request for proposal. This was the best thing that had ever happened to my company.

I accepted the offer to bid on the contract. But I would need help getting that whale into my boat. So I called my husband Curtis, who was a finance guy, and he worked on the proposal along with a peer, who had experience working on multimillion dollar projects, and our new partner. Everything was going well until my peer started encouraging me to try to win the contract alone without the other partnering company. I felt that such would be an act of betrayal and so unnecessary. It was stressful to have my peer attempt to get me to do something that I wasn't comfortable in doing. I needed his help in writing the proposal, but, unfortunately, he brought with him an underhanded way of doing business. I did not want to cut the proposed partner out of the opportunity because I felt that there was enough to share. My peer that was advising me decided not to help us any longer since I would not do what he wanted. So it ended up with Curtis and my team working on the proposal in collaboration with the proposed partner. That was really tough because none of us had experience in writing multimillion dollar proposals.

We worked around the clock to pull this off. We submitted the proposal and we all crossed our fingers. In a matter of weeks we were selected to win the contract. Now the heavy lifting had to begin. I hired Curtis to be on my leadership team as my COO and to help me manage that contract. He was eager to join the contract because his company was all but out of business based on the downturn in the finance/mortgage industry. We started hiring for a project manager, program manager, and several other people to fill a variety of positions. My company more than tripled over night. That contract had consumed my company. We spent an inordinate amount of time building and managing the program. It was wonderful!

Success had its price

Whether I admitted to having bipolar disorder or not, I had the classic textbook symptoms. My paranoia ebbed and flowed without warning. Over time, I did not trust my husband as my COO. I started to think that he might try to siphon money. Also, I would ask him for financial updates that I never received. I then asked him to shield me and deflect things from me so I could focus on the things that I did best, which was working with clients and speaking to the masses. However, our relationship became less about supporting one another and became more of a competition. I could tell that I was becoming disruptive and that something was wrong with me, but I still was in denial about having bipolar disorder. I simply knew that all I needed was my husband, who was my COO, to protect me, and he didn't. I felt exposed and vulnerable for some reason. Kay Redfield Jamison relays this feeling from her book *An Unquiet Mind: A Memoir of Moods and Madness (pg. 67)*:

> *There is a particular kind of pain, elation, loneliness, and terror involved in this kind of madness. When you are high it's tremendous. The ideas and feelings are fast and frequent like shooting stars, and you follow them until you find better and brighter ones. Shyness goes, the right words and gestures are suddenly there, the power to captivate others a felt certainty. There are interests found in uninteresting people. Sensuality is pervasive and the desire to seduce and be seduced irresistible. Feelings of ease, intensity, power, well-being, financial omnipotence, and euphoria pervade one's marrow. But, somewhere, this changes. The fast ideas are far too fast, and there are*

Moving from an Entrepreneur to a Small Business Owner

far too many; overwhelming confusion replaces clarity. Memory goes. Humor and absorption on friends' faces are replaced by fear and concern. Everything previously moving with the grain is now against—you are irritable, angry, frightened, uncontrollable, and enmeshed totally in the blackest caves of the mind. You never knew those caves were there. It will never end, for madness carves its own reality.

My company had won a multimillion dollar contract with the Department of Dependability. I was on the path to great success and total madness. I moved into a larger office space. All around me were new employees. As we settled into the contract, we had about 20 people working for the company. Many of the employees were working on the Department of Dependability project and stayed out of my way, but there were still people in my space. Everything was seemingly fine on the surface. Curtis was an ex-military officer who was great at managing people. I still had Frances, London, and Sherry with me who were considered the seasoned employees of the company. They experienced growing pains too. It seemed that our culture had changed overnight. We were so accustomed to struggling and working long hours and weekends, but that was no longer necessary. We had money coming into the company whereby our jobs were not always on the line anymore. Curtis was doing an okay job, but I always felt that his performance could have been better. For some reason it felt as if he resented me for being his boss and he would not allow me to manage him. I knew so much more about the government and things that should and should not be done, but he would refuse to listen to me. We often argued about the smallest things. But, if the truth be told, I harbored ill will towards him because I felt as though he never helped me in growing my business.

He only joined the company because his company failed as a result of the finance and mortgage industry collapsing. But the reason I was angry with him was because he had a finance background, but he never shared with me ways to improve my company. Throughout the years I struggled with no help from him, until I was able to offer him a job with great compensation.

Several years ago, I tried to purchase a nice copier. I remember talking to Jeff, a copier sales guy, about buying a high speed copier from his company. "Indigo, I could put you in this copier, but you'll need to finance it," he said to me in a matter of fact way after showing me a state of the art copier.

I needed that copier because we produced all of our workbooks in house and it was time to step up our game. "That is fine," I said without hesitation. He then informed me that I needed good credit to get the copier on credit. "Oh, that's no problem. I have great credit," I said with pride.

He had me complete some paperwork and he went to another room to speak with his finance people. He came back with a look of disappointment. "Indigo. You do not have credit," he said.

I argued, "Yes I do. You see all this furniture. I paid for this. I pay all my bills on time, and I don't owe anybody."

"How did you pay for this furniture and these computers?" he asked.

"I either paid cash or used my American Express," I explained.

"Indigo. That doesn't build your credit," he said with a look of concern on his face. "You know that I sold your husband this exact same copier and he has credit. Doesn't he have a finance background? He hasn't shared with you what you need to do to build your credit?"

Moving from an Entrepreneur to a Small Business Owner

"Hell, no. He's never mentioned anything to me," I blurted out with disdain.

Jeff began to share with me how to build credit and got on the phone with his company to pitch me as a new customer. I leased the copier and started building a credit history. But I was terribly hurt that my husband withheld information that could have helped me with my business. When I asked my husband why he never shared with me that I needed credit he said, "You never asked."

How would I know what I do not know?

As fate would have it, years later Curtis was working for me, and I felt that I was there for him when he needed me, but I could not depend on him. I tried to block such negative thinking out of mind because we had work to do and there was no room to allow our differences to get in the way. However, it was at the right time, I had enough money to pay him a very good salary and bring him on board to help me manage the new contract and my finances.

As he became more entrenched in the contract, Curtis would become overly protective of "his" employees on the Department of Dependability project. There was a distinct division between my seasoned employees and the rest of the new team. I would ask things of the Department of Dependability team that would be met with resistance. On a couple of occasions it was said to me "let me run this past Curtis to see what he thinks." I found Curtis becoming less like an employee and more as if he were in charge. I started disliking the dynamics and I knew that I needed help in managing not only the contract but Curtis, as well.

My knight in shining armor

I hired Richard on a temporary contract basis. He was a very dear friend, colleague, and confidant who had an extensive background in corporate America. He brought with him leadership skills. Often when Richard was between employment, he would come and support me on a temporary basis. He came to do a cultural audit and identify where we could improve and streamline. A couple of months earlier, I'd hired a new employee named Bernadette to be my business manager. Bernadette was not a good fit, but she brought other things to the table that I thought could be useful at some point. In fact, the job was over her head, but I felt that she could learn the ropes based on her project management background.

Within a couple of months, I was very unhappy with Bernadette who became very close to Curtis. I did not know how close they were until he was named as a witness in her lawsuit against me when she quit. I was having difficulties with Curtis and hiring Bernadette was a big mistake. My behavior would become more bizarre than usual when I felt upset or threatened. I was becoming verbally abusive and insulting around the office. I was really hard on Bernadette, and she eventually quit, and in her resignation letter that she sent to Curtis she mentioned that I was abusive and a terrible example of a leader. Later we received a letter from her attorney. The letter listed Curtis as someone who could testify on her behalf. I was not shocked by her letter, but I was angry that my husband Curtis was named as her witness. I was further enraged that she was able to give examples of things that could hurt me based on what she had learned from Curtis divulging information. I cannot recall a lot about that time period, but I was not on medicine and nothing seemed right with my employees.

Around the same time as her departure, Richard had decided to join the company as a full-time employee serving in a leadership and executive capacity. I made Curtis the CFO and Richard became a primary player on my leadership team as the COO. It was a nice honeymoon period. Curtis would take Richard's direction and guidance. (Things that I asked of Curtis or required of him did not happen until Richard came onboard.) Curtis seemed fine with having Richard as his boss, and our relationship improved.

Everything was working well, but something changed. I believe that I was becoming manic again. Richard was working hard at doing everything he could to protect me and make me happy. Richard's first real order of business was that he had to go to the Department of Labor to represent us in the case filed by Bernadette. I was so disgusted and angry with Curtis for being named as her witness that it eventually contributed to the challenges that led to our divorce a couple of years later. He felt that he was trying to help an employee survive. I wished that he would have shared with me that someone was so upset with me that they were looking at quitting.

Even though Richard won the case, I needed to clear the air with Curtis. One day, I entered Curtis's office, grabbed a chair, and asked if I could have a seat. He nodded in agreement and I sat down. "Curtis, why didn't you share with me that Bernadette was so angry that she wanted to sue me?" I asked.

"I knew she was upset, but I did not know that she wanted to sue you," he said.

"But she did, and thanks to you, I could have really been in a lot of trouble based on the shit that you told her," I yelled in a rapid speech pattern.

"This is why I do not share things with you, Indigo," he shouted back and added, "You go into your dark cave and you pull anyone around you into it."

I just sat there and looked at him. I knew exactly what he was talking about and I could not deny that some days I would spend the entire day in the cave. He went on to tell me how difficult it was working with me, and that I could be so much further along if I did not go into my cave and pull people in.

That really hurt because I often did not know that I was in a cave. I knew that darkness surrounded me, but it was not something that I could change or help. I felt all alone at that very moment. I often felt that I had no one on my side or that anyone understood me. I still did not attribute this or past problems to having bipolar disorder. I just saw that the person who was supposed to stand beside me actually threw me under the bus. This deepened my distrust of Curtis, and quickly I came to trust Richard, although everything always seemed like a battle for us as well. I felt as though I trusted him, but I did not know how to show it. What I found that I needed most was shielding from people who did not understand me or what I was trying to create. According to Dr. Ronald Fieve in his book *Bipolar II* (pg. 28), with Bipolar II it is common to have coexisting conditions (one or more psychiatric or medical disorders that co-occur with the illness) that can complicate the diagnosis and treatment. For example, it is not uncommon for the Bipolar II patient to also have coexisting Generalized Anxiety Disorder, panic attacks, phobias, social anxiety, conduct disorders, eating disorders, substance abuse, sexual addiction, ADHD, and problems with impulse control, among others. I would later find out that I had impulsivity issues and a lot of anger. This impacted my relationship with my two leaders and across the organization, in general.

The Department of Dependability project caused my company to grow exponentially. It was one of my most difficult times. Having all these personalities and people around me daily was difficult for me to deal with because of my mood swings and angry fits. I was not firing people, but my behavior was erratic and volatile at times, while at other times I was the life of the party and people enjoyed working for Careers In Transition. We were doing meaningful work within the government, and I was pleased. But something had to change. According to Ronald Fieve in his book *Bipolar II* (pg. 83), bipolar mood disorder is primarily biochemical and genetic in origin, and there is no other "primary" reason for it. Environment and major stressors, however, may trip off the complex genetic vulnerability and biochemical mechanisms that are responsible for the mood swing. I was beginning to spiral out of control from the constant stimulation of people and the many changes in my company.

Richard had an extensive background in corporate America and brought with him leadership skills. A true sign of leadership is being able to supplement and augment what you are lacking, so to some extent I demonstrated leadership, but I had so much work to do in the area of managing my emotions. And anyone who understands leadership knows that managing one's emotions is paramount to being a great leader. Richard was excellent with the employees. He urged me to stop managing the employees and allow him to do so. He wanted me to continue growing the business externally. Richard recommended that I spend most of my time in DC, which was why and how I moved to DC full-time. He spent months on repairing the organization. That was when I realized that I was actually responsible for leading the organization and that I was doing a God-awful job.

Something had to give: I can learn to lead

Leading the company meant more than just getting the business; it also meant retaining employees in a healthy environment. That was when I decided to let go and completely turn the reigns over to Richard, and I buckled down to learn how to be a more effective leader. But that came with its own set of circumstances. It was less than a few months after the Bernadette fiasco that I was accepted into a doctoral leadership program. Ironically, Bernadette inspired me to become a better leader. I felt that her resignation letter was very intense and scathing, but there were points that were true. I needed to learn how to be a leader. Initially, I was really nervous about whether I would be accepted or not, and then upon being accepted I started to wonder if getting my PhD was really the answer to my problems. I was in search of something to move my career in another direction. Also, it became painfully clear based on the many and most recent incident of an employee leaving that I needed to learn how to be a leader.

I woke up very anxious but sluggish the day after receiving an email stating that I had been accepted into the program. I was feeling overwhelmed and basically fearful of my decision to go to school for my doctoral degree. I canceled all my meetings the next day; I just could not pull myself together. I was fearful of what I would learn and that I would be exposed.

Same me in a new environment

In 2011, I was 47 years old with a goal of attaining my PhD by the time I turned 50. I arrived in Lisle, Illinois to attend my first class at Benedictine University. When I began the course with a cohort (an intact group that stays together) I felt out of place because everyone seemed so happy, while deep down I either felt nothing or scared. I wanted that particular university program because it had a cohort. I believed that I could learn more by being with other people versus an online program. I instantly found that I was different than the rest of the students. My peers were either military leaders, professionals groomed in organizations to lead, or students who simply did not have a mental illness. I did not realize how different I was until the first week wherein I felt ridiculed for my thoughts and work by several peers. I was shocked at the many strong personalities and, unlike being in my company, I was not the boss. I had to accept whatever they dished out.

The first introduction to the class was through an eight-day intensive session. The first week I did not feel accepted. I was placed in a group to discuss our authentic selves and our sacred stories whereby we shared our beliefs. I felt very uncomfortable with this exercise. I recall one particular Sunday being a truly emotional day for me. There were many conversations around leadership that actually moved me a little closer to my goals and objectives of being a better person and leader. I openly talked about Shirley Borel and how much she meant to me. I lost all composure because Shirley was a woman who was my instructor, mentor, and a believer in me. She was a journalism instructor at Waubonsee Community college where I received my Associate of Arts Degree. She impacted my life so greatly; however, she passed away several years ago. I would often be reminded that I was alone in this world when it came to people who accepted me unconditionally.

Based on all the exercises and activities, I walked away with a new way to control and modify my behavior. So I thought. I would simply ask myself whether Shirley Borel would be proud of this behavior. But I needed actual medication unbeknownst to me and not just a technique to change my behavior. However, I started to see growth each day by discovering self-awareness on a higher level. My time in class and the homework assignments allowed me to have self-understanding and self-knowledge that was moving me closer to self-acceptance.

I became very transparent and curious about myself. It was intriguing watching the teacher become the student. For the past 20 plus years, I had been the teacher in a variety of settings ranging from an adjunct faculty to a speaker at conferences. But now I was at a phase in my life where I was learning, and much of my learning was about me. That was exactly what I needed at that point in my life. I started to believe that maybe I could heal what I had broken and fix what was broken in me. There was a legacy exercise that included a retirement speech. I wrote about the changes I would make based on the recent lawsuit without mentioning the lawsuit. When I finished pouring out my heart through a very introspective paper, two women in my group tore me and my paper apart. They seemed to take offense to what I had said. I became very confused and through tears explained that this was my reality. They argued every point with me.

Later that day one of the women came and apologized to me because she felt that she took what I said personally. Later I found out that she was having difficulties on her job with her boss. But the other woman came to me and said that she would not apologize and did not feel that the other student should have apologized. I felt such venom in her voice. We never seemed to get past that day.

That evening I asked the professor to look at my paper and share with me what I could have written that incited such emotions and to tell me what I did wrong. He read the paper and gave me kudos for such an introspective, thought-provoking paper. He suggested that I change one word. He recommended that I change the word employee to associate. Over the next few days, we were to make changes based on the feedback. I did not make any changes aside from the one word. A few days later the groups were asked to go to their separate rooms and present their papers again. I read my paper and the same two women had the nerve to say that it was much better. "Well, this is the exact same paper that you attacked a couple of days ago," I said angrily. They insisted that I had to have made changes.

All that proved to me was that the attacks were personal. I could admit and accept that I was crazy by normal standards, not the insane crazy, but rather an unusual thinker. I saw the world entirely differently than everyone else. I was not sure that I could go a couple of years defending my thoughts at every turn. I knew my craziness got me to this level of success and clients actually paid to hear my crazy thoughts.

I could feel that I was slowly withdrawing in the class.

One day in class a classmate said, "Indigo, you have to love yourself." She said it with such compassion as if she was looking through me. I do not know what I said or did for her to approach me with such a request, and I am not even sure that it made me feel better. I have three years to work on me, I thought to myself. I wanted to be transformed by the time I was fifty. So I needed to put on my big girl panties.

Each cohort session was very difficult for me. Sitting for long stretches and interacting with the many personalities was very taxing on me. I believed that I was making significant progress as a result of my leadership classes back at the office, but in the class things were intensifying. I felt like I was on a reality show, and I was brought on as the antagonist.

I just wanted to go and learn.

Over the years, I took a lot of assessments that would pinpoint my personality. In class, I took an assessment titled StrengthsFinder® and it revealed that I was an Achiever, Learner, WOO (Winning Others Over), Command, and Strategist. This combination made for a strong personality that did not seem to fit well with the cohort. This revealed to me that owning my own business gave me the freedom to be me. I was able to engage and interact with others in small dosages, which led to my success. People paid to hear what I had to say, which was often novel. However, being in a cohort was difficult based on the new role that I had to assume. I was not the CEO or the expert in this new environment. I share this because it was a significant part of my journey.

Time flew by. I was becoming a leader, but I felt the journey was too emotionally draining. When I first got home from the eight-day intensive session, I was thinking that I wanted to quit the program. All I needed was for someone to support me in quitting and that would have been enough to justify letting go of a long held dream to get my PhD. But everyone encouraged me to stay in the program based on the changes that they were already seeing in me. I shared with my employees what I had learned and I put a lot of the principles that I learned into practice. I could actually see some changes in terms of my behavior. I started reading books as a part of the classes and independently. I started learning what leadership was all about and that was an eye-opening experience for me. In the meanwhile, Richard was handling the day-to-day operations of the company while I focused on marketing and public relations in the company. However, my biggest task was being a student. I spent a lot of my time focusing on school.

I continued my trips to class once a month. School started to consume me, and I spent an inordinate amount of time focusing on it. I was in my apartment in DC and I had just sent in my two assignments a few days earlier than their due dates. I really felt that maybe this leadership program was not for me. There was a nagging feeling that the cohort was not the right fit for me. I promised myself that I would give it the "ole college try" and if I felt differently by the next class I would stay. Reading the books and feeling good about finishing the assignments, I started to feel better. And people around the office already started seeing a difference in me when I would visit headquarters. I felt calmer or maybe just exhausted. I became a little more deliberate in what I did and what I said, which was a good thing. This came as a result of one student asking me in class, "Do you hear what comes out of your mouth? We think these things but we do not say it." I remember just looking at the student and thinking shame on him for not expressing himself. I had grown accustomed to sharing my thoughts and beliefs, which was my job as a consultant and CEO. But after becoming ostracized I learned to keep my thoughts to myself or at least not be so vocal about what popped into my head. In fact, I read a book that mentioned that leaders can say too much. So, not speaking my mind was a lesson that I had to learn. If two years of this could help me leave a lasting positive legacy and lead an authentically good life, getting through the class and my cohort would be worth it, I thought.

I thanked the universe for the opportunity because I believed that I had been afforded a golden opportunity and something special through the program. I felt that I had a cast of 1,000 rooting and cheering for me. This may have been the bipolar disorder trait of grandiosity, but I felt that I had so many people in my corner, real or imaginary. I was learning so much about me that I welcomed meeting the me that I would become based on the program.

Time was passing, and I shifted from running the company to studying and preparing for class. I wanted to focus my time and energy on school because I wanted to become a better leader. School became more to me than mere classes; it was an opportunity for growth. I found the readings and papers that I had to complete relatively easy. I thoroughly enjoyed writing the papers and exploring my own behaviors. I became very introspective and open in my ability to examine my thoughts, behaviors, and actions over the years. I wrote very creatively and often was praised for my writing, but not my inability to attribute my papers to the source. That was because I was often the source. I intuitively knew things and understood things from a perspective that did not come from text. On several occasions my professors would ask where I gained my information. Unfortunately, I couldn't cite anyone because what I wrote were my own ideas and opinions. I often had a different and creative perspective on things that came to me through an insightful intuition. This did not serve me well in research, but it allowed me to see things slightly differently, even if it was momentary. Eventually, I learned how to conduct true research and cite my sources.

As a result of incidents at school and growing problems at work, I started taking Symbyax, a mood stabilizer that would calm me. I did not take this medicine because I was bipolar. Having bipolar disorder was still the furthest thing from my mind. I was taking the medicine because I shared the story about school with my general practitioner and he recommended that I take something to take the edge off. I was feeling euphoric, and I could not sleep. I was feeling better, but different. According to Dr. Ronald Fieve in his book *Bipolar II* (pg. 59), the course of Bipolar II disorder is marked by relapses and remissions. When four or more cyclical mood episodes of illness occur within a 12-month period, the person is said to have Bipolar II disorder with rapid-cycling. I was being treated by a physician, not a psychiatrist, so I was not truly being treated for what truly ailed me. I needed help and I was spiraling out of control.

A chance to change with medication

It was mid-2011 and my career was doing extremely and fantastically well. I was pretty happy for the first time in a long time. I wrote in my journal that I was still taking my medication. I was speaking all over the country on my books and everything was good. One month later I was really irritable and angry even on medication. I had gained a lot of weight being on the medication. It was hard not to eat because I craved food. I would go to class and during lunch I would need to go to my car to sleep. I could barely keep my eyes open in class. The two side effects were being lethargic with incredible weight gain. I started thinking that maybe I would stop taking my medicine because I was too uninteresting when medicated. I was not as on edge and emotional, but I needed my over-the-top personality for my speaking engagements. I knew that I had to change so I withdrew mentally from the class and sat in the back of the room to manage my behavior.

Curtis, Richard, and I were attending a conference in Las Vegas. I missed most of the conference because I kept falling asleep, even during sessions. At one point, I had to leave the conference because I could not stay awake. I could not believe how strong that medicine was and how it affected me. So I stopped taking that medication. I simply could not function. But I just knew that I would be alright. An incident that happened with a student in class would not happen again because I would change me. I would be low key and keep quiet in class. I would sit in the back row off to the side, by myself, to keep out of trouble. I devised a perfect plan to make it through the program, and I would minimize my time with employees.

A slow unraveling

I was on a trip back to Atlanta. I had one of the most productive and successful trips that the leadership team had ever taken. Curtis and Richard accompanied me, and we won a million dollar contract with a long-term client. Then we finished up that meeting to meet with another high profile client to discuss another project. The universe was raining business for my company.

I was a little nervous because it was far more than we could handle, but this was what growth was all about. We were experiencing phenomenal growth and I was becoming a better leader as a result of my doctoral program. Unfortunately, in the mix of all of this success I wished that I could make all the pain that I felt go away. Having bipolar disorder allowed me to experience both highs and lows, known as a mixed episode. I was soaring by day and crashing by night. This allowed my company to grow, but it shrouded me in darkness.

I wished death was the answer, but it was not. I could not shake an overwhelming sadness that I felt day in and day out. I really did not feel loved or liked and that would hurt so much. Often I would think about taking all my sleeping pills, but I was afraid of what happens to people who commit suicide, as I mentioned earlier. If someone could just assure me that I could and would just go on to a peaceful place, I would have checked out of this world. I felt that being me in this life was too hard.

I wrote in my journal that I was crying, looking at the clouds out the window, wondering *Why me? It hurts so badly*. According to Dr. Ronald Fieve in his book *Bipolar II* (pg. 13), as life progresses and episodes recur without stabilization, the prognosis for unmanaged mood swings is not nearly as good as the first episode. That is why education, early diagnosis, and effective treatment of the Bipolar II patient with medications that stabilize mood prevent the worsening of the illness that would otherwise occur. I did nothing to alleviate the problem and kept the diagnosis a secret in hopes that it was an error that a psychiatrist made years ago. But my thoughts of suicide became more frequent and more vivid, especially since I lived alone in the DC area. It would be less complicated with my kids not around and I had no one to give me a reason to live while there. It was Sunday evening when I wrote in my journal:

I'm so sorry! But I can't live this life as the bad guy. I gotta find a way out. This is just too much pain. Sometimes I feel nothing but darkness around me. Sometimes I feel that I am darkness. No matter how much light I try to shine, people see the darkness. I need courage to die, not to live. But how? All my life I've wanted out, but I lacked the courage. I gotta be stronger to turn off the lights and fly away. I wonder how many people are sitting somewhere moments from taking their own life. I wonder what they are thinking. I can only imagine how they are feeling because I feel the same way.

I refused to take medication. "Can anything save me?" I often thought to myself. Things were very difficult, even at work. My leadership team had a difficult time working with me. I had discovered that I knew about leadership methodology on a superficial level, but I needed to move it from my head to my heart. I so desired to become a better leader. I had led since I was a teen. People always flocked and followed me, but I would push them away either intentionally or unintentionally with words, behaviors, etc. The real reason for never allowing others to get too close was out of fear that they would discover that something was different or wrong with me. In fact, I never wanted to be a leader or follower, and now I was leading and following at the same time.

For the first time, I consciously and willfully wanted to lead. The employee who wrote the scathing letter really got into my head and heart. I wanted to be the kind of leader that this employee would willingly follow. I needed to modify my behavior. My biggest problem was how I treated people when I would become hypomanic and/or depressed, which had been a part of me since I was a young adult. Now that's either revealing or just pretty darn sad.

Moving from an Entrepreneur to a Small Business Owner

I was becoming more of a danger to both me and my company's reputation. I had established an excellent reputation in the field of HR with my clients and even with my employees, some of whom simply thought that I was a quirky entrepreneur who fit the mold of many highly successful business owners: a go-getter and butt-kicker. But that was slowly deteriorating, and I couldn't see it or understand what was happening. As my behavior became more erratic, my leadership team became concerned. They needed to keep others away in an effort to maintain my persona and the integrity of the company. This impacted my company greatly because I moved from being the face of the organization to the "crazy aunt in the attic." I was no longer visible or meeting with clients. According to Kay Redfield Jamison in her book *Touched with Fire: Manic-Depressive Illness and the Artistic Temperament* (pg. 13), these depressive symptoms include apathy, lethargy, hopelessness, sleep disturbance (sleeping far too much or too little), slowed physical movement, slowed thinking, impaired memory and concentration, and a loss of pleasure in normally pleasurable events. Additional diagnostic criteria include suicidal thinking, self-blame, inappropriate guilt, recurrent thoughts of death, a minimum duration of the depressive symptoms (two to four weeks), and significant interference with the normal functioning of life. I was not manic. In fact, I don't know what I was but there was growing concern about me by family members who saw my life unraveling.

The truth comes out

It was the fall of 2011, and I was off my meds again, and not even the appropriate meds at that. But I had learned to embrace a huge game changer for me. In class I found that some people were put off by my comments. Things would escalate until I became the bad guy. So I took my own advice from my own books, *Playing by the Unwritten Rules*. In essence, I started to play the game. Therefore, I began to say very little to my peers, I did not ask for clarification, and I appeared to be in agreement by keeping my feelings, thoughts, and opinions to myself. Mostly everyone around me became comfortable and pleased. Some people would ask me if I was okay as they took notice of the change. But that was the answer—just play along to get along. All my life I have found that it was okay for people to hurt me, but when I reacted or responded then I was the bad guy. So I isolated myself at school partly to protect myself and to protect the other students.

I knew with a certain amount of clarity that I was enrolled in the doctoral program not just to increase my credibility but to truly become a better leader for my organization and employees. I read two books during the holidays, *Don't Sweat the Small Stuff* and *What Got You Here Won't Get You There*. I read both books to discover that I had my work cut out for me. I planned to spend 2012 truly developing as a person and a leader.

Here is what I know and this is what I think I wrote in my journal:

> *I need to simplify. Life doesn't have to be so hard or complicated.*
>
> *Where is my there? A place that is beautiful, peaceful, and accepting of me. I will get there by:*
>
> *Becoming more patient with others.*

MOVING FROM AN ENTREPRENEUR TO A SMALL BUSINESS OWNER

Being less judgmental, and definitely not voicing those judgments.

Not trying to prove that I am smart and good-hearted.

Forgiving, forgiving, forgiving and then the pain will go away.

Letting go of the past by embracing the gifts that came from each experience and moving on.

Opening my circle to others and not being afraid to befriend on deeper levels.

Letting others be themselves and stop wanting to change others, which will allow me to be me authentically.

In other words:

Stop being irritated and annoyed so quickly which will lead to patience.

See people as unique individuals and embrace them, and when a negative thought surfaces, keep it to myself.

I'm smart and it is dumb to try to prove it. I'm good and kind and time will reveal so . . . not me telling such. Allow time to speak for me.

I'll stop hurting when I stop living in the past. Most of my pain is behind me, so I need to leave it there and enjoy now.

Resenting only hurts me the most. I'll forgive even when others do not apologize.

Become less self-absorbed and be a real friend to others. The spirit requires it. Stop shutting people out.

Dueling Dragons

If others allow me to be me, then out of respect I will allow others to be themselves. I will stop trying to change people. Let others be, so I can be.

Wow, just think what and who I could be by accomplishing this. It was the first of the year in 2012 and the books that I read revealed that if I changed me, my world would change. Hell, it had become way too difficult to be me. There were too many dos and don'ts that I placed on myself. I was very hard on myself and others, and my expectations of whom I should have been were far too difficult to live up to. Everything from my dress, hair, and mannerisms became a battle to uphold. I was living an ideal me, which was strenuous and taxing. I did not allow for mistakes and I was a perfectionist with myself and others. Nothing could leave the office without being perfect. We worked long and hard hours and many weekends and holidays to often pull things off. I believed that a great part of my success was due to my tenacity and dogged precision. I always presented a perfect image in terms of dress, hair, etc. and my work was a reflection of me with every "i" dotted and "t" crossed. Nothing was ever right or good enough, which was truly a heavy burden for both my employees and me to carry. I started looking everywhere and in everyone for peace and comfort. I had already started incorporating things from the books and I started to feel good about who I was and where I was going.

The night that Richard gave me the books, he told me that I was on a journey and everyone knew but me. He was right, I was on a journey, but now I had a map. I wrote things down that I needed to do and if I were able to accomplish 10% of what I wanted to achieve then I would have been well on my way, even though 100% was my goal. Things were truly looking up for me and my company. For the first time, I felt that I was moving in the right direction.

Richard submitted an application for our company to be considered for the Inc. 500|5000 List of Fastest Growing Private Companies in America. Everything seemed to be in place with me and for my company with Richard managing the day-to-day operation of the company. I had a semblance of peace and I felt that I was finally doing things right.

When others stop and take notice

A team from my company was in Detroit, Michigan attending a major federal employee conference. I was a guest speaker invited to speak on several topics. I was scheduled for several workshops based on my books. I arrived at the conference venue with my team and we went to the speaker's lounge. I found out where my classes would be held and we began to proceed to the rooms. Once we found my room to set up, a couple of people split up from the group and went to the exhibit hall where they set up our exhibit. So each of us had our own jobs and things to do to make the company's conference attendance a success. After a full day of speaking, exhibiting, and book signing, we all went to a local restaurant for dinner. I noticed that Richard went back to the car and came into the restaurant with a package, and everyone was smiling.

I asked, "What's in the package?"

He smiled, and said, "Indigo Johnson, we have a surprise for you."

I could not even imagine what he could have been talking about, but I would play along since everyone seemed so giddy.

"Indigo, Careers In Transition placed 239th on the *Inc. Magazine* 500|5000 List of Fastest Growing Companies in America," he said as he pulled out a letter from a white folder that held a special double issue of the 2012 magazine.

"Oh, my God!" I sighed in disbelief. "239th?" I asked. Then I reached my hand out to get the package.

Richard said while handing over the package, "Yep. 239th. Do you know what this means?"

I just smiled and clasped my hands like a little girl opening a present on Christmas day. I placed the folder down in front of me and started rifling through the package. "This is a cause for celebration," I exclaimed, and Curtis, my husband and CFO, called over the server. "I needed a drink anyway after today, but this will make the drinks even that much sweeter," I laughed as we ordered several different types of tropical drinks that could be shared around the table. As I took out each piece of literature that ranged from the magazine to the logo order form, I became more and more ecstatic. Richard nominated us for the Inc. 500|5000 Fastest Growing Private Companies in America, and we made the list. We ranked at number 239th with a three-year growth of 1,500.4% and revenue of $5.2 million.

This was indeed an honor in and of itself, but the true honor came when *Inc. Magazine* wanted to write an article on how we grew so rapidly. I did not feel that we grew rapidly. In fact, I believed that it was a long and difficult journey. It took 17 years to grow to this size, and I knew what kept us from growing aside from the high turnover. And that "something" that kept us from growing was a who and not a what. And that who was definitely me.

142

Moving from an Entrepreneur to a Small Business Owner

I shared in the article titled *Why I Stopped Firing Everyone and Started Being a Better Boss* that I would blame others for their failure to deliver when it was really me not leading them effectively. I believe that I learned a lot being in the school, but I could not solely attribute my newfound success to the school because the list was based on the previous three years. I could not even attribute my company's success to Richard who recently joined the company. We made the list despite my mental illness. We made the list despite me. My disorder gave me the audacity to think that a small HR firm could compete against the large HR corporations. I believed that we had the best products and I often worked around the clock to forge relationships. That is how we made the list. I forged relationships that are still intact today. However, what was going on in the backroom—i.e., high turnover—was preventing us from having momentum.

Then I opened up the magazine, and what did I see? There was the article about me. I recall the many interviews that I had with a variety of journalists from *Inc. Magazine,* but I never anticipated that there would be a whole page devoted to me. My story was told on page 87. This was quite impressive because out of 500 top CEOs only 12 were selected to have their stories featured aside from the number one company. I quickly read over the story and tucked everything away and placed everything back into the package. I remember becoming agitated. The mood at the dinner table took a slight turn. The smiles, laughs, and sheer bliss became thick and heavy as my mood changed. I was feeling really awkward.

"Is everything okay?" Sarah leaned over and asked me. Surprised that she asked, I stammered and said, "Yeah, everything is fine." But I was really feeling crummy about the article. I made myself smile and rejoin the chatter of the group, basking in our glory of making it to the Inc. 500|5000 List. However, all that night I became a little more distant. I could not put my finger on what was wrong about the article, but I knew something was not right. Could I have simply felt tired and overwhelmed about the entire day? After all, speaking takes a lot out of me sometimes. We finished our dinner and left for the hotel since I had an early day ahead of me. I was speaking again in the morning and I had a television appearance to make on Fox Network News that evening. I wanted and needed to get my rest.

Days passed and we were back in the office. At the Monday morning meeting we shared with the employees that we made the Inc. 500|5000 List of Fastest Growing Private Companies in America and that I had been featured in the magazine. I pulled out the package and passed the magazine around the table. There were oohs and ahhs around the room as we discussed the significance of being on the list.

"Inc. is the premier magazine for entrepreneurs in the world," Richard explained. He went on to say, "It was a privilege and honor to make the list, but to break into the 500 rank was phenomenal and to add to such an achievement to have our CEO featured is incredible."

Yes, we ranked in the top 500 which was awesome, but having a story that featured me firing people was not something that I was exceedingly proud about, I thought to myself. But I smiled and welcomed the good wishes and congratulations. Everyone was on a high, and for once I would hide my true feelings because this meant a lot to the team. But I could not help thinking about what was written:

Moving from an Entrepreneur to a Small Business Owner

Even as her company advised federal agencies and businesses on how to train and nurture employees, Indigo Johnson, a former Marine, ran her team like a drill instructor. She fired employees so regularly that few of them ever lasted longer than a year. Until finally she realized—she was the problem.

The story goes on to read that I hadn't fired anyone in a year and that I learned to allow people to utilize their strengths. This was partially true. I did not fire anyone because I hired Richard to manage the day-to-day operation of the company. Richard was a mild-mannered charismatic man who took on the task of cleaning up my mess. As Richard was being hired, he had to represent us at the Department of Labor wherein a past employee was attempting to sue us. He won the case, but he had a lot of damage control to put in place because turnover was beyond what was reasonable for any small business. That was the real story. I felt as if the magazine story was a fraud. The only real truth in my opinion was that I started a PhD program and within that program I came to realize that I needed to become a leader and started acquiring those skills. The real success in terms of retaining employees was due to Richard's efforts. But, what was most unsettling to me is that the article referred to me as a "new woman." I was anything but that as I struggled with behavioral problems.

One day I was sitting in my office working on training materials when Richard popped up in front of my desk. Richard was exceedingly proud of what "we" accomplished through Inc. and had yet another surprise for me. I saw in the hallway that there was a large package and I asked, "What are you up to?"

145

With the biggest smile on his face, Richard grabbed the package and said, "Here. This is for you, and you deserve it with all of the hard work that you have done over the years."

I stood up and walked around to the side of my desk and retrieved the package. As I pulled the brown wrapping from the item, I could see that it was me. Richard waved his hands like jazz hands and said, "Ta Da!" He had the article mounted in a beautiful gold-framed picture box with the magazine cover, the story, and our ranking.

It was absolutely beautiful. I humbly accepted the work of art and thanked him graciously. What a surprise. I started looking around my office to locate a place where the picture would be prominently displayed. I could not hang it just yet because it was too heavy for the nails that I had available so I promised that I would get the right size nails and would have the picture hung over my desk. Richard left looking pleased as punch. But I sat there feeling uncomfortable as the picture stared back at me. I was uncomfortable because I had not stopped firing people and I hadn't changed necessarily. I'd been trying and I had grown, but much of the credit belonged to Richard. Sure, no one had been fired, but that was because Richard was a master at retaining employees. I was still struggling with behavioral issues due to my constant mood swings.

After a couple of days of the picture sitting on the floor simply staring at me and reminding me that I was a fraud, I took the picture over to Richard's office. In a rapid speech pattern and elevated tone I asked, "Can we talk? We need to talk." I closed the door and sat a chair in front of his desk. "Richard, I'm not comfortable with all of this," I said with a gut-wrenching look on my face.

"All of what? What are you talking about," he asked looking really bewildered.

Moving from an Entrepreneur to a
Small Business Owner

"This. This article. This picture. All of it," I rattled off quickly. "I did not turn this company around. You did! The only reason people stopped being fired is because they worked for you."

"Now that's not true, Indigo," he tried to reassure me. "You are still in control of what happens and who ultimately does or doesn't do something around here. Sure, this is about you and this is your story," he continued.

We talked a little more as he attempted to show me how I have changed. However, I simply felt that I was a fraud when it came to the story. Yes, I built the company, and the increase in sales that ranked us 239th was due to my efforts. But the firing of people just kept nagging at me.

After that article was published, I had hired some marketing employees to help further my career and speaking engagements, and to leverage the article. The article received a lot of mileage. People wanted to interview me and reprint the article. I was amazed at how people referred to the article especially the part where I mentioned, "Pulling on grass doesn't make it grow faster." I discovered this saying while conducting research for class. This was an actual article in the Servant Leadership Journal that really touched me. I remember reading that article and simply crying. I truly felt bad about the many people I brought on and terminated so quickly. Aside from feeling bad, I felt a sense of shame. How was it that I hired quite competent people, but in a matter of months I managed to cut them down and discard them? I was no different than the school that fired me. In fact, I was worse because I provided a service that taught employers to value their employees.

It never occurred to me that something was truly wrong with me mentally even though I had been diagnosed as bipolar nearly ten years earlier. Even the article mentioned that I realized that I was the problem. Unfortunately, I believed that the problem was merely my not having leadership skills. What I came to understand was that I never learned leadership skills in the military as many would assume. I entered the enlisted ranks. My only encounters were with young corporals and sergeants who were abusive. They would yell at me to "motivate" me and give direction and instructions. In fact, most of my conversations with anyone who was responsible for me were threats. I did not have interactions with true leaders, i.e., officers. I had young immature men constantly yelling, berating, and abusing me. This was what I learned as a technique and effective way of managing and leading. After all, it worked on me. I really believed that tearing people down to build them up was a method that led to success. That was the Marine Corps way: tear you down and build you back up.

Because my active duty time was limited and there were only brief encounters during my reserve time, I was exposed to a process that was meant to create strength and hardness. I carried that methodology into my profession. But that was soon to be resolved since I was working on my PhD in Values-Driven Leadership. What I thought was happening to me and within my company was that I lacked leadership skills, and that once I learned the many aspects of leadership from reading books to taking assessments, I would be better equipped to deal with my employees. But such was not the case.

Within the year, I would officially be diagnosed with Bipolar II disorder. It would become clear that I needed more than leadership skills. Aside from having Bipolar II, it was determined that I am impulsive with rage and Post Traumatic Stress Disorder (PTSD). It was as if I could not help myself when it came to controlling my actions.

There was an incident a few years ago when I fired nearly everyone on staff in one day. However, I kept two employees, Frances and London, because they had figured out how to work with me and set boundaries. But firing several people at once was pretty impulsive. I did not do it without cause. Each person was not performing at the level that I would have liked, but I can now see how drastic a step firing nearly everyone in a small business could have been. What I have come to learn about being bipolar is that people impacted with the disorder can work at an amazingly fast pace and think several steps ahead of people. This would cause me to become very frustrated with employees because I could not understand why they could not ever outthink me or be as insightful. This would lead to me finding their weaknesses and picking them apart. This would go on for a matter of months and they would either quit or be terminated. It was an ongoing process that led to a revolving door in my company.

Having bipolar disorder does not make sense and many of my actions did not make sense to me or the people around me. Now, being on medicine to control my bipolar urges and impulsiveness, I can see how detrimental my condition was to my organization. Unfortunately, every time I fired someone would mean hiring someone else to replace that employee, which took time and resources. It meant time loss in performance since no one was in the position to get the work done, and it placed an incredible amount of strain on my remaining employees who had to do that work in an effort to make sure nothing fell through the cracks.

Truly reflecting on the Inc. scenario, I realized that I did the right thing as a leader. I hired someone who could do what I was incapable of doing. Richard knew how to retain employees, while I did not. A leader cannot be excellent with strengths in everything. I had the wherewithal to know that there was a problem with our high turnover, and I hired someone to fix the problem. That was accomplished in headquarters, but the issue traveled with me to DC.

Chapter 6

A Private Mess Living a Public Success

So much was starting to happen. The company was receiving a huge award from *Inc. Magazine*. Everyone around the office at head-quarters was buzzing. I purchased tickets for London, Frances, and Richard to attend the conference. I felt that they deserved to be with me when I accepted the highest honor that the company had ever received.

Leading up to the conference I shopped for the most beautiful gown. "This would be really sexy," said the woman who waited on me at the gown boutique. "No, it's a little too flashy," I said as I thumbed through the dresses looking for a gown to wear to the Inc. 500 Award Gala. I did not know what I wanted, but I knew that I wanted to look elegant. Everything that the sales associates kept showing me were too revealing. "I do not want people to think that I won my award or got my business by sleeping around," I said without giving too much care to the many dresses they held in their hands.

I was very concerned about the image I would project at the conference. I wanted to be respected for what I accomplished, so I wanted to pick something that would make a statement with class. I found just the right dress; it was gray with sequins and sheer in the mid-section and flared out with layers and layers of fabric that touched the floor. My chest would be out, but it was very tasteful with a shawl and Swarovski jewelry around my neck. The dress reminded me of something from a Disney fairytale movie. It was truly a ball gown. For the first time I felt like royalty, a princess of sorts.

At the conference, I participated on a panel for a session, and I was interviewed by both *Inc. Magazine* for their online videos and the Kauffman Foundation for a video that they were shooting. Everything had come together for me. I was at the top of my game and all of my hard work was being rewarded. There were no worries of employees, mood changes, or even losing clients. For the first time, I did not have a worry in the world. And then the evening of the gala I wore my gown, and I felt as if I'd finally made it. At our table, we joked and laughed. My primary team was with me soaking in the entire affair. The evening was long, but waiting to hear the emcee call our name was well worth the wait. When they got to our name, the entire team went with me because I wanted them on stage with me. There was no doubt that I was there because they were here for me. It was our brightest moment ever.

It was a week after the conference, and I was tired, physically and mentally. I spent the weekend preparing for Hurricane Sandy that was ripping through the Eastern Shores. In preparation, I equated how going through a career storm was similar to going through an actual storm. So I wrote an article about preparing and weathering the storm in your career. It was very profound and later published in a professional organization newsletter. I was very prepared for the storm and what would inevitably hit my career. I was on a high for days, so I took sleeping pills to sleep. As far as I was concerned, the world was all right with me. I wished that I could bottle that feeling to unleash it whenever I felt depressed, angry or insecure, which happened all too often.

Things seemed normal around the company, but I just found out that another employee quit. Our Human Resources Manager implied that I was the reason for him quitting although the employee assured me that he was experiencing family and personal problems that were impacting his job. I did not know how much I believed his excuse, but I had to take his word for it. Interestingly, he became a contractor, which worked out fine for both him and the company. But I hated losing an actual employee. I had become very sensitive to the turnover. Ever since that article was published in *Inc. Magazine*, I felt that I had to live up to what was written. Yes, there was a drop in turnover thanks to Richard, but there were the employees who worked directly for me who were in harm's way. I tried to be mindful of them and I worked extra hard at being a good leader and boss.

Close encounters of a disruptive kind

During all the events that were happening with the company, I was working and living in the DC area. I was not flying back and forth, but rather living there. I set up a home office in an apartment in the DC Metro area. I had an office in one part of the apartment and I set up two work stations in one of the other bedrooms. I was very happy to finally be in the DC area and pursuing my career in delivering more speaking engagements and television appearances. I started to hire people to work directly with me, up there. I had brought on four people over the course of a year to support me and, without fail, each one either quit or was fired. Even though this was after the Inc. article and award, I knew that I had a problem with retaining employees but I did not know what to do since Richard was down in the main office. This was a small environment to work in and it was my home. Initially everything was wonderful, but slowly I became different. I now realize that I was entering into a severe manic episode. I shut myself off from headquarters and wanted to focus all of my attention on the employees in the DC area. Not recognizing that I was actually bipolar and becoming manic, I did not know that everything I was doing would be detrimental. When I was manic, I would often yell at the employees when things were not done, I did not trust them to do their job, and I was highly critical.

On average, there would be one or two employees working with me at a time. There were many days that an employee would leave the office very upset or sit at her desk with tears flowing down her cheeks. I cannot even describe what I was doing, but I was out of control. When I experienced a hypomanic stage I would rage. I couldn't see that I was abusive, bullying, or intimidating. I was not aware that I was bipolar or what bipolar really meant since I was still in denial. I can't emphasize that enough and I'll explain the importance of awareness in-depth later. It is the lynchpin to mental wellness. My behavior was erratic as I would throw things, swipe everything off of my desk with a sweeping of my hands, or curse and scream under my breath while sitting in the other room.

This went on for weeks and months, and slowly people would quit or I would terminate them over that one-year time frame. When I was not manic, I would have deep depressions that I would attempt to hide. This usually came in the form of being very quiet and not really caring what the employees did or did not do. I was consistently sending inconsistent messages, not even aware that I or my behaviors were abnormal.

I was living a seemingly double life, but it all was bipolar. I was giving away money to nonprofits and a variety of organizations. I gave away over $47,000 in 2012. Little did I know that spending money recklessly even for a good cause was a sign of hypomania. I was creating scholarships and donating money for a variety of initiatives. This led to a lot of recognition from organizations that I was affiliated with both in DC and Atlanta. I received awards from organizations based on my charitable donations, but I also received awards for the work that I accomplished in the Human Resources arena. I was a public success, living a private mess.

From first class to jail cell

It was December 2012, and I was traveling back to Atlanta to work at the home office. Rhoda, a new employee and dear friend, was accompanying me to meet the other employees, and I had my 13-year-old son with me. He would visit me occasionally while I was in DC. Our routine schedule was to catch the 6 a.m. flight from DC to Atlanta. We arrived at the airport and met Rhoda there. She was excited about meeting her peers down in Atlanta, and I was hyped up about going "home" and being with my other employees. In fact, I had scheduled a "forced fun" for the entire company. A forced fun was my way of either giving back to the community through community service or just closing down the company to do something meaningful together. It's called forced fun because that was a term I picked up in the military; however, no one ever felt forced because we had such a great time and often employees had a say and voted on what we would do for that day. So this was going to be a special trip filled with fun mixed with work.

I started my morning at 4 a.m. to get ready for my day, arrived at 5 a.m. at the airport and sat in first class at 6 a.m. to travel to Atlanta. I had a very important meeting scheduled for 10 a.m. at a high profile corporation with a prominent executive. The plan was for me to get picked up at the airport, dropped off at my office, and Richard and I would go to meet a potentially new client together. However, things took a turn.

As usual, I would have one of my sons pick me up from the airport and serve as my driver. He had a full-time job with my company but some of his actions were too volatile for the organization, which caused people to fear him, and thus it forced me to agree to have him terminated. He is very intelligent, tall, and attractive, but a volatile young man and I attribute that to his disorder. Being a mother feeling somewhat responsible for the well-being of her child, I gave him the assignment of picking me up and dropping me off at the airport with a car that I left at the office. He picked me up as usual, with Rhoda and my youngest son who piled into the car. Rhoda and I placed a large blue trunk between the two of us on the back seat. I spoke to my son and so did Rhoda. Before making it off the airport property, I turned to Rhoda and asked her whether my son spoke to her. She said, "No," in a low whisper. My son looked in the rearview mirror and snidely stated that he did speak. Rhoda and I looked at each other and giggled under our breath like little girls as she shook her head, indicating that he didn't.

It was now around 8 a.m. and we were driving to my office. I began telling Rhoda that I heard that my husband had purchased a live Christmas tree and decorated the whole house to prepare for his family to visit from out of town. I made a few comments about the situation that upset my son. I could tell that he was already irritable and agitated, but I continued to talk to Rhoda because she was my friend and I wanted to share with her my thoughts about my husband whom I was divorcing and for all practicality was separated from. We laughed and chatted about marriage and that perceivably damn live Christmas tree. After a couple of minutes of our giggling and talking, my son yelled, "Don't talk about my dad. He doesn't talk about you!" I reminded him that I was a grownup and could talk about anything I chose to talk about. He then threatened to turn off the expressway and head home and not take me to work if I didn't stop talking.

Well, we were pretty far from my office so I stopped talking about his father. But as we got closer, I started talking about the divorce and the live Christmas tree, which was a source of contention because my husband was adamant that we wouldn't have a live tree when we were together even though I grew up with live trees. He grew up with artificial trees and being the controlling passive aggressive person that he was, I went along with his tradition. (Okay . . . I think that was a dig, but I'm trying to bring clarity to why I obsessed over the tree that, by the way, turned out to be artificial.) I felt really pissed that he would get a live tree to impress his family once I moved out. Well, my son wasn't having it. He started saying things such as I wasn't a good wife or a good mother. We began to argue about his dad and I shouted, "He's not your real dad, anyway. In fact, both of your fathers ain't shit."

This was the straw that broke the camel's back. Even though he knew that Curtis wasn't his biological father, he was very loyal to him. He sped by my office park without stopping. I was yelling for him to take me to work. I was screaming that he was going to make me late for my meeting. He simply tuned me out and kept driving. This terrified me because this 28-year-old young man had totaled several cars, to include two of mine, and he was diagnosed as bipolar. For the first time in my life, I was afraid of this person driving me off to God knows where because he was angry that I talked badly about his father, two to be correct. When yelling and screaming at him didn't faze him, I started hitting him, which didn't even cause him to blink. So, I continued hitting him in the back of the head, and then I started choking him, to no avail. I was panicking and the more I panicked the more he became detached. With my heavy winter coat restricting my movement, I quickly climbed from the back seat to straddle the middle console and continued hitting him to get him to pull over. He just kept driving, so I slid into the driver's seat with him and began wrestling with the steering wheel and trying desperately to stop the car and turn it off. I was switching the gears, stepping on the brakes, and hitting him all at the same time.

As we drove down the road, with me feeling as if I was being kidnapped, I saw a police vehicle in the parking lot of a church. I started to honk the horn and turn the car into the parking lot. As soon as we got into the parking lot, my son jumped out of the car and ran over to the police. I put the car in park and got out screaming that he was trying to kidnap me. I was terrified. I learned later that the event brought up traumatic past events of being controlled, detained, and once actually mugged and accosted by someone at gunpoint who attempted to get me to drive from an area many years earlier. The police came over to ask a few questions, and I hysterically told him that my son was crazy and that he was kidnapping me. I told the officers that I worked several miles back the other way and that my son would not let me out or stop the car. The police left and went back to my son and they talked for a few minutes more. One officer came back and said that your son wouldn't kidnap you. Then another officer walked up and said that I was under arrest and to put my hands behind my back.

I was shocked. How was I the criminal? I could see that I would take the hit for this. I started to take off my nice coat and other items that I didn't want to have lost in jail. With the look of shock on my face, I turned around and put my hands behind my back. As the officer was handcuffing me, I quickly turned back around to give Rhoda my purse. That startled the officer and he yelled that I should never make sudden moves like that. I apologized and was read my rights. I told Rhoda to share with my leadership team what happened and to still make the scheduled meeting that I was there to attend. It never occurred to me that Rhoda had a front row seat to my madness.

My husband showed up and just placed his hands on his hips as he made sure that my sons were okay, not once inquiring about my well-being. I slipped into the back seat of the squad car nonchalantly with no real emotions. What I now realize is that the thought of being controlled triggered me. As I slid into the car, I looked to the left of me and there was a young woman in the vehicle crying hysterically. I tried to talk her into being calm and suggested that she breathe. I then sat back and took the ride to the police station.

It was a very surreal trip. How did I get here, I thought to myself. Things got real real fast . . . I was really on my way to jail. The officer drove through the gates, and upon our arrival I was placed in a holding cell after being searched. I was dressed in a Brooks Brother's suit, I had on my expensive jewelry, and I was dressed for success because I was on my way to a high power meeting that morning. From flying first class that morning to a jail cell hours later.

The jail guard placed me in a cell by myself. I was able to come out and make a phone call. I struck up a conversation with the jail guard and other police officers in the area and they were appalled that I was arrested. Some officers would come through the holding area and ask me whether I was a celebrity or someone famous. They kept saying that I didn't belong there. They allowed me to stay outside the cell as I talked to them about their careers and allowed one particular officer to discuss what it was like working as a police officer, especially as a woman. And of course I talked about my son and how he was the reason for me being arrested. They were troubled that a son would do what he did, and had no explanation of what I could have done differently. I really connected with one officer who actually started crying as we discussed the harassment and unfair treatment that she had endured on the job. I became the professional coach which was my natural role so I didn't feel scared or overwhelmed. I was okay because I was being treated with respect and genuine concern.

I was charged with misdemeanor battery and reckless conduct. I had a lot of the officers supporting me and guiding me on things that I should and should not do during the booking process. For instance, I didn't want to take what I believe was a TB shot because I recently had that same shot in preparation for my trip to China. But the jail guard shared with me that if I didn't take the shot I would be placed in isolation, and inmates in isolation weren't seen by a judge for days, which meant I would be there until God knows when. Later that day, I had to take a mug shot, which I smiled for because I was still in disbelief that I was actually in jail. Frances, from my company, tried to make bail but they wouldn't allow it to go through, which meant I had to stay overnight.

It was now evening, and the jail officer was apologetic as she brought me inmate clothes. She proudly shared with me that she found new items such as underwear for me to put on. She had managed to allow me to stay in my own clothes all day, kept the cell unlocked and treated me with the utmost dignity and respect. Unfortunately, her shift was ending and she came over to tell me good night and reemphasized that I didn't belong there. I was grateful for all that she did and the kindness that she showed.

Later that night, I was taken to the actual county jail where I was given a mat and placed in a cell with a woman who had been there for a year. The door slammed and locked behind me as she pointed to the top rack. The space was just like the movies with a toilet at the foot of the bed. We introduced ourselves, and we talked. I was very curious about everything. The lights shut off and everything became quiet. I was lying on the top bunk wondering how I got there. I was freezing because the vent was directly in front of my bunk. My cell mate showed me how to cover the vent with spit and paper, and I went to sleep but not before hearing the many echoes of crying throughout the place.

So much pain crept throughout the jail. They told you nothing there, which was hard to deal with considering I needed information. They wouldn't talk to you through the intercom or glass/metal doors, it was extremely cold, the holding cell was filthy, people were sick, which was difficult to handle since I have serious issues with germs, and the pad on the steel bed was painful. I was lying there thinking how just a few months ago I paid $5,000 to stay at a destination spa and now this—a jail cell.

That next morning my cell mate woke me up for a head count which meant getting up and standing outside the cell in a general area by making a circle. After the count, we returned to our cell and I climbed back up on the rack. Then she told me to hurry for breakfast. It was still dark outside, and I was not interested in eating that early or eating in general. I stayed in the cell and she left as the door slammed and locked behind her.

That was an awful feeling. I began to worry about all the what ifs—what if there was a fire, what if something happened, how would I get out? And the big what if . . . what if they forgot I was in here?

She returned after breakfast and I felt a little better. I did not like being alone in that cell. Everything seemed so dark and gray. It was like a heavy dark cloud hung over the cell.

Time passed and we had to come out and clean up the central area. I was pleased to be doing something. I cleaned like I was being graded or paid. Then it was time for us to socialize. This was actually interesting to me. I had a chance to talk to a lot of the women who bared their souls. They respected me, and sought my counsel. Ironically, the young woman who rode in the squad car with me came over to me to apologize for her behavior. I expressed that no apology was necessary and that I was glad to see that she was doing better. I just showed the many women kindness and gave them a chance to be heard.

A Private Mess Living a Public Success

My heart quickly connected with them. So many of them were there for stupid stuff but they couldn't pull themselves out of a destructive cycle. Some of them were very intelligent and my heart went out to them. All I could think about was how could I help them. Later that day, the booking officer came by to see me and make sure that I was alright. I also went before the judge who gave me a court date, and all I could think about was a pending trip to China. I asked whether I could leave the country for my internship, and he stated that such was fine. But, his answer came with a very puzzled look. The look of disbelief. I looked and behaved nothing like the other prisoners.

The day went by slowly and my cell mate shared with me what to expect. She told me that I wouldn't get out until late that night because the county makes money on prisoners the longer they are there. And she was right. I didn't get out until 11 p.m. or so. And my loyal employee Frances was there to bail me out. My husband showed up, but I could care less about him being there. I was processed out and I hugged Frances, but I rode home with my husband. I got to the house and showered for what felt like a lifetime because I hadn't done so at the jail. For the first time in a long time, I slept in the bed with Curtis. For years, I had been sleeping in a separate room, but that night I didn't want to be alone.

The next day, I returned to work and had an all hands meeting to learn about my company's experience at a motivational seminar, as their forced fun excursion. They were in disbelief about my experience and so very grateful of the event that I sent them to. I was remorseful that I couldn't share what turned out to be a very meaningful event for them. They talked about the many suggestions that the speaker shared about turning their lives and careers around.

Was I exactly where I needed to have been? I touched several lives while I was in jail, and I too was touched. I discovered that there are a lot of broken people and that maybe God was calling me to hear their voices to one day be their voice. That was a life-changing experience that opened my heart to becoming more compassionate. However, again I did not see the whole ordeal as a call for help for myself and that I was experiencing my own mental breakdown. In fact, employees kept asking whether I was okay. I thought that I was fine. I didn't have a clear sense of reality. I remember being upset that I missed our forced fun more than anything. Looking back, it was actually very traumatic.

Dr. Fieve states in his book *Bipolar II*, "I've seen numerous hypomanics who overestimate their abilities, and while their minds are sharp, their judgment is sometimes poor, resulting in impulsive decision-making, job loss, reduced income, broken relationships, and even suicide." It is commonly known that people who battle with bipolar disorder often have encounters with law enforcement. I was no different despite being a business leader and highly respected citizen. It is not uncommon for people with bipolar disorder to have a history of explosive behavior. In my case, I was later diagnosed with rage, but some people may have mania, violence, anger, etc.

There is diversity in mental illness, and none of us are the same. There is a distinct scale and range in which people behave. What is important to gather from this incident is that when your behavior involves law enforcement you are probably dealing with a mental disorder. In my case, my brain betrayed me by causing me to be out of control, needing law enforcement to keep me and others around me safe. Had I known that I was mentally ill, maybe I could have shared that with the arresting officer to receive an alternative treatment. However, I can assure you that jail was not the answer. It only forced me to get a good attorney to have everything cleaned up, but my mind was still amiss. Four months later, I was in treatment with a peer who spoke of her experience in jail.

There should be training or more understanding about mental illness so that law enforcement can better handle a situation. When someone is suffering from a mental disorder they should be taken to a mental health agency for evaluation instead of a jail cell. I needed mental health care, not jail. I recall going before the judge the next day and all I was concerned about was my one month trip to China and all he was concerned about was my court date. Nothing was solved and the time bomb to my mental meltdown was slowly ticking away.

The beginning of the end

It was a few weeks later when I would leave for China. A few months ago, I'd enrolled in an internship program that would take place in China. One of my sons was accepted into the program, and, coincidentally, my school required that all students attend an international conference or some sort of venue that would further our leadership and international exposure. I asked my son to put me in touch with the program that had accepted him into an internship over in China. This program would have me in Beijing, China for 30 days starting in late December and ending in January. I went through the entire application process based on being a PhD student. There was a cost associated with it that ranged from accommodations to a variety of fees. But there was no payment afforded for this "learning" opportunity.

I was accepted and I then began all of the legwork needed for me to be in China. I received a series of shots and made many preparations to be away for an extended period of time. I was excited about the opportunity, especially since it would give me a chance to be with one of my sons whom I seldom saw since I was living in Washington, DC.

I arrived in Beijing, China in the middle of the night after a lengthy flight. I took sleeping pills and I drank vodka all the way there as a way to relax and sleep. I packed several trunks for my stay. I was well-prepared based on one of the Marine Corps' sayings: "Hope for the best, but plan for the worst." I had everything that I felt would be the comforts of home.

We were picked up from the airport and transported to a condominium that was supposed to be an upscale apartment. I shared an apartment with two other young ladies. I was the oldest student in the entire program, but I felt that I would learn a lot being with these other students from all over the world. The apartment was not comfortable and my room was cold, but things would get better once there was daylight. I always felt that a new day would bring clarity to any situation.

The next day we were taken to our perspective employers. I interned for an American-owned logistics company with all the employees being Chinese. Only one person within the organization spoke English, and she was my boss for lack of a better term. I will call her Sun. We got along very well. I shared with her who I was and what I was capable of doing. That was all it took for her to realize that she struck gold. I wasn't your ordinary intern who was there to learn.

A PRIVATE MESS LIVING A PUBLIC SUCCESS

I was assigned to the HR Department of this organization, so there were many projects that I could be a part of. However, instantly I was asked to work on a project based on something that Sun was struggling with. She asked me to help her with performance appraisals that the corporate office required of her. I quickly assessed that she needed more than performance appraisals. There was so much that she needed to build a foundation of performance and productivity. Many of the employees needed a career map and other developmental initiatives. I started working with Sun on determining job tasks and functions which led to writing job descriptions.

In the meanwhile, I had to figure out how to get from the office back to the apartment. It was an indescribably horrible commute to and from the office. It was bitterly cold there and the mass transit system was nothing like anything I had ever experienced. You would wait for the train, and when the door opened, people would literally fall out onto the platform and be trampled over as others got into the car which was more packed than a can of sardines. I have never witnessed anything like that in my life.

After a couple of days of doing that, I opted to take a taxi to work. That was not feasible. The taxi cab drivers simply would not stop for me. I stood in the freezing temperature for nearly an hour with taxi cab drivers waving their hands at me and moving their mouths at what appeared to be a yelling gesture. Was I encountering racism or nationalism? It was both. I was denied transportation because of my race and being American. It was a terrible experience as I walked to the subway to catch the train. The experience of catching the train was too stressful for me, and I was miserable. I would make it to the office frazzled and sit at a lonely desk that was assigned to me. I would sit there and just observe the other employees.

No one talked to anybody, and it wasn't until lunch that they would all gather to eat together while an Italian intern would teach them English and geography. It was a sight to behold. All day not a word to one another or breaks, and then they would gather together for an hour or so of communicating, laughing, and being together. Then we would go back to work without looking up from our computers. I was working on things that did not inspire me but came as second nature. Then the day would end and I would have to walk a long distance in the 10-degree temperature to the subway and be pushed and shoved onto the train.

I was completely unhappy and depressed after a few days. I finally came in to the office and sat down with Sun and shared with her that the work that she had me doing was actually a task that I would ask of one my employees. I shared with her that I was so far removed from that kind of work that it was not something that I was willing to continue doing, but that I would finish the task that I was working on. I told her that I would work from the apartment and then come in twice a week to update her and share with her what I had completed. I then left for the day to avoid the evening rush hours and I went back to the apartment. I had to get out of there; it was a freezing hell in China.

That evening my son came to my room and asked if I was going to accompany him and the other young adults on a trip to get groceries. I recalled how one day an older Chinese man walked up to our group and began yelling and cursing at us in Mandarin as people started moving away from the scene. It was a frightening experience and I vowed that I would never be placed in a situation where I couldn't protect myself. So I told my son that I would stay in my room. He said that I needed to get groceries. I shared with him that I had plenty to eat. I took him to my kitchen and opened the drawers and fridge and said, "See, I have plenty to eat; I'm good," as I pointed at bottles of liquor, coffee, chocolate-covered nuts, and chips. This was what I packed in my trunk. That was pretty much all that I had been eating and I felt that it was enough to sustain me for a few weeks. But, my son disagreed. He said, "Mom, you can't live off of wine and nuts. You need food."

I was slowly losing it mentally. That place was the most difficult environment I had ever encountered. Even when it snowed, the snow looked like white charcoal that glistened like crystals due to the extreme pollution. It was the nastiest place that I have ever been with feces, vomit, and phlegm all over the sidewalks and even indoors at some places. Beijing was a God-awful nasty place to be, let alone live.

Another few days passed, and I went to Sun and shared with her the work that I completed. She was overjoyed at how fast I could work and how in-depth my work was. She learned a lot from what I presented her. At that point, I shared with her my two books *Playing by the Unwritten Rules*, and I left for the day to go back to my apartment.

I found myself in the Far East as a VIP

The next couple of days I went back to visit Sun, and she was all afloat about my books. She had read them cover to cover. She had a thousand questions that I answered as we sat and talked for hours. She asked if I would be willing to speak to a group of her HR peers throughout Beijing. By this time, I had become very ill because my room did not have heat. I complained to the landlord, but to no avail.

So on Christmas day my son and I moved out of our apartments into a four-star hotel. Fortunately, it was only a few blocks from the office, so I was able to walk to meet with Sun.

Things had change drastically for me based on my books. I met with Sun's peer at the hotel where I was staying for a coaching session. Then I spoke at this magnificent place that was similar to a spa and homeopathic center for healing. I spoke to Sun's HR colleagues on the book. I was completely in my element. I spoke with passion, purpose, and insight. The audience loved me, and that breathed life into me. I was humorous, relevant, and compassionate. I was able to share with these professionals a new way of thinking about their careers. It was wonderful. That led to Sun arranging for me to fly to Shanghai where I would give the same presentation to HR professionals enrolled at the University of Hong Kong.

By this time, I was living in the hotel, eating real food, and getting my rest. I was now being treated like a VIP. Sun arranged for her husband to take my son and me on tours throughout the city, and a woman whom I coached took us out on the town, as well. Things had turned completely around for me in China. I had use of the company's driver and everything was going well with me. I also started meeting people who could speak English and Mandarin which made things so much easier for us.

The day came that I traveled to Shanghai and presented at a conference center that was packed. I was on a complete high! Everything went so well that the director of a business program at the University of Hong Kong asked if I would speak with him about my teaching courses that would be offered in English. That evening Sun treated me to an evening of sheer fun. I was exposed to the night life of Shanghai and treated like a VIP.

A few more days passed and it was time for me to return to United States. I can honestly say that I was a little sad and definitely not ready to leave. I was in a place where I was valued for my thoughts and ability to touch lives. I gave them what I had to give and it felt good. I was doing what I loved and what I was a master at doing, and that was presenting my ideas and opinions as they pertain to career success and progression. The people whom I engaged absolutely loved me and I returned that love. I was on a perpetual high.

Thrown back into reality

When I came back from China, I was a little more agitated than usual. I'd had the experience of a lifetime, and I wasn't ready to come back to my boring world of responsibility for a company. But what I had experienced wasn't the real world and it was time for me to get back in the saddle. I believe that I was suffering from depression and the disenchantment of being back at work and things became so chaotic that no one could function in that work space.

The most wonderful hire and then heartbreaking employee encounter was when I hired a very close friend, Rhoda, to come on in a senior leadership capacity. The first month or two was fine right before I left for China, but without warning I became cross and more paranoid upon my return. I am not sure whether she was ever the right person for the job, but I shared with her that I needed someone I could trust because I started to not trust Richard or anyone at the headquarters. I brought her in for all the wrong reasons. She was hired to truly market me as a speaker and entrepreneur, and then the company. However, my mental illness constantly got in the way.

I built a fortress around me in DC, with limited exposure to the headquarter office.

Looking back, this was truly an example of psychosis as I became leery of people and stayed in my apartment for days without leaving. The only real access to the outside world was through my newest employee, Rhoda, who became the target of my irritability and anxiety. It was just a matter of time before she would quit under the pressure. I had limited communications with her while I was in China, and upon my return home I became very abusive because I felt that she hadn't accomplished anything meaningful during my absence. I could tell that she became frightened, and she limited her time in the office. Within weeks of my return she resigned, and when she did, she did not notify me, but rather Richard. I was deeply hurt by her resignation. In her resignation letter to Richard she spoke of abuse.

I can definitely see that such occurred now that I have gone through extensive therapy, but at the time, I felt betrayed by her. I could not understand why she went to Richard instead of coming to me. In fact, several employees had gone to Richard to resign out of fear of coming to me. This was very painful and it felt like betrayal. As people quit, I felt shame and resentment because I could not understand why they would leave me. I often felt alone and misunderstood.

Nothing would stick, including employees

What was very confusing for me was that I continued to study leadership, and I was reading all the books, taking the assessments, and attempting to do the very things that would attract, develop, and retain employees, but it just was not happening. It was so frustrating to want to do the right thing by my employees, but because of my impulsiveness and rage tendencies, I was unable to control myself. Unfortunately for many of my employees, being my employee was more like being in an abusive relationship. I would belittle, yell at, and accuse employees of things that were ridiculous. They often tried to explain but I would poke holes into their stories. This was often where their tears would develop and I would retreat to my office. After I cooled off and calmed down, I would approach them with a genuine apology. I often felt bad about how I treated them. I felt like a puppet on a string with a cruel puppet master.

According to Dr. Ronald Fieve in his book *Bipolar II* (pg. 24), sometimes the Bipolar II hypomania goes too high, which becomes evident in increased physical activity and more rapid and irritable speech. The elated disposition becomes hostile and angry, resulting in explosive words and actions. I ran everyone who was closest to me away until I was all alone in my apartment.

As an entrepreneur in a growth capacity, it is imperative that you have people with some corporate knowledge. It was fortunate that I had isolated myself and not destroyed my company, but my career continued to stall and become static because I could not retain the people who were hired to help me launch a television presence and maintain my speaking career. In fact, I stopped communicating with my clients altogether.

This was troubling for me personally and for Richard, who had to work twice as hard, as people would call him for counseling and consoling about working for me. Even though we were separate from the headquarters, the employee issues took their toll on the company. Financially, the company took a hit because I hired all of these people with substantial salaries, but they did not produce anything measurable. Part of the reason they did not produce was because I often got in their way. Also, it takes a while before a person is truly performing and contributing, and since several employees were with me only a few months we did not see a return on our investment in terms of the expenses associated with hiring new employees. This truly negatively impacted our bottom line.

It was said that there were rumblings at the headquarters about how the money being used for me could have been better used in other parts of the business. This had a rippling effect on the organization because it frustrated employees to see that we were running through employees, again. Also, headquarters employees interacted with the DC area employees. When they would quit or be fired that created tension throughout the organization. It was a chaotic time for me and the organization.

Interestingly, when some people would quit they would remain in contact with me and wish me well. They often spoke of how they believed in me and what I was trying to do, but that they needed to move on. Rhoda resigned and sent a scathing memo to Richard, and within the body of her message she mentioned that she knew that I had a kind and good heart. It was as if people knew that I cared, but for some inexplicable reason, I was difficult to work with. This is often a signature mark of people with bipolar disorder. They have difficulties in working with people and often lose their jobs. In my case, I would not be fired because I owned the company.

I know that if I had worked for a company and these behaviors manifested there and people would quit or leave a department because of me, I am certain that I would have been fired. But I was the owner so I was able to keep my job. I think that I, personally,

and my company would be so much further along if I did not run so
many people away. It was disappointing that I had no control over
how I treated people when I raged. It was if something took over my
ability to rationalize and reason.

Chapter 7

The Beginning of the End of Darkness

I was alone in my apartment and the office space was empty. I had no plans to hire anyone and I had no plans for my career. Each day blended into the next. Even though I pushed Rhoda away unintentionally, I became very depressed with her resignation. I could not make sense of anything any longer. I was having a true psychotic episode all alone in my apartment. I tried talking to Richard, but he was at the end of his rope with me. As hard as he tried to protect me and keep our employees intact, I managed to undermine his efforts based on my paranoia.

I could not understand what was wrong with me. I lost interest in everything. I had filed for divorce, distanced myself from family, and disconnected from what few friends I had left. In fact, I was an official member of the NFL (No Friends Left).

I think one of the most major events that sent me over the edge was my divorce of a 20-plus-year marriage. My husband was threatening to take half my company, which by law he was entitled to in the great state of Georgia. My husband was my Chief Financial Officer for the company so he knew exactly what my company was worth.

In an effort to not lose everything and the one thing that I built over the years, I asked him for his terms and conditions that didn't include my company. I even agreed to see a mediator to come up with something fair that didn't involve my company. He arranged for us to meet with an attorney who kept going back to my company as a viable option. What I figured out was that my husband tricked me and arranged for us to meet with someone who was supporting him in taking my company. I was so pissed, but I had to work through this calmly.

What no one seemed to understand was that taking half the company really meant dissolving the company to get to the assets, so this was devastating to me. After weeks of back and forth negotiating, he submitted his terms in an email to me. He required the house fully furnished, primary custody of our youngest son, our time share, season tickets for our Atlanta Falcons, half a million dollars, child support, a two-year contract to stay connected with my company, and a commitment that my company would mentor his company so that he could get government contracts upon returning to his company. Many days I cried, asking him what I was getting from the divorce because none of it was fair. His reply at one point was, "You get to keep your company." But I felt as if I was losing everything including my mind. He stripped me of everything he could get based on his need to take care of himself.

I agreed to his terms because I wasn't in my right mind to fight, thus I was taken advantage of, and this sent me over the edge. I was able to complete an assignment for school and attend a class, but everything felt as if I was just going through the motions. I cannot describe what I felt; it was a place I had never been before. I was filled with rage and depression at the same time.

I found myself distrusting everyone, especially Richard, who was making unscrupulous deals that would be revealed months later, that eventually cost me my savings and reputation, and my paranoia heightened. Those closest to me saw that I was unraveling and actually took advantage of the situation. Not to mention, Rhoda's quitting really rattled my cage. But her quitting was merely one link in a long chain of events. After all, she was a dear long-time friend, and if I could not sustain employment with her, what did that say about me, I thought to myself. I would obsess over all the employees I lost and the relationships I destroyed. I sank deeper and deeper into my cave. I was still the leader of the company, but I was leading in total darkness at this point. I was sending out bizarre and hostile emails that often did not make sense. I also made reckless financial decisions based on Richard's recommendations that would come back to haunt me.

My breakdown was a breakthrough

It was January 2013 and the walls caved in on me and my world came tumbling down around my feet. This was what I would call a break in reality. I was experiencing a major episode. I just got off the phone with Richard. I shared with him that I was going to seek therapy or counseling. I was feeling at my wits' end and I did not understand all of the emotions that I was feeling. I just knew something was terribly wrong. I went online to research therapists and found Dr. Shield. I called her immediately. "Hello, Dr. Shield, my name is Indigo Johnson, and I'm calling about your services," I said as I left a message for her. I left messages for at least a dozen psychotherapists, but Dr. Shield seemed to resonate with me based on her bio and YouTube Video. A day or two later I received a call from her.

"Indigo, this is Dr. Shield. What is going on that makes you believe that you need a therapist?" she asked.

"I do not know. I feel awful and my world seems to be falling apart," I told her with the typical rapid speech that was indicative of bipolar disorder. She shared with me when she had an opening, and I took the next available day and time. I felt some relief the morning that I was on my way to see Dr. Shield. I was thinking, as I drove to her office, there was finally someone who could help me. I was in the lobby of the building looking at a scrolling screen that listed all the offices and floors. I was frustrated because I forgot to bring the actual directions. In fact, I was a little late because I got turned around since I relied on my memory.

"May I help you?" a gentleman asked me.

"I'm looking for Dr. Shield's office," I said.

"Hmm . . . I believe that office is on the 8th floor," he said confidently.

I hurried on to the next elevator and pushed the button for the 8th floor. When the doors opened, it opened to a dental office. I was furious at myself for listening to that stranger. I never take the advice of strangers because they often will want to help even if they are unsure about something. I stepped back on the elevator and went back to the lobby to look at the screen and waited to see Dr. Shield's name. Bingo. She was on the 5th floor.

When I arrived, I was a couple of minutes late, but it felt like an hour. I became really anxious about time. I looked at the clock and went over to the receptionist desk. "My name is Indigo and I am here to see Dr. Shields," I blurted out.

"Thank you, please have a seat," the young man said as he gestured for me to sit in the waiting area.

I took a seat near the receptionist desk and just sat there watching the people come and go. I was confused about the office because there were all kinds of people who did not seem to have a common look. Some of these people did not appear to be there for mental problems. I do not know what I expected, but it did not fit into my thoughts of what a counseling waiting room would look like. What I found out later was that it was a shared environment with everything from social workers to counselors.

Now ten minutes had passed and I grew concerned because no one called Dr. Shield to let her know that I was there. What if she came out at the top of the hour and assumed that I was a no-show? I approached the desk and said, "Can someone let Dr. Shield know that I am waiting?" I was feeling real anxious.

"She comes out to get her clients," the receptionist stated.

"Okay," I said hesitantly because I felt as if I was being overlooked or that I would miss valuable time to meet with the doctor.

After a few more minutes, the doctor came out and dropped by the receptionist desk. I could see that the receptionist directed the doctor's attention to me and she walked over to get me. It was now 15 minutes after our scheduled meeting, and I felt really anxious. We walked back to her office, and I shared with her that I was anxious about being late.

"You aren't late," she said.

I thought to myself that I may not be late, but she definitely was. She took some forms out of her file cabinet and began telling me a little about her practice. She then asked me to describe why I was there. I did not have any specifics. I just knew that I had been feeling really angry the last few months. I knew something was wrong because I should have been floating on air after receiving the Inc. 500|5000 award, but I felt worse than I had ever felt in my life. I actually felt like a failure and I was angry with everyone. She asked me questions such as how long have I felt that way, what did I think was the cause, and so forth. I shared with her that I had been feeling agitated and depressed for weeks, and it was getting worse. I was becoming incapable of working or doing anything. I was just tired of being sick and tired.

We talked for about 45 minutes as she laid down the law of what she expected in the relationship and of me, her compensation, and overall, how the sessions would be held. I was fine with it; I just wanted help. I asked her if we could meet twice weekly, but she refused. She stated that such would be too much for her. I knew that I needed more time with a therapist because I was carrying a lot of anger with me, but if one day a week was all she was willing to commit to then that would have to suffice. I wrote her a check, scheduled my next appointment, and thanked her for her time. I left the office feeling the same but hoping there would be a light at the end of the tunnel as I continued to see her.

Too much for a mere mortal and therapist

I managed to get through to the next week by staying in my apartment. I did not interact with anyone. I just became a recluse. The next week I visited Dr. Shield, again. I arrived on time and headed straight for the office. I checked in with the receptionist and took a seat. I thumbed through a few magazines, as I watched the clock.

"Hello, Indigo," Dr. Shield said as she approached me. We walked back to her office. I let out a long sigh as I took a seat. "How are things for you, Indigo?"

"Not good. Not good at all," I said with little to no energy.

"Tell me what's going on," she said.

"Everything. I'm crazy!" I said with a smile. For the first time, I truly felt as if I was either crazy or going crazy. I was unraveling at the seams, and I needed help. I did not attribute my current state of mind to being bipolar because I'd never accepted the diagnosis. I just simply thought that what I had been trying to control and hide for years was simply coming to the surface and that was that I was crazy. During my session with Dr. Shield, I repeated that I was crazy.

"You aren't crazy and you shouldn't refer to yourself as crazy," she said with a little attitude.

"No. I am crazy. I know what I am. That's why I am here," I exclaimed. She discussed some things with me and I shared with her that many years ago I was diagnosed as having bipolar disorder. I did not know exactly what that meant, but I knew that it made me moody. But what I was feeling was beyond moody. I was feeling hopeless and desperate.

We talked for the remainder of our time, and as we were finishing up, she shared with me that I actually scared the receptionist when I came there the last time. I was confused by her statement. First, why did she wait until we were almost finished meeting to bring that up? Second, I did not say or do anything to them to cause alarm. Here we go again, I thought to myself. I become the bad guy whenever I say anything. I shared with her how I was feeling at that time, and that I was only bringing to his attention that I was waiting for her. She shared with me that my mannerisms can be threatening. I was shocked and hurt because I did not intend to be threatening. In fact, that was the first time that someone actually said that my mannerism was threatening.

Thinking back over the years, I have caused people to become uncomfortable and I have a look that can kill. I guess that is what a student who felt threatened in class experienced. What a kick in the butt that conversation became. It merely confirmed that I needed help and she really wasn't helping.

The sun was going down on me

In less than a week, things became intolerable for me. That Friday I sank into a deeper depression. For the first time, I went to the very bottom of my dark cave. This feeling was so scary that I started thinking that I should commit myself into an institution or hospital of some kind. That next day I started making calls to mental institutions all over the country. I called everywhere with the question, "Do you have an inpatient service?"

"Do you feel like you are going to hurt yourself or someone else?" the voices on the other end of the phone would ask me.

The Beginning of the End of Darkness

I was locked in my apartment alone, so the answer was no. I was not going to hurt anyone unless they came in the apartment. I isolated myself with no plans of going out for any reason. I stopped taking phone calls or reaching out to people. I felt like I was going crazy and I could not even describe the feeling. Every hospital seemed to only help people who were deranged. I was not deranged, just hurting.

I called a mental health clinic in the Georgia area. I finally got someone who would listen to what I had to say. I shared with the voice on the other end that I was crazy and that I needed to find a hospital that would admit me. She chuckled at the things I was saying. I have always been known as someone who was funny, but I was not trying to be funny. I was quite serious even though I would laugh at myself during the conversation. She asked me several questions, and recommended that I call a psychotherapist by the name of Dr. Broddy who was located in the Atlanta area who would be able to refer me to a hospital. I did not care if she was on the moon. If she could help me I would give her a call.

I called her and, oddly enough, she answered her phone over the weekend. I shared with her information about my career and that I needed a discreet place where I could get help. She recommended Sierra Tucson, a treatment center out West. I called the facility and they scheduled a time to conduct an intake questionnaire. I cannot recall if it was the same day or the next day. But I spoke with someone who asked me what felt like a thousand questions.

Based on that conversation, I was scheduled to check in within a week or two. I basically committed myself. I flew out West where I was picked up at the airport. I remember walking though the airport in such a daze. I was hoping that nothing would go wrong because I was on the verge of exploding! I also remember hoping that I would be diagnosed with a brain tumor which would answer everything—the crazy thoughts, the bizarre behaviors, drastic mood changes, and a crumbling world. I felt that a brain tumor was more palatable than a mental illness. At least with a brain tumor they could operate and I would be cured.

When I arrived at the treatment center, I was escorted to a hospital-like setting where blood was drawn, a body search was conducted, and other things happened that I cannot even remember. I had to stay a night in the hospital under observation. There was a girl attempting to break out and the place reminded me somewhat of the movies that depict mental institutions.

What had I gotten myself into, I thought to myself as I made myself comfortable in the white-painted patient room. However, for the first time in a long time, I got a good night's sleep. I finally felt safe even though the place was truly a residential treatment center.

I had a physical exam conducted and I found that my body was basically shutting down. You wouldn't have recognized me because I was so frail and ill. I have read that people with bipolar disorder die 25 years earlier than normal people on average due to the mental illness. I believe that this is attributed to people not taking care of themselves, not eating properly, not getting their rest, and then there is the issue of suicide. According to Dr. Neel Burton in his book *The Meaning of Madness* (pg. 143), episodes of depression and mania are difficult to live through, and in some cases can lead to death through suicide, self-neglect, or accident. I was fortunate to be alive because I stopped taking care of myself for months, which actually became apparent in China and continued until I arrived at the treatment center.

THE BEGINNING OF THE END OF DARKNESS

The next day or so I met with my psychiatrist who ordered me 25 mg of Lamictal because he diagnosed me as having Bipolar II Disorder. Unfortunately, I had two aggressive encounters within my first few days of being there. I verbally attacked another resident who annoyed me and then I verbally threatened and physically intimidated an employee whom I felt was not taking me seriously. I wanted to change my behavior and ability to go from 0 to 60, but I learned that change would be a process. I hated feeling as I did and ruining relationships. While there, I found that people were scared of me and that was not what I wanted or who I wanted to be.

It was my seventh day anniversary at the treatment center. I learned about forgiveness through an exercise. During the exercise, tears ran down my cheeks, and I felt lightness in my chest as I forgave. This was a huge breakthrough for me because part of my anger was based on so many things that had happened to me since childhood and I'd held on to those memories and relived them often. I had been carrying around resentment and pure anger from being abused as a child, not just from my mother but society in general.

I was starting to learn how to modify my behavior through a variety of methods such as breathing techniques to mindfulness. I could feel that the medication was starting to work. I was not as tense, sleepy, or irritable. For the first time in forever I was grateful and hopeful. I started feeling a sense of peace. My psychiatrist actually diagnosed me as having Bipolar II Disorder and Post-Traumatic Stress Disorder accompanied with rage. He explained in detail what that meant and I attended classes to learn more about my condition. For the first time, I was knowledgeable about the disorder, and things started to make sense. I had a team of therapists along with my psychiatrist, and I was making huge progress.

187

My life-changing experience

My actual breakthrough came when my primary therapist had me reenact a painful childhood memory during a group therapy session. The reenactment came as a result of writing a letter to my inner child or rather myself as a child. I read the letter in front of my entire therapy group. My therapist then encouraged me to take Debra (my child self) out of the closet. I remember sitting there frozen at the idea of acknowledging my child self was still in a dark closet, let alone bringing her into my present life. I remember asking one of my group members named Peggy to walk over to the closet with me. Peggy held my hand as I walked over to the closet, weeping. When we stepped in front of the pretend door, I actually stepped into the constructed closet in my mind and sat down on the floor. I actually became that scared child again in the closet.

My therapist came over and explained that he wanted me to bring my child self out of the closet. So I sat there for a few minutes trying to process what he was asking of me. I then stood up and he coached me through the steps of taking Debra's small hand into mine and leading her back to my seat where I was then asked to hold her. I lifted her up and sat her on my lap where we both cried, and I asked her forgiveness for leaving her in the closet all these years.

As I matured, I saw no other way of moving on with my life as Debra. I thought that I had to leave her there in the darkness alone. I needed to become someone else other than that vulnerable little girl. But boy, was I wrong on many levels, and I found myself by finding her again. I learned to embrace and accept that little girl who I thought was too black, ugly, dumb, bad, and a host of other negative characteristics based on what I was constantly being told, not just by people, but society in general. The 60s was rough on a little black girl growing up in a predominately white environment. But seeking Debra's forgiveness and reconnecting with that child spirit was freeing for me. I had a life-changing experience that was phenomenal!

Over the next couple of weeks, I would become aggressive, but overall, the medication and all the techniques I was being taught to control my behavior, temper, and actions were starting to take effect. In fact, I was starting to feel again. For some time, I had felt empty.

People within the treatment center started to see a change in me after being there a few weeks. I was beginning to laugh and have fun. It was so refreshing to have emotions that did not include anger, fear or hopelessness. I was so embraced and loved there. Things were going so well, that I even entered a talent show. I was so pleased that I did a comedy act. I was a huge success on the stage. You know that you must be pretty funny to have a room of people laughing without the effects of alcohol. I was coming out of my shell. I was expressing love and allowing others to love me. I even stopped having problems with my leg circulation that was debilitating for me.

When I arrived I was wearing compression stockings for the pain. I was a mess when I was admitted to the center. I was anemic with a host of other ailments. My health was on the decline from not sleeping or eating, and I was a mental, emotional, and physical wreck. While there I started to eat properly, take vitamins, and build back up my health. I would talk to Frances and London who sent cards, flowers, and well wishes.

Even though I made a lot of progress, it was decided that I would not return to work until June—three months away. I knew that my office needed time to heal, as well. I had become so destructive leading up to that manic episode that those closest to me seemed to need time to recuperate, too. My team canceled all speaking engagements on my calendar and they let people know that I was on a sabbatical. I would just focus on me and getting well.

I spent so many years taking care of and worrying about everyone else that I now had to focus all my strength and energy inward. Here was a place where it was alright to focus on me. The treatment center had a program wherein family would come to visit to reconcile. I asked my husband (soon to be wasband), my oldest son who had me arrested, and my mom to attend with all expenses paid by me. I really didn't think that they would come. A side of me wanted to heal our past, but another side of me was completely angry with each of them for the many things I "felt" that they did to me over the years. When I found out that my family was coming to visit I became really aggressive and agitated that my medicine dosage was increased. My family came and went, but I knew that there was some serious work that would need to take place once I arrived home.

The last stretch

I cannot describe the intensity of the kinds of therapy that I was subjected to. I was always in some kind of therapy that helped me to release fear and anger and I learned how to regulate and manage my emotions. I participated in intense therapy with a couple of therapists that included Dialectical Behavior Therapy (DBT), which teaches mindfulness, interpersonal skills, distress tolerance, and emotional regulation; Eye Movement Desensitization and Reprocessing (EMDR) to help heal the effects of trauma; Somatic Experiencing® to increase awareness and help release trauma-related tension; Biofeedback, Neurofeedback, and Mindfulness to teach relaxation and skills for coping with stress; Somato-Emotional Release massage for release of stress, depression, and fatigue; and Integrative Therapies such as Acupuncture and Massage Therapy to offer mind-body approaches for healing. I was putting in the hard work and it was paying off!

I recall a vivid conversation I had with one of my therapists. I shared with her that my mug shot was beautiful and that I was smiling. She shared with me that I was not in my right mind at that time, that most people would have been crying, and, with my status in the community, even worrying or having some sort of fear about the consequences of being in jail. But I shared with her that I held up my booking numbers and smiled with a devil may care look.

So much was brought to the surface for me to deal with during my therapy sessions. I spent a lot of time recounting my childhood and healing the inner child that I had abandoned. I went through some of the most extensive therapy throughout the day, nearly every day, and educational sessions at night. It wasn't an easy journey. In fact, there were a couple of incidents where a committee met to determine whether the treatment center was a right fit for me based on my aggressive behaviors. Fortunately, I had advocates and supporters who fought for me, which has been a part of my script my entire life. This gave me a chance to heal, develop, and emerge from the darkness.

Life is becoming worth living

The treatment center was a life-changing experience for me. I became a leader on the campus, and I became very resourceful in the group therapy. One morning, I attended a community forum where I was presented with a prestigious honor: the spirit stick. The spirit stick was bestowed to members of the treatment center community who displayed spiritual leadership and demonstrated significant growth. I felt a profound sense of humility and pride as I accepted the actual stick which had personal items and trinkets from past patients. The stick also had a journal for each recipient to write their thoughts as it related to the spirit stick, recovery, and the center. I became a true leader on the campus and many sought me for encouragement and words of advice.

My primary therapist came to me and said that he believed that it was time. What I, too, started to realize was that it was time for me to leave. I was becoming someone who no longer had to live in her emotional mind, but rather in her wise mind. I transformed while there and became the actual "new woman" that *Inc. Magazine* wrote about. I did one final standup comedy act and I was prepared to go home and start a new life. I experienced an outpouring of love. The treatment center, as well as all the people, would be missed, but it was time for me to move on. The treatment center had served me well and I was prepared to enter the real world again. The treatment center saved my life.

Chapter 8

A New Life in the Light

I took a couple of months off from work and called it a sabbatical. I could not think of school, work, or anything. I was still recovering from the episode that initially caused me to seek help. In short, I was in recovery. Basically, I spent a lot of time reading and working in my self-help workbooks that came from the treatment center. I was not ready to talk to people, so I kept to myself for a while.

I just needed some alone time. I didn't feel like I was on firm footing. Everything seemed so different to me. This feeling could have been from my medication but it could also have been from trying to reintegrate into society after being gone for nearly two months. I had to rediscover who I was with this new diagnosis. I was a new woman, a better woman, a changed woman, which meant I needed to be doing things differently. I felt that my crazy got me where I was, be it good, bad or indifferent, but it was through loving support that I would find my way out.

I spent an inordinate amount of time with my youngest and middle sons. I really felt as if I was able to connect with them. For years, I had been physically there off and on, but I had separated myself mentally from them, too. I knew how to feel positive emotions and spend time with them that did not include agitation and irritation. They were so pleased to have their mother back, and I was glad to be back. I was now divorced; it actually happened while I was at the treatment center. That even gave me a sense of freedom. I was finally free from feeling pain and I was in a position to live life to the fullest. Everything was coming back together for me, and I had vowed to stay on my medicine as a new way of life.

I had a real difficult time finding both a therapist and psychiatrist in the DC area. No one could compare to the professionals at the treatment center. Eventually, I just relied on my primary care physician to prescribe my Abilify, and I then called Dr. Broddy and asked her to be my therapist, which meant taking trips back to Atlanta. Everything was going well. I was balanced and hopeful. More importantly, I was taking my medication every morning as a part of my daily regimen. I knew that I could not miss a day without feeling agitated. I also put into practice mindfulness and spiritual consciousness. Earlier on when I started my company, I had become very spiritual, but I lost that along the way. It was time to get back to the basics. I began meditating to calm my nerves and focus my thoughts. I was truly becoming the new woman that *Inc. Magazine* wrote about.

I finally felt that I was out of the darkness and in the light. I'd spent a lifetime in darkness and led my company while in the dark. I had put in the hard work for recovery. After a couple of months of convalescing and continuing the work of becoming mentally well and balanced, I returned to work. According to Kay Redfield Jamison in her book *Touched with Fire: Manic-Depressive Illness and the Artistic Temperament* (pg. 17), psychotherapy, in conjunction with medication, is often essential to healing as well as to the prevention of possible recurrences. Drug therapy, which is primary, frees most patients from the severe disruptions of manic and depressive episodes. Psychotherapy can help individuals come to terms with the repercussions of past episodes, take the medications that are necessary to prevent recurrences, and better understand and deal with the often devastating psychological implications and consequences of having manic-depressive illness (pg. 17). I spent an inordinate amount of time reflecting on my life experiences and the things that I put my family and coworkers through. I was deeply remorseful with some deep levels of shame that I had to work through.

I was quiet initially and much calmer than I had ever been. I could tell that people saw me differently, but there was some hesitation in how they would approach me. Employees would make comments that I looked more at peace and seemed calmer, but I knew that they had to learn to trust me before being comfortable in my presence. As for friends and business associates, that was a different story. I contacted a close business associate and we arranged to have dinner and go to a concert. During dinner I shared with her that I had bipolar disorder. This was the first and only person in the business community that I shared my condition with and became vulnerable. I felt that I needed to explain why I suddenly resigned from a board that she chaired. But our conversation about my mental illness was rather brief.

I said, "Hey Sue, I needed to leave the board because I haven't been well."

She replied, "I know and I understand. You have to take care of yourself. That's what's important."

"I know, but it's a little more than that. I have been diagnosed as having bipolar disorder," I said as I sipped on a glass of wine.

She looked at me, smiled, and said, "Girl . . . you aren't bipolar. You are just under stress. Don't be claiming that! We're not going to claim that in the name of Jesus."

The look that she gave me included a period, as if to say that we weren't going to talk about that anymore. She just looked at me with the "I can't believe you bought into that crap." I really felt misunderstood and unheard. I think what people want more than anything is to be heard and then understood, and I got neither. She was in denial and needed me to get on the same train with her. I knew then that I was in this all alone when it came to the business community. After all, she was an ordained minister and a wildly successful entrepreneur. If she couldn't accept me, then who would?

What I had laid on the table I scooped up and tucked away and finished our dinner talking about "more important" things like dating, making money, etc. But I really needed someone who could empathize with me and just hear me out.

I'm wondering how many people reach out to their church or minister about their mental illness and are told that it is either the devil or something that they simply shouldn't "claim"? What a tragedy. The church and family are the two most frequent places where many people seek mental health help but are shut down. The

196

church will treat mental illness as if it is a demon that possesses you and will attempt to use prayer to make you whole.

But I have news for you! Mental illness is no different than physical illness. Yes, I believe our thoughts can manifest certain illnesses, but then there are illnesses that have nothing to do with your thoughts. Sometimes it's just faulty wiring, a bad valve, poor circulation, etc. and all the prayer in the world will not repair the heart that has had two massive heart attacks. Prayer will comfort and even place you in a state where you can manage your health better, but you need a doctor.

The same goes for a brain that has a mental illness. You need a doctor, and yes, I believe you also need prayer, but it's not something that you can ignore away. You see I did that for over ten years, to my demise. I'm certain that if I said that I had breast cancer, Sue would have been concerned and offered prayer for healing as opposed to telling me to not claim it which is the same as saying ignore it in this situation. No one would tell a woman with breast cancer to not claim it.

Then there is the family. Bipolar disorder can be hereditary, so you may not receive the counsel that you need when you go to someone who actually has the same disorder and is also in denial. If you were to go to your mother about some extreme behavior that you have demonstrated, she may tell you that you are fine because she would have done the same thing in the same situation. In short, if the person you are going to for help is sick in the mind, you will get sick responses that you may not see as bizarre. I guess I was thinking that the rational business woman would have shown up in our conversation, but I got the southern Baptist minister who simply couldn't wrap her head around my mental illness.

DUELING DRAGONS

Recently, I read an article that discussed how churches are often unprepared to deal with mental health issues, even though church members will seek their help. How disheartening. This says, more than anything, that people must become advocates of their own health and mental state. People who have a mental illness are no different than someone with a physical illness. We want to be heard, understood, and free of judgment. We want to know that you will support us in whatever way you are able to be there for us. But rarely is that the case, which causes so many people to stay in the closet, in the darkness and in denial.

Chapter 9

Recovery: A Current State of Affairs

After a month or two of allowing the employees to get reacquainted with the new me, I held an All Hands meeting. I invited everyone who worked at the headquarters to the meeting. I decided not to involve people who were elsewhere because they either did not work with me or they didn't actually know me. Also, I was not ready to divulge my condition to everyone.

Everyone from headquarters was in attendance except Richard, who was on a two-month paid sabbatical. He was burned out and we agreed that maybe he just needed some time away to reenergize. I started the meeting promptly. "I'm sure you all are wondering why I invited you here," I said with a half-smile. I was very nervous about what I was about to say because you cannot un-ring a bell. Everyone started looking around at each other. The only time we have an

All-Hands meeting was for our weekly Monday Morning Meeting or if something happened.

"Well, I invited you all here because I need to share something with you," I said with a quiver in my voice. "I was not on sabbatical these past few months. I was in a treatment center for mental illness because I have Bipolar II disorder," I confessed. People looked confused as they listened intently. "What this means is that I'll be on medication for the rest of my life. I need to take a tiny pill that keeps me from having drastic mood changes. I'm sure you had to wonder what was wrong with me. Some days I would be laughing and fine, and then the next minute I was angry. Bipolar disorder has two polar opposites—mania and depression. When I was hypomanic I would rage and when I was depressed I would often isolate myself. Bipolar disorder creates extreme mood swings from high to low. I could be happy and ecstatic and then slip quickly into depression," I said with some embarrassment. "But I now see a therapist, I have gone through intensive psychotherapy, and I am on medication," I continued. "While all of you thought I was having fun at a spa I was actually at a treatment center wherein I had a team of doctors, therapists, and medicine to get my life in order. I'm so glad that I have my life back, and I hope that you all will support me," I concluded.

The staff all looked relieved that the company was doing fine and the meeting was not bad news, but there was a look of hurt in some of their eyes.

"What do you need from us to support you?" asked Mike.

"I just need you to treat me the same, but realize that I may be in a bad mood and that it has nothing to do with you. I need you to understand that I have a mental illness, but I am okay. However, I do not have a casserole disease," I said, a little resentful. Heads went to the side like the RCA dog listening to the phonograph. "What I mean is that mental illnesses like bipolar disorder do not get any sympathy. I will not receive a casserole for my disorder like someone who was diagnosed with cancer or had a heart attack. That is what I mean by casserole disease," I said with a smile.

I was trying to convey that having a mental illness is like any other illness and needs compassion, but people with mental illness often receive the opposite reaction than other diagnoses. What I shared with them was that when other people at the treatment center would cry because they were depressed, people would wrap them in their arms with love. When I would rage, I would become ostracized. People would turn their backs on me rather than embrace me and reassure me that it would be alright.

"That's hard to do," said Curtis, my wasband (ex-husband).

"I do not expect people to hug me when I am upset, but I do need them to be understanding that I will have good days and I will have bad days, and to understand that it may be because of the illness." I further explained that I did not need people to be different around me, just to understand that I may need space and time to get back acclimated.

We talked a little more and everyone seemed appreciative of my transparency. They asked several questions and I answered them willingly because I was pleased that they were interested in understanding me and my disorder. For several weeks, people would drop by my office to see how I was doing. It was as if they were checking in and up on me. That was fine. I never got tired of their concern. I can't even begin to know why I became vulnerable and transparent with my colleagues. Maybe I simply couldn't hide any longer that

I had changed. Maybe I simply needed to reconcile. I don't really know, but it was a heavy burden lifted.

I spent many days speaking to employees individually to apologize and reconcile whenever I felt that there were past incidents that needed cleaning up. Since being medicated and having extensive therapy, I have contacted some of those employees to explain what happened. I needed them to know that the things that happened during their employment was not a reflection of them, but rather because I had a mental illness. I explained to them what it meant to have bipolar disorder and I asked for forgiveness. I feel that it was important that there was positive closure for some past employees.

As for the picture that Richard presented to me and the article, the picture still hangs in Richard's office, but I can now embrace the article. I now know that I did exactly what I discussed. I was becoming a better boss. Each day I work at treating my employees with kindness, respect, and fairness. The article did not say that I had it all together, but rather that I started being a better boss. That is true. I broke some eggs along the way because I was battling with having bipolar disorder without realizing that such a war was going on in my mind. But now that I'm on medication and practicing several techniques for wellness, everyone is safe and happy as employees with the company. It is amazing what one pill and extensive therapy have done for me. However, what is most telling is that all the heavy lifting and hard work that I put in is serving me well. I am now working with some of those ex-employees on a contractual basis. Our working relationship is based on respect because I allow them to do what they were hired to do. In essence,

I now tap into their strengths and that has proven to be a win-win relationship for everyone.

I eventually came to realize that my decision to move to DC was part of my bipolar decision making. I was running away from everything, including my family, but now being sane, I needed and wanted to be around my family. So I traveled back and forth from DC to Atlanta to rejoin my family and to assume full responsibilities of my CEO duties. That was very difficult because my company had changed. It was like taking over the command of a ship that was re-designed and outfitted with a new technology that I was unfamiliar with as the captain. I slowly started reaching out to clients. It felt so refreshing to be in the light and leading the company. However, my memory was shot and my drive was less than before because of the medication.

This could have meant that I was just trying to get my sea legs after being gone for so long or the reality was that the medicine and therapy changed me. I was less assertive, more introspective, and very calm. I also talked far less than ever before. This was very notice-able because people with bipolar disorder tend to talk incessantly. Either I simply did not have much to say or the medicine caused me to be truly reflective based on the built-in filters. Interestingly, I did not have much to say about anything, which was something that I had never experienced. A characteristic of bipolar disorder is being talkative with a need to talk. I had become somewhat reserved. I can now see why I stayed in trouble most of my life. I think a lot and I think about a lot of things, but I am not inclined to discuss what runs through my head. I simply do not feel the need to share what I think unless it pertains to a conversation or discussion that is relevant.

One day an employee dropped by my office. "I worry about you, Indigo," Frances said, very concerned as she stood in the doorway.

"I'm fine. Really, I am. Sometimes I miss the me that was quick to think and had something to say about everything. But I can't risk not taking my medicine. I lost so much by having bipolar disorder. In fact, I attribute my divorce and many foolish decisions that I made because I was either manic or depressed," I dumped on her because I needed to share how I was feeling.

"Yeah. I get it. But sometimes you are too quiet," Frances said with a deep look of empathy on her face.

"I'm fine," I reassured her. Most of the time I would just listen and not interject when people met with me, as if nothing fazed me. I was so unlike the me that they had grown accustomed to before I left—the fire was gone. I may not have that burning desire to make things happen, but at the same time no one was getting burned by being near me. My fire is not a roaring flame burning down everything in its path.

Two months after I returned, I received an email from *Inc. Magazine* stating that we had made the 2013 Inc. 500|5000 list. This would be our second time making the list. It was Monday morning and everyone was around the conference table. "I have some good news, "I said as I pulled out a white package with *Bravo! You are in the select company of America's Fastest-Growing Companies* written in silver embossed lettering on the cover. I opened the package and read the first paragraph of an enclosed letter. *On behalf of Inc., I am delighted to inform you that Careers In Transition has earned the position of 430 on the 2013 Inc. 500.* "Yes, we made the Inc. list again," I said with a bright smile. "This means a lot to me, but I would like to hear from you all on what this means to you," I said as I looked around the table.

"It means that our first listing was not a fluke. We are the real deal," said Martha.

Another employee chimed in by saying, "It means that we are doing the right things."

Other employees expressed how they felt and there was much laughter and kudos that circulated the room. As for me, it meant that there was a light at the end of the tunnel, and that light was not a train. I could now enjoy the fruits of my labor with my colleagues. I would hear giggles and laughter filling the office when walking down the hallways. This was something that we experienced before, but now I did not worry about my mood shifting, thus causing the laughter to end.

A couple of days later, I received an email stating that there was an error with the ranking from Inc. The email stated that we were actually 428, which was even better. Everything was right on track with my leading the company. There were the usual ups and downs that go along with owning a company, but I was in a much better position to handle those ups and downs by not having the mood swings and bouts of depression.

Richard resigned after taking his two months paid sabbatical. He decided not to return partially due to how much stress I had supposedly placed him under due to my mental illness. However, I later learned that he may have accepted a job elsewhere while on sabbatical. Since I left the treatment center we have not worked together nor have we seen each other except for twice, and those encounters were brief. Once he went to DC to visit me immediately upon my release from the center and then the second time to resign. I was shocked and dismayed, and I would be lying if I said that I understood. I felt that when I needed him most he abandoned me. Sure, I was destructive and disruptive over the past year, but I was all better now. But I could not change the impact and strain that my mental illness had on him. He was not around to see my transformation. He did not know who I had become. But I had to accept his decision and assume the role that he left behind. I was a little nervous about what to expect, but I could now lead the organization and I was prepared mentally for the task. When there is light you can find your way.

All was not nirvana

Four months passed since I returned, and everything was not okay. I discovered a few unethical things that Richard did that placed the company in a terrible contract with another business, and he made changes and promises that we weren't able to keep. I learned over time that Richard actually caused a horrible rippling effect with the company's finances, too. I took full responsibility for this because I placed him in the role of CEO without him having ANY small business experience, and then I walked away to let him be in charge. I must have been crazy (no pun intended . . . well, maybe a little bit). I spent a lot of my time putting out fires that were created while I was gone or cleaning up things that just happen as part of owning a business. I was much more aware of what was going on around me. Just recently, I had to scramble to raise $200,000 within a day to cover a retirement plan that was a bad financial decision that I made while being manic a year ago and trusting Richard's judgment. It is common knowledge that people with bipolar disorder can and often do cause risky behavior in business ventures. I was now having to deal with the consequences of having bipolar disorder and not having been on medication. Each day I got stronger in dealing with the challenges that I created. But what was magnificent is that I was totally in love with my employees. Each Monday we started our All-hands meeting with a round robin discussion about a variety of topics ranging from what we were grateful for to why we loved our jobs. I found in my employees a sense of belonging and unconditional love. I had never experienced this across the board before. I was very close to Frances and London, but now there was a genuine love for all my employees. It might be because I shared with them something life-altering and personal and they embraced me, or it might be because I was now walking in the light. I did not obsess with the thought of firing anyone any more. I treated my employees with kindness and compassion. I found myself dropping by their desks to simply see how they were doing because I genuinely cared. The same attention that I would give clients I now gave to my employees. I thanked God for them and my company. My life had totally changed.

The federal government, which represented 90% of our client base, was experiencing a Sequestration, budget cuts, the threat of a shut-down, and all sorts of things, which were directly impacting my company. This negatively affected my company, but I was leading us through this storm. Things became so difficult for the company over the last few months that everyone, including me, had to take a 15% pay cut. I simply refused to let anyone go. No one resigned, aside from Richard, and everyone expressed how much of a family we were and that we would weather the storm together.

I found joy in coming to work even through these tough times. The company was experiencing its darkest days, but as long as I was in the light, I was able to navigate us through it all. I told my employees that I loved them very often, and they often came by my office to just let me know how much they appreciated me. Life was good and being the owner of Careers In Transition was a gift that I shared with my employees. It was not my company but rather our company. Clients were starting to call me for speaking engagements and I was working at a moderate pace these days. I made sure that I did not work too late, and I made sure that I got my rest, which was essential with this disorder. There had to be a complete lifestyle change in order to lead effectively and have mental balance. I had to forgive myself for the chaos that I caused, and embrace the new woman that I had become. My journey continued, but now it was with balance, harmony, and peace. I continued to practice mindfulness, meditation, and prayer along with my medication and therapy. That was what was missing all along. I would sometimes take some form of medicine but I did not seek therapy. I realized that it took a combination of things to turn my life around. I continued to read about leadership and incorporate techniques to be more effective. Each day I had to make decisions that impacted the lives of my employees and each day I attempted to make the right decision that would help my company to grow while protecting the interest of my employees too.

Something unheard of happened! The federal government shut down. I started my company as a result of being hired to help federal employees transition out of the federal government in 1995. It was unheard of that the federal government would ever lay off workers, but I was hired to offer transitional assistance. In 2013, I was right back where I started, but in a much more vulnerable place.

RECOVERY: A CURRENT STATE OF AFFAIRS

Eighteen years ago all I had to concern myself with was maintaining a job for myself. In 2013, I must be concerned with employees, their livelihood and their families. I couldn't afford a government shutdown, but that was exactly what happened. My clients closed their doors and sent everyone home, except those in critical work capacities. I went home early on the eve of the shutdown. My son came home and asked why I was home because he had never known me to be home before him. I walked over to him and said, "The government is shutting down," as a tear welled up in my eye. I could tell that he had no idea what I was talking about at his young and innocent age. So I decided right then and there that I would not worry him and place an adult issue on his mind. I told him to do his homework so that we could go out for pizza later.

I slumped back on the couch and continued watching CNN in hopes of hearing something that would sound like hope. Every news station reported on the impending shutdown and commenced to having a countdown. I couldn't find hope on television, which was the last place I would have expected to hear anything positive anyway, but I was drawn to it like a moth to a flame. All I kept hearing was how the government was shutting down for the first time in history. But in an instant my soul said, "God is still working. God hasn't shut down." That gave me a moment of peace and I turned off the television to ignore the inevitable. There was nothing I could do to change what was happening, but I could change how I would handle the situation. I decided to trust in God and spend time with my son.

The next day the federal government closed its doors. I continued to allow my employees to work and receive payment versus sending them home without pay. I felt that this was the right thing to do even though no money was coming in. As the days peeled off the

209

calendar, I felt so overwhelmed about everything. So much to do and handle that I often wondered when things would turn around. One employee said that I looked peaceful. I was not peaceful by any stretch of the imagination. I was like the duck that appeared to be moving effortlessly across the pond while paddling like hell underneath the surface. Often I was just void of feelings. I didn't want my employees to know how bad things were with our financial situation. But if I had one word to express how I felt most days I would have used either the word nervous or scared. I made some huge mistakes in regards to my personal life and within my company by having bipolar disorder and being out of control, which finally caught up with me.

I seemed to fret about a lot of things and I didn't feel like myself anymore. I was often nervous and worried and I didn't know what to do with myself since there was no work to be done. I had been gone basically for a year as Richard ran the company. Our philosophies were totally different. I believed in building the business by establishing and maintaining relationships. He believed in proposal writing. So I let all of my relationships slip away except for the occasional outreach, whereby I would share with my contacts our accomplishments via email. So at this point in time the phone didn't ring and it was as if we were out here alone.

I had to start developing new business but I was not sure where or how to start. I would often say that once you build a business to a certain level, you could lose it all and do it all again because success would be in your DNA. I started to think that I needed to get back to the basics. I needed to do what used to work; however, things had changed so drastically in the government space. I could no longer go door-to-door peddling my products and services. After 911, it was virtually impossible to get into a federal building without an escort, so I couldn't just pop in on potential clients any more. Then there was the dreaded email that allowed people to not have to answer their phones. I couldn't just call people and expect them to pick up with a pleasant surprise of me being on the other end. Nope, things had changed, which meant my way of jumpstarting the company will need to change, as well.

During the shutdown, the office vibe was slow and heavy. I was trying to stay of good cheer, but it was darn near impossible. My entire team was working even though we weren't being paid by our clients. This presented a problem for me, i.e., the company. We invoiced for several jobs right before the government shut down, but all of those recent and past invoices were not processed. Therefore, I had to pay employees and contractors with money that was already in our bank account. However, that was a problem because we had cash flow problems. We had to pay into a retirement plan that required me to cash in my stocks and the company had used its line of credit completely. We had to make payroll for employees and contractors with no accounts receivable.

London came to me with the vice president to discuss our cash flow problem and that we had not received any money based on outstanding invoices sitting on some government employee's desk. They walked into my office very cautiously and talked about our current financial state. I put my head down and lifted it back up with a smile, and asked, "What is the gap?" They said that we were short by $50,000 in making payroll. I asked London to contact our financial representative to have papers drafted up so that I could move money from my personal account into the company. I thanked God that I could pull my company from the brink of disaster, but my personal reserves were becoming depleted. The company was bleeding out and I was running out of personal bandages.

We continued to keep things as normal as possible around the office, but things were getting darker and darker in terms of not being able to speak to our clients, no new business coming in, and there was the impending completion of some substantial contracts.

I decided that we would close the office one Monday after our Monday morning meeting and we would have a forced fun. Under normal conditions, we always had forced fun whereby I would force the employees to have fun by going somewhere to either volunteer or just play. This was the highlight of everyone's experience at the company and we would do it quarterly. Often they would say that it was amazing to be paid to have fun. But I felt that this activity builds loyalty, esprit de corps, and rejuvenates the employees. We had volunteered at Habitat for Humanity and Project Open Hand and competed against team members at Dave and Busters and other places. But I wanted something different that would get us out of the office to get our minds off of what was not happening, which was that the business was not growing. I decided that we would go to the park for a great deli lunch and then play kickball.

Once again we were competing against each other, which seemed to excite us. We let go of all of our frustrations and just became kids again playing a real game of kick ball. It became so competitive that the vice president had to be carried off the field and escorted home. He attempted to slide into the base and everything unraveled from there. That pretty much ended the game as employees passed around pain relievers walking to their cars.

For a week I was sore, but I felt really good about our forced fun and all of the laughter that followed us from the park into the office.

But that only placed our problems on temporary hold. When we arrived back at work we continued to work on the current projects, but the phones were dead silent from clients and potential clients not calling us. This was the kiss of death for an organization, if things remained the same.

A couple of weeks passed and the government went back to work. Similar to a large machine, it would take a while before that engine was moving at the same pace and things would be flowing freely again. Then a month passed and payments still had not been made. I remained calm and positive when I engaged my employees, but on the inside I was sad, nervous, and anxious. But the upside was that I was having normal emotions to life circumstances and not bipolar episodes.

Things wouldn't have seemed so dire if a prime contract worth millions of dollars wasn't ending in a couple of months. That contract was a significant part of my business and there was an unsteady and uncomfortable feeling knowing that things might change. I would say to my therapist that things seemed so much easier when I was manic or experiencing bipolar disorder. Before I was treated, I would know of negative situations but they didn't seem to faze me as much. In fact, people would tell me things that should cause me to give pause, but I would often smile and say, "Okay."

The days of saying okay and not really paying attention to situations were long gone. I saw more clearly now and everything was so real now that I was mentally balanced. The only problem was that I couldn't seem to do anything about these situations. My therapist said several times that I was now seeing and experiencing the world like normal people. As she would say, "Welcome to our world." I had to be honest . . . I didn't like this new world in which I found myself, but I realized that it was for the best. Everything seemed so much more simple when I was "crazy." But through prayer and constant meditation I was learning to stay in the moment and deal with situations with grace and peace. I was practicing mindfulness as opposed to having a mind full of mess.

For the last few years, employees within the company had given a statue to an outstanding employee during our Monday morning meeting. Recently, during one of our regular Monday morning meetings, the team voted for me as the recipient of our "Together We Can" award. This statue has three people holding up a bowl that holds three silver balls with motivational inscriptions. The statue was given to one person who had gone above and beyond the call of duty in the company. If no one was voted or if everyone seemed to have excelled that week, then the team was nominated and the statue remained in the conference room with the other awards. But during a dark week in October, my name was nominated and many others chimed in stating that I was worthy of the award. I was nominated because of my "leadership."

I was shocked and honored. I had never received the award because of my leadership. That felt so good. It confirmed that I had been doing something right. Then a few days later, the vice president thanked me for my leadership. I kept hearing that people really appreciated me and what I was doing with the company.

It was now mid-October and I was on my way to my second trip to the Inc. 500|5000 Fastest Growing Companies in America conference. I really felt as if this would be our last year, at least for a while. My team was convinced that we would win again. But reality said to me that things would have to change drastically for my company to make the 500 ranking again. Last year, I played a pivotal role at the conference, while this year I was one of the many attendees who was there to celebrate, network, and learn. What I learned by attending sessions was that I had truly succeeded at something that many have been unable to do. Entrepreneurism is a hard and arduous journey. It is not for the faint at heart. There are long hours, inherent risks, lonely moments, and an absolute roller coaster ride that you sometimes hold on to for dear life and then at other times raise your hand and enjoy the ride. I left the conference a little perplexed. I felt a sense of pride, but was also energized to figure out how to make it on the list again and not allow my company to be a statistic in terms of failure.

Acknowledging being bipolar has its consequences

What the government shutdown had revealed to me was that my company needed to diversify. We needed to diversify in terms of products and clients. We needed to offer something other than Human Resources products and services, and we definitely needed something other than the federal government as our client base. But this would be taxing for me now that I was medicated. I no longer had that flash of genius. I had lost myself along the way and I often didn't know who I was anymore. The fire that I had seemed to be gone. That scared me because I needed my hypomania now more than ever. I needed to work my magic. I needed to network with zeal and finesse and I often didn't have the energy or interest because of my meds. I had become very docile and sedate. Everyone loved the new me and the many relationships that I had ruined were now stronger and healthier. I couldn't accept that it had to be either-or.

I had to be balanced in my mind while reaching out to the masses. So I *was* really cautious about moving forward. I didn't want to take on too much, but I needed to turn this ship around before we ran aground.

I had spoken at engagements and I was not as animated. I gave a solid and profound message, but the burst of energy was gone. I received accolades and emails that mentioned that I was awesome, but I did not feel awesome. I just felt as if I was going through the motions. Was this the new me that I could expect to be for some time? If so, give me back my crazy.

After weeks of feeling disconnected and powerless, I decided to reach out to my employees. I held a couple of brainstorming sessions to discuss a possible new name for the company, new products and services, and new clients. That seemed to breathe life into our organization and made everyone feel as if they were part of the change that was just around the corner. What we decided to do was offer my speaking engagements publically and leverage my being an Inc. 500 award recipient twice. We would offer sessions on growing a small business, workshops around my book, and hold networking events for professionals. I started reaching into my contacts and network to arrange meetings to discuss the potential change. I started getting out of the office which helped, but there was a great sadness that I could not shake. I didn't feel that I was having a bipolar-induced depression, but rather a reaction to the stressors of the business and life.

As an example of how things had changed and the impact of having bipolar disorder, I recently had a vivid wake-up call that I was no longer in Kansas anymore. My financial planner realized that my company was not insured if something catastrophic happened to me. He advised me to get some additional insurance that would pay out to my family who would incur all sorts of taxes in the event that I died. I was pretty well covered by a variety of insurance policies, but this was one that we really needed now that my company was worth millions. My financial advisor set everything up, and I received a call from a particular well-known and established insurance company, which I already had a policy with.

I was scheduled for an in-depth physical examination, similar to one that I received two years ago for another policy. At that time, I was so physically healthy that I received a discount on my insurance as the underwriter marveled that I was extraordinarily healthy for my age. I didn't take any medications for any physical symptoms; I was remarkably healthy.

The day came that I was given a full physical right in my office. Everything was sent off and about a month later I received a letter that read, "After careful consideration, we regret to inform you that we are unable to issue an insurance policy. This decision was made because of your recent hospitalization for bipolar disorder."

Seriously? I was healthy in every way, aside from my mental condition which was manageable. I now realized more than ever how bipolar disorder had impacted me in every way imaginable. I could also understand why people were unwilling to get treatment. There was a legitimate fear of getting a diagnosis. Heck, I refused to accept my initial diagnosis over ten years ago. And I'd been mentally ill forever, and I had tons of insurance, but once I sought assistance and help . . . now I was penalized.

Let's be real here, a diagnosis can affect your employment, relationships, and being insurable. But I would add that not being diagnosed and untreated can ruin and possibly end your life. So, I had more to gain than to lose by coming to terms with a diagnosis. But I'm a little salty with that insurance company.

Dealing with depression like a mere mortal

One day I was sitting at my desk with my back turned to the door. I was thinking about the many hurdles and situations that my company was facing, i.e., that I was facing. Tears began to stream down my cheek. I couldn't hold the pain in any longer. Then I heard someone behind me. As I turned around an employee saw my tears and rushed over to hug me. She asked, "What's going on, Indigo?"

I tried to say that I was fine, but I burst out with, "This is so hard."

She asked, "What is hard?"

I sobbed on her shoulder and said, "Work . . . this is so hard."

She tried to console me by saying, "We know. And we are here with you." She continued to talk as I took my seat. She went on to say that the employees were 100% behind me. She said, "No one has jumped ship. That should tell you something. We are all here to stay and everything will be fine."

I smiled between the last few tears that trickled down my face. I never thought about it that way. She was right. No one had quit and everyone was working just as hard. There was a blind faith that we would win another multimillion dollar contract and that everyone would be okay.

As she left my office, I turned back around and allowed myself to really cry. I simply needed to let go of the fear and anxiety. I then wiped away the tears and got back to work. I began emailing people to set up meetings and focusing on how to rebuild relationships.

RECOVERY: A CURRENT STATE OF AFFAIRS

Ironically, it was October which was the month that my treatment center offered an alumni retreat. I called the treatment center to see if it was too late to attend and I was informed that the retreat would be happening a week from my call. I hurried and registered and bought a plane ticket to go out West.

I went to the alumni retreat in search of answers. I don't know what I was going for, but I felt the need to be there. I attended workshops and sessions and fellowshipped with people who had received treatment around the same time as I had entered the treatment center.

For the first few days, I learned that I needed to let go of some things. I needed to forgive myself for all that had happened and then move on. I learned that I needed to be at peace with myself. I figured out why I was so sad. I hadn't truly embraced the new me. I was afraid of having bipolar disorder even though I knew more about the condition than ever before. I was fearful that the old me would return. I was living in fear of myself. At that point, I just let go and surrendered.

Over the course of the weekend, I also learned that I was in actual recovery. I swear that never occurred to me. I would say that I was in recovery but I didn't truly allow myself to understand it. I wasn't allowing time to work things out in my mind and life. In essence, I didn't really know what was meant by the term *recovery*. I felt that I went in for treatment and came out healed. But as it was shared with me, I went through a life-altering experience and it would take a little time to be completely "cured." In essence, I needed to treat what I was going through like any other recovery.

We hear about 12-Step Programs and other initiatives that deal with alcohol and drug abuse, but I didn't have a problem with abuse per se, even though my mental illness caused me to self-medicate. But I questioned what recovery was needed for a mental illness. So I went to Google, the modern day sage, and it stated:

Recovery:

1. *Return to a normal state of health, mind, or strength.*

2. *The action or process of regaining possession or control of something stolen or lost.*

This definition piqued my interest because I never knew what a normal state of mental health was for me. I knew that I felt better, but what was normal? For God's sake, I thought that I was normal all the while. So I could only deduce that normal was based on what the average person would do, think, or say, and I was now doing that. I was engaging others in an acceptable manner. I had filters, did not have suicidal ideations, did not obsess, or have abnormal thoughts. And I knew that I had taken the action of regaining control of my life which I'd lost along the way. Heck, I was regaining possession of many things that were lost such as family relationships, career direction, mental stability, and the list goes on and on. Yes, I was in recovery.

What is so refreshing and enriching about recovery is that it gives you the courage to walk in the light, be completely authentic, and totally transparent. According to the Substance Abuse and Mental Health Services Administration Center for Mental Health Services, recovery is:

RECOVERY: A CURRENT STATE OF AFFAIRS

Self-Direction:

Consumers lead, control, exercise choice over, and determine their own path of recovery by optimizing autonomy, independence, and control of resources to achieve a self-determined life.

Individualized and Person-Centered:

There are multiple pathways to recovery based on an individual's unique strengths and resiliencies as well as his or her needs, preferences, experiences (including past trauma), and cultural background in all of its diverse representations.

Empowerment:

Consumers have the authority to choose from a range of options and to participate in all decisions—including the allocation of resources—that will affect their lives, and are educated and supported in so doing.

Holistic:

Recovery encompasses an individual's whole life, including mind, body, spirit, and community.

Non-Linear:

Recovery is not a step-by-step process but one based on continual growth, occasional setbacks, and learning from experience.

Peer Support:

Mutual support—including the sharing of experiential knowledge and skills and social learning—plays an invaluable role in recovery.

Respect:

Self-acceptance and regaining belief in oneself is particularly vital.

Responsibility:

Consumers must strive to understand and give meaning to their experiences and identify coping strategies and healing processes to promote their own wellness.

Hope:

Recovery provides the essential and motivating message of a better future—that people can and do overcome the barriers and obstacles that confront them.

Recovery is so liberating that it has the potential to make someone an even better person. I would recommend that everyone recovers from something and simply go through the recovery process. What if classes in high school could be offered on recovery? What a wonderful world this would be. However, recovery misses one quintessential step, requirement, or whatever it is called, and that is forgiveness, which I will discuss a little later.

I needed to give myself permission to relax, grieve without shame, and laugh without guilt. I had been so consumed with my company, my dissertation (an autoethnography based on my leading a company with bipolar disorder), and having bipolar disorder that I had actually lost my way. As one person shared with me, I needed to stop identifying myself as being bipolar. He stated that I have bipolar disorder and that I am not bipolar. That made me smile because I have been saying that I am bipolar. I now know that I am Indigo, who has bipolar disorder, and that it does not define me.

Recovery: A path to recovering

Over the past few months, I had been depressed about the many bipolar decisions I made that had impacted my company. I drove a top of the line Jaguar with payments that were simply stupid. I bought that car when I was manic and now I cringed whenever I thought about the wasted money for a car that wasn't even important to me. I looked at the money that I had lost over the years through bad deals and decisions, some of which were due to my not being active in the company and allowing Richard to be in charge. But all of it was par for being bipolar. I had to forgive myself for that too. Similar to someone who was an alcoholic or drug addict, I was now taking each day at a time. I couldn't do it all alone or in a day any longer. I was learning to utilize the team around me and to allow them to help me.

I came back from the treatment center's alumni retreat completely rejuvenated. I slept that entire following Monday. I missed work for the first time in a long time. I simply could not get out of the bed because I was so emotionally drained from the retreat.

That Tuesday, I came in and began doing what I used to do. I was calling people, emailing people, and reaching out to my contacts for help. I attended functions where I could network and I arranged for many meetings. The federal government was back to work, and I had been reaching out to people for meetings. I felt really good about my recovery and I now knew with certainty that there would be difficult days. My days seemed to be a little more difficult than for most, but nothing that I couldn't overcome. And I now knew with certainty that I was going to be okay. I kept telling myself that I just had to keep moving.

I couldn't say that it had been easy since returning. In fact, this had been really difficult, but I had been able to do the right things by being focused, clear-headed, and balanced. Every day I woke up and thanked the Universe/God for my mental well-being, my eye sight, and health. I then prayed and meditated. This was a part of my daily regimen that I practiced in the morning when I awoke and before I went to bed at night. That gave me a sense of peace, joy, hope, and love. This was my journey and I continued this journey realizing that the universe had great things planned for me and my company.

I sometimes thought about having bipolar disorder and the life sentence that I had been given. I was learning to live with the disorder by increasing my knowledge about it and sharing information about it with those in my inner circle. One day I would be able to look back on this phase of my life and appreciate all that I was learning and experiencing, but for now I was taking each day at a time. There were days that I literally cried from having to acknowledge and recognize the havoc that I caused all these many years. I had to now work on not beating myself up, but this had been a very sobering journey, but one that I had to take. Fortunately, I was not on this new journey alone. I had a support base both in my personal life and in my company. I knew that my cave was not far away so I was mindful to stay on my path to healing. I could now be the leader that others wanted and expected of me, now that I was out of the cave and leading out of the darkness.

Rebuilding a life in recovery

As things became clearer, and I was able to live life with clarity, I purchased a home in Atlanta and moved back. I really wanted to be in my company full-time and, more importantly, be with my children. I felt very overwhelmed with the move and writing my dissertation. I couldn't think of any other topic and I became consumed with understanding and living with bipolar disorder. I was finding it very difficult to research let alone write my dissertation. Maybe my medicine was too strong or something, but I simply could not do this, I would think to myself. My thinking was slow and plodding, and I couldn't even comprehend the literature or hold any train of thought. So I made the decision to get off my meds so that I could focus on my dissertation. It was the fall and I was very nervous about what to expect because I was pretty bad off before I started my medication. Within days, I was able to read without falling asleep. I vowed that I would pay close attention to my behavior. I made an appointment with my therapist to share my decision with her.

I met with my therapist, who was quite understanding. I didn't think that anyone could tell that I was off my meds because I was so mindful of being calm and I continued to stay quiet. I continued to practice meditating, praying, and going to bed at a decent time to manage my emotions. I was thinking that such would be enough to keep from becoming manic or depressed. I really wanted to be on my medicine, unlike many people with bipolar disorder. However, I needed to write my dissertation to earn my PhD, and I simply could not do it on medication. Over the first few weeks, employees commented on how calm and peaceful I appeared, which was really encouraging because I knew that I wasn't on any medication and that I was managing my disorder single-handedly.

Life was catching up with me. A new house, recent divorce, ups and downs of owning a business, and a dissertation to write. I was feeling overwhelmed, drained, and depressed. But my depression,

I could honestly say, was not a bipolar byproduct, but the result of living life. I was learning to distinguish between what was a bipolar emotion and a reaction to life.

I spent an inordinate amount of time working on my dissertation and researching. I discovered so much about me and my disorder while in the treatment center, but my research on bipolar disorder and leadership took my understanding of what I was battling and experiencing to a whole new level. I truly believe knowing is half the battle to mental wellness. The more knowledgeable I was of my condition the more manageable it had become. Unfortunately, the entire dissertation process caused great anxiety and stress, and over the last few months I had been off my medicine to sharpen my thoughts and remain focused. I was hoping for mania but I just seemed calm and balanced. That wasn't so bad, but what I wouldn't do for a little mania.

I found that I fretted a lot during this time of change and transition. In terms of my mood, I was feeling pretty good these days and I believed wholeheartedly that everything was working for my highest and greatest good. However, whenever I traveled back to DC for business development, I felt drained. Hustling, building, and developing the company simply wasn't in me any longer. Or I was realizing that this company wasn't what I wanted to do as a career anymore. I was working harder than ever to keep my company moving forward. Interestingly, now that I was sane I couldn't believe what I used to do to build and maintain my company. No mere mortal could continue at that pace before burning out or breaking down. Maybe my condition was calling me to do things differently or to do something different altogether. Mental illness can bring about a lifestyle change, but it may cause you to change career, as well. Maybe it was time to select something that would support my mental well-being.

I was closing out 2013, and everything was coming together. My company got an extension on a multimillion dollar contract, my therapist was pleased with my progress even while being off meds, I spent time with my entire family, and I was given the ultimate compliment by my general practitioner's staff. They said that I looked really healthy and at peace, even though my doctor warned that I should get back on my medicine. That was huge considering they had seen me totally out of control during past office visits. Heck, I must have been doing something right. Everyone commented on how at peace I appeared. I attributed that to my praying and meditating twice daily, and putting into practice the many techniques and tools that I learned while in treatment.

It was now 2014, and the clock was ticking in terms of me completing my PhD by the time I turned 50 years old, which was a personal goal. What an unnecessary goal and expectation that I placed on myself. I had to keep reminding myself that a PhD wouldn't define me, either. Writing the dissertation was exhaustive and overwhelming. However, I think that such was because I was writing about myself and my journey with bipolar disorder. So much was revealed and I had to deal with each and every incident as I pulled back the many layers of both the disorder and actions that I had taken that didn't always serve me well. I was often thrown into dark memories and experiences that proved to be emotionally draining.

I realized that it was only a matter of time before my company folded. I could see the writing on the walls. It might be because I simply didn't have a passion for it any longer, or that I could see that we weren't winning contracts any longer and that the federal government was doing business in an entirely different way. I decided that I would offer a networking series in Atlanta to reintegrate myself into the Atlanta market in hopes of discovering corporate contract opportunities for my company since going to DC wasn't as productive and the government simply wasn't spending money the way it used to. The game had changed and I wasn't enjoying it any longer. So I'd been working diligently in creating a new source of revenue.

Your slip is showing

It was mid-January and a very rough week for me. I was juggling writing my dissertation, running the business, and creating a networking series. I was burning the candle at both ends. I was in my office when Curtis, my wasband, came into my office and asked if we could talk. We had a really special and good relationship even though the divorce was a little messy. He still worked for my company on contract and I interacted with him on a daily basis. He said that my youngest son came to him and complained that I was always angry. Then he brought to my attention that he noticed that I was explosive.

I had to be honest that I was feeling agitated and angry, but, heck, I had a lot on my plate. But let's be honest. The disorder was rearing up its ugly head again. Then later that same day someone who held a leadership position in my company came to me and mentioned the same thing.

Okay, I couldn't ignore it any longer or deny that I was slipping into mania accompanied with anger and agitation. I sat there feeling not just angry but saddened that I wasn't controlling my bipolar disorder like I thought I could. It was controlling me. My slip was showing . . . people were seeing a change in my mood and behavior despite my best efforts.

I was so upset by this that I went to Frances's office. I shut the door and took a seat, and began telling her that I was going to have to get back on my medicine. I broke down crying, telling her that I didn't want to be on medicine, but I also didn't want to be angry with outbursts! She tried to console me as I wept, feeling depressed and like a failure. I really thought that I could manage the disorder without meds!

For the next several weeks, I was agitated and depressed as a smaller dosage of the medicine was recalibrating me. What I was doing differently than ever before was staying at home when I felt volatile or really angry. This allowed me to keep a safe distance from my employees and I gave myself permission to mentally heal.

I continued to work and drive the business. I launched the networking event which was a huge success. I was so pleased that it happened and it worked. However, I attributed the success of the event to my bipolar disorder—I was manic. Each night I fell asleep quickly and then woke up within hours wide awake and completely alert. I'd been taking sleeping pills, but nothing seemed to work. And I knew that I was hypomanic because I was giddy, happy, optimistic, speaking fast, and using sexual innuendos to express myself. I didn't understand it because I was back on my medicine, but if the truth must be told, I was taking half dosages.

I was bursting with ideas. In fact, I started hosting a radio program. I did three shows that were really awesome and then quit. I was jumping from idea to idea, and I finally completed my dissertation. Now, I needed to be patient and wait for my committee to read it and provide guidance. That was the most agonizing process.

In essence, this was a period of finding myself. I was no longer the person who went into the treatment center and I had grown significantly. Along the way, I realized that I wanted something more in life than my business had to offer, but I didn't know exactly what that was as I went through each day attempting to reintegrate into the company.

It was mid-year 2014, and I was turning 50 and completing my dissertation on time. This was the first real goal that I had ever made and achieved. Most of the things that I had achieved in life came as a result of living and moving forward, but not necessarily planning. This was the most magical time of my life. I threw myself a huge birthday party that included a magician who was incredible, a live band, etc. at a swank hotel. I even commissioned an artist to paint a picture of me. The story behind the picture was how I came out of the darkness into the light and learned to manage my bipolar disorder. That picture now hangs over my bed as a daily reminder of my journey to wellness.

The last few months had been great in planning my birthday party and having it be a huge success. But as I wrote, I was manic. What could go wrong when there was a positive spin to mania?

The bottom fell out

It was now June, and my world was being flipped upside down again. Last month, I was on top of the world and this month I felt the weight of the world on my shoulder. What I thought was my greatest challenge was what to do with my career. I no longer felt passionate about my company, radio didn't fulfill me, and I felt as if

I was drifting. I had just earned my PhD and I was eager to achieve something meaningful with that degree.

I learned that a multimillion dollar contract that my company held for many years would not be renewed. This contract was with the Department of Dependability. There was nothing that we could do to salvage or keep that contract because my company had graduated from a program that the contract required. However, I was miserable, and as it sank in that I was losing 50% of my company, I became very depressed. I was hopeful that everything would work out over time, but I was sad, ashamed, and remorseful about losing the contract. I had to lay off everyone attached to the contract. It felt like a scene from *It's a Wonderful Life*. Here I was, a person that gave thousands and thousands of dollars to help people, I created jobs for people through my company, I became an excellent leader, and I walked in love and light, and one day I was operating a multimillion dollar business and the next day I had a small business struggling to keep its doors open. There was nothing I could do as my company bled out. But there was one move that I had at my disposal. That was to get off my meds again. I needed to be creative with energy to weather this particular storm. What I had come to learn was that I had to be crazy to build a business the way that I did, and that it would take a touch of crazy to rebuild the business, jump-start my career, and save my company. I needed the daring tenacity that mania gave me whenever I was natural and not on meds. I just knew that I had to watch myself carefully to make sure that I wasn't having any emotional highs or lows. So I got off my medication, again. This time I told people, aside from my therapist, what I was doing so they could help me monitor my behavior or any mood swings. Often, others can see a change within someone who has bipolar disorder long before they realize something is actually wrong for themselves.

If things weren't bad enough, we hired an attorney to be released from another multimillion dollar contract that caused us to be in a very abusive relationship. This time the abuse was coming from another business owner who held the contract. Richard brokered this deal which was disastrous from the very beginning, and we simply could not stay in the relationship. This was the nail in the coffin for my company. We lost over 75% of our employee base and finances. I felt so lost and alone, but I continued to walk boldly with courage and optimism.

Nassir Ghaemi, in his book *A First-Rate Madness: Uncovering the Links between Leadership and Mental Illness in Times of Crisis* (pg. 2), states that in times of crisis, we are better off being led by mentally ill leaders than by mentally normal ones. The people who were left were watching me to see how I would lead. I kept cool and calm at all times, but I cried uncontrollably once I got home. Nassir Ghaemi (pg. 4) continues to say that depression makes leaders more realistic and empathic, and mania makes them more creative and resilient. I was definitely depressed from the soles of my feet to the top of my head. I often hugged employees and told them how much I appreciated and loved them as they packed their boxes to leave the building for the last time. But I was rapid cycling, which caused me to be both manic and depressed, so I put on my creativity hat to stop my company from bleeding out. I would spend hours and sometimes an entire day just thinking about how to save my company.

Climbing out of the hole, but still in the light

There was a family reunion in Chicago that I attended with my brother. A distant cousin walked over to me and said to her daughter, "This is Indigo. This is the woman that you researched and wrote your paper about." The young girl gleamed with a bright smile and I stood up to hug her. She was starstruck as she shared with me my many accomplishments. She talked about the New York Times Article, the full page exposé in Ebony magazine wherein they termed me as the *18-million-dollar woman*, and she then asked questions and just beamed as we bonded. However, as she talked I felt smaller and smaller with shame.

I told my brother on the way home that I never felt so embarrassed. He couldn't understand why I felt the way I did. So I broke it down for him. I said that I wasn't that person whom she talked about. I felt like a complete failure. I felt lonely, hopeless, and lost. I was in a deep depression that I was hiding from everyone, especially my employees. Yes, I was the great pretender because I felt like a fraud. My brother pointed out that no one could ever take away what I'd accomplished and that I would always be the person they wrote about even if I never did another thing . . . because what was done was done by me. I spent months in that deep depression even though I was trying to move forward each day.

Things continued to go downhill in terms of my company and my mental well-being. Despite all of the failings my company was experiencing, I was notified that we made the Inc. list again. We didn't make the top 500, but rather the top 5000 Fastest Growing Companies in America.

This did nothing to make me feel better. In fact, I felt horrible because it was a reminder of how far I had fallen. I would pray and meditate daily knowing that everything would work out, but I felt so lost. I didn't know what to do with myself in the meanwhile because there was absolutely nothing I could do with my company since so much had changed in the federal government contracting arena. I would toss around whether I should focus on a bleak speaking career, stay the course, or get a job. I started reaching out and meeting with recruiters and executive search representatives. But deep down I knew that I didn't need a job and that I wasn't "mentally" wired for a job.

As my depression deepened, I stepped up my practices to remain balanced. I was attending church and the pastor spoke of shedding things and letting go. I learned that very instant that I needed to let go of how my business was and embrace what it was to become. The pastor shared a story about a snake that he saw while walking his dog, and his story really resonated with me because I had a snake in my front yard that lay coiled right under my bedroom window. Every day I would see this snake with fear. In fact, I went to the next door neighbor's house and asked her husband if he would kill the snake for me. He came over with his hoe and stabbed at the snake (in my opinion, hoping to miss). But he gave it the ole college try as the snake quickly slithered for cover under the bush. Each day I saw the snake I realized that maybe nature was trying to tell me something. Snakes must shed their skin to grow. Maybe the snake was there to teach me a life lesson that I needed to shed my company to grow and move on. I started embracing the idea and in a matter of a month or so the snake was gone. The black snake that I saw every morning and night as I would leave the house or look out of my window was gone. I believed he was there to teach me a lesson. I was starting to feel less afraid as I could see that there was a rainbow in my storm.

Through my spiritual beliefs I started having hope and faith that God was blessing me with something that would surpass what I felt that I lost. One day I was doing everything and anything to be busy at work even though I didn't have any real meaningful work to do. At one point, while sitting at my desk, tears came to my eyes and I was ready to walk out, but I knew that I had nowhere to go. So I kept working as hard as I could. I was making calls to connect with clients, creating marketing pieces to sell our products, sending emails pitching our services, and combing emails dating as far back as 2009 to look for leads. I started saying to myself that I had to keep swinging. So every day I went to work and swung my bat knowing that someday I would hit something. As I started reaching out to more and more people, someone planted a seed that I should consider nonprofit as my next career move. The client was referring to a nonprofit job, which could be nice with the right one in the right position. So I spoke to a few nonprofit recruiters.

I was asked to speak at a women's conference at the Philips Arena in Atlanta. I was going to speak on my books *Playing by the Unwritten Rules*, but something told me to focus on resilience, which is a topic within the book. I found myself really connecting with the energy of resiliency. I shared with the audience how my wasband Curtis took everything that he could possibly take from me. I overcame what he did to me, forgave him, and continued to live my life, but now losing my company was something much greater than I could have ever imagined. I felt that I was losing a part of me, if not all of me. I had identified with my company for so long that I didn't know where

I began and where it ended. I mentioned this early, but it became more obvious and clear that my journey included resiliency.

According to Nassir Ghaemi in his book *A First-Rate Madness: Uncovering the Links Between Leadership and Mental Illness in Times of Crisis*, depression makes leaders more realistic and empathetic, and mania makes them more creative and resilient. The resiliency that accompanies my disorder has served me well. Nassir Ghaemi goes on to say that what psychologists mean by resilience is defined as "good outcomes in spite of serious threats to adaptation or development." Resilience isn't simply something one is born with. It grows out of an interaction between factors that promote it (like hyperthymic personality) and harmful life events, producing a good outcome in the end. I seemed to have gotten stronger with each disappointment and perceivable setback, and that became the focus of my journey that I began to share with others.

Chapter 10

Living Courageously by Becoming Public

Robin Williams' suicide rattled my cage

These had been the most difficult past two years anyone could ever encounter as I struggled to remain optimistic and mentally well. I'd been making trips up to DC, but each time that I went I became very ill. I got these splitting headaches, nausea, and felt sick in general. I just didn't have the desire or drive to rebuild the business up there. This led me to start thinking of other things that I could do to transition from the company.

One day, I was walking past a television and I heard that Robin Williams committed suicide. That really rattled my cage because I had always thought that he was bipolar and this was one more reminder of how unforgiving mental illness can be. Some said that he had physical illnesses that caused him to be depressed, but come on. How often have we heard of people with terminal illnesses and they fight tooth and nail to live? No, people with mental illnesses often commit suicide and it was so much easier to blame his death on anything but reality. He was mentally ill, and that mental illness is a serious condition that needs to be addressed with compassion, understanding, and support in America.

At that very moment, the spirit said to me that it was time. I knew exactly what the spirit was speaking of. And no, it wasn't just a voice in my head. It was God tapping me on the shoulder, saying that he had other plans for me. And these plans meant that I needed to become public about my disorder as a way of changing the conversation about mental illness.

It was revealed to me that I could heal others by sharing my story and leading others into the light. I went to work the next day and started writing a blog. This was the very blog that people have asked me to write for years. I just hadn't felt like I had anything to say. I sat down and wrote with passion and courage. However, I couldn't post the blog. I was still afraid of what people would think because I became transparent in my blog and shared that I had bipolar disorder.

That Sunday, while at church, the minister spoke about Robin Williams. I can't even recall what he said, but I felt that he was speaking to me at that time. So after church I went up to him and mentioned that I, too, have a mental illness and that I actually blogged about Robin Williams and my situation. I also shared that I didn't post the story out of fear for some reason. He simply said that I needed to post the blog.

LIVING COURAGEOUSLY BY BECOMING PUBLIC

The next day I hit the send button to post my blog on www.indigotriplett.com. I felt so free with a sense of purpose and complete clarity for the first time in a long time. People wrote to me directly through my emails as opposed to the blog. I got a lot of kudos, support, and even questions. Then I started writing about resilience, courage, fear, and many other things that caused people to reach out to me. I felt so good about the responses that I was receiving and the newfound freedom I had from being honest and open about my diagnosis. I knew that I was on the right path to true recovery and healing.

I'd felt dead over the past two years, and disclosing my mental wellness made me feel alive. There was something exhilarating about being open, transparent, and honest about who I was on life's journey.

Over the next few weeks, one person after another kept sharing with me how my blog moved them. This gave me the courage to be real with others across the board. I was starting to date this guy whom I really liked. He was "spiritual," handsome, and successful, but what attracted him to me was that he watched Super Soul Sunday with Oprah. Now, that was a man after my own heart. He was everything that I wanted in a man. We met through online dating, and we would talk every day, text all day, and just connect in ways that were refreshing.

One weekend, we went to a concert and the next day attended church together. Everything was perfect, but I knew that it would be a matter of time before he read my blogs since I talked about it with him. We talked about everything and I knew it was time to share my complete self with him. So I decided to share with him that I had bipolar disorder. I didn't want him to stumble upon the information or find out any other way than from me.

I looked at him and said that I had something to share with him. That moment became serious. I simply told him that I had bipolar disorder and I explained what it meant in simple terms. He then asked was I on lithium. I looked at him and said that I wasn't on any medications and that I had learned to manage the disorder, and that I had Bipolar II disorder, which was mild for me. I further explained that I didn't have extreme disturbances. I discussed how through a lot of internal work, spiritual guidance, and therapy I had learned to manage my condition. He listened intently and we talked about it candidly.

That evening he had to leave to drive to North Carolina, and we said our goodbyes. I thought that I had found the man who could accompany me on my new journey and support me. I finally had someone who accepted me for me and I could be open and honest about myself. I felt special for the first time in a long time!

Hell, I haven't seen or heard from that man since. I called and texted him for a week, to no avail. What I had to come to terms with was that I spoke my truth and it wasn't a good fit for him. I did what I needed to do for me and he did what he needed to do for him. In his defense, he had a brother who committed suicide. I was sure that weighed heavily on his decision to bail on me.

I then began to wonder whether I would ever meet someone who could embrace me totally. I was the total package, i.e., beautiful, caring, intelligent, successful, loving, and spiritual; however, my brain sometimes had a mind of its own. Things became surreal about mental health and wellness based on that encounter and experience.

Living Courageously by Becoming Public

There was such risk associated with being open. But living in the shadows was so unnatural and I absolutely preferred standing in the light as opposed to slumping in the darkness, even if it meant standing in the light alone. Interestingly, being in the light revealed that I was not alone. I could now look to the left and look to the right and see so many people walking alongside me, and then when I was still enough I could feel the many hands on my back pushing me forward.

However, that particular scenario kinda knocked the wind out of me, but I kept pressing forward with acknowledging and sharing my condition with others. I really developed an appreciation for seeing the condition for what it is . . . a health condition no different than someone with heart problems, diabetes, or any other medical condition that has degrees and variances. But I also came to realize that the more you acknowledge and embrace it, the more you heal despite the stigma associated with mental health. I could no longer be ashamed about myself or my condition. I was at peace with all of me for the first time in my life.

At this point, I decided that a nonprofit that I was already working on launching would be recreated to help people with mental illness. For two years, I had been working on establishing a nonprofit. I had the 501(c)3, but it had no real purpose. I actually created the nonprofit to mirror my company Careers In Transition. I would offer career services to veterans, women entrepreneurs, and students at Historical Black Colleges and Universities (HBCU). I felt a rush come over me to live a life that included not only embracing my mental health challenges, but leading others out of the darkness into the light through my nonprofit, Indigo Insights (www.indigo-insights.org). I galvanized my remaining employees in Careers In

241

Transition and we worked on coming up with a mission and vision for the nonprofit. Interestingly, the remaining employees were my loyal and long-term employees who had weathered many storms with me over the years.

For the first time in months, I had a sparkle in my eyes, which energized my employees. The mission for the nonprofit is to *provide mental healing by nourishing the spirit and the mind of people who are challenged on life's journey.* I had come to realize that absolutely everything that I had experienced and lived through had been for this very mission. In essence, I reinvented myself and I felt that I had found my purpose. I once heard Steve Harvey quote Mark Twain to Oprah. He said, "The two most important days in your life are the day you are born and the day you find out why." What I had learned along the way is that there are a lot of broken people who are in darkness seeking to be led to the light.

The nonprofit is called Indigo Insights and its purpose is to assist those individuals with mental health challenges on their life journey, so that they may live the life they want despite a diagnosis. Services are not designed to replace therapy or psychological help, but rather to support people who need a little extra guidance in managing their lives and careers. I'd seen therapists who couldn't help me with my career or truly identify with how I actually feel because they'd never walked in my shoes. I believed that my wealth of experience in owning and operating a small business and being a success could be instrumental in career coaching individuals who have mental health challenges. I was bringing to a coaching relationship, workshops, and speaking engagements years of experience of being in denial, being in darkness, and living a destructive life due to my lack of managing the illness. Many people hear about one side of mental health. Who better to identify and support others by sharing all sides of mental health? I understood the journey for people with mental health challenges because I was on the same road: I'd walked along their path. And even when things were at their worst I was able to effectively manage my mental well-being.

Being public about my mental state was one of the scariest things that I had ever done. Coming forward and sharing with the masses who I was was frightening. I feared losing friends, scaring off romantic interests, and just being viewed as crazy, but offering services to heal others was much bigger than I was. I was here to help heal others. In fact, I had been a healer and care provider all my life. Now, I could do it as a career. I prayed daily that I heal and that I heal others.

I threw a nice launch party for Indigo Insights, which everyone who attended thought was a great success. I shared my story of denial to recovery. I showed my dissertation, *Leading out of the darkness into the light: my story of building a business as a leader with bipolar disorder*. I gave some stats and figures about mental illness, such as one out of four adults—approximately 61.5 million Americans—experiences mental illness in a given year according to National Alliance on Mental Illness (NAMI, 2014). I discussed how I had been wildly successful and that I attributed a great deal of my successes and failures to having bipolar disorder. I told the audience that if someone could cure me with a pill, I wouldn't want it because I was what and who I was because of the illness, which had actually been a blessing in some regards.

After I shared my journey with the audience, I allowed people to ask questions and come to the mic to make any comments. There was an overwhelming response of appreciation as people shared their personal stories of connection to mental illness either through a family member, self, or friend. I felt like I was making a difference right then and there. One lady whom I did not know came up and shared with the audience that she had heard and seen me speak several times and that she was always in awe of me because she thought that I was "perfect." She kept saying that she thought that I was perfect and that now knowing that I wasn't had allowed her to feel free because she had lived in shame since she was a child because of her mom, who had a severe mental illness, which caused her embarrassment. I kept jokingly saying that I was perfect, but I did embrace my imperfection, knowing that I was beautifully human.

After everyone who wanted to speak finished coming to the mic, I asked for a donation or love offering, and I closed out my discussion. As I was walking from the podium and mixing with the attendees, a successful guy who was a television personality pulled me to the side and shared with me that his dad committed suicide and that his family believed that maybe he had bipolar disorder. I could see the pain in his eyes as he shared his personal experience with mental illness. This was further confirmation that I was on the right path, finally. We raised a little bit of money that basically covered the launch party. But I was encouraged by knowing that there would be provision for my vision.

The next day I had to take the day off to relax and rejuvenate. I was mentally exhausted. I gave of myself in such a way that I depleted my energy. What I had learned along the way was to listen to my body and spirit. When I needed to rest, I rested. I didn't feel guilty about needing to rest my mind because that helped me to stay balanced. So I rested all day and just thanked the Universe for such a liberating and rewarding evening. I knew that my life had changed that very night and that the heavy lifting was to begin the next day. I was now on a mission that would consume me if I were to be a success. I had to lose nearly everything to find myself and my true purpose.

Over the next few weeks, I worked diligently in building the organization. I attended functions, called prospective partners, researched, and did a host of other things to share my vision with others. I always heard from nearly everyone that my service was greatly needed! It was amazing how many people are impacted by mental health challenges in one way or another. I knew that the only way to make this thing work was to become very vocal about it and to be a true advocate about mental health. I hadn't worked this hard in years, and at the end of each week I was drained. I didn't actually see any real progress, meaning that no money had come in, but I knew that I was moving the chain. I shared with people how I coached a woman years ago who attempted suicide and I helped bring her back into the light. I now realized that this was a calling for me. However, one Friday I left the office and I went home. On the way home I started to feel lonely, like a failure (all over again) and afraid about my decision to be public about my mental health challenges. I was getting wonderful responses, but no donations, no clients, or speaking gigs. What if all this was a mistake and I outed myself for no reason?

I walked into the house, went in to my bedroom, and undressed. I climbed in the bed and began to weep. I said aloud, "God help me! You asked me to do this. I didn't want this. This is something you asked me to do and I need your help." I truly surrendered at that given moment knowing that none of this was about me and that I needed to walk by faith and not by sight. I couldn't depend on how I was feeling or focus on what didn't appear to be happening. I had to keep pushing forward.

I lay there as tears ran down my cheeks and dropped onto the pillow making a soft sound. I started seeing how things were evolving. I could see how every door for my company had closed but doors for mental healing were opening. I could see how people were supporting me and rallying around me. I had to simply rest my mind and know that God would take care of the details. When you leap a net will appear. I drifted off to sleep and awakened to continue writing this book.

It was only a week later, and I met some incredible people who were willing to support me. People were sending resources my way and I began building a consortium of counselors/therapists and coaches to align with Indigo Insights. This would allow us to provide government contracting with organizations such as the Veterans Administration, as well as work with churches and other nonprofits, and the potential was unlimited. I'd also been approached by youth organizations which was quite appealing. As a resource shared with me, there was a great need to work with youths. What I thought was going to be an organization that worked with professionals was now moving in many directions and I was allowing myself and the organization to be tapped into and pushed wherever we were needed most.

Mental healing didn't have to have a limitation. I'd been a leader since high school and now I was leading a 501(C)3 which had true meaning and purpose. It was as if every step I had taken had led me here to lead others out of the darkness. I was finally at peace because

I was not only living my purpose, but I was here to heal others and lead people into the light. I hoped that those that I led to the light would become public and that we would create a ground swell across the country bringing positive awareness to mental health challenges. But more importantly, I was creating a place where people could find solace and refuge.

One day I was sitting at my desk at my home office and the day began to turn dark and I had been writing all day, along with answering emails for my primary business, working a little on the nonprofit, and even working on a new venture that I started to generate additional income. As I sat there, it occurred to me that I had never worked this hard in all my life. And even in working hard I hadn't seen the direct fruits of ALL my labor. I started to feel overwhelmed. At that very moment, I even started to say to myself that I could not continue to live like this, day in and day out working so hard and swinging my bat without seeing anything go out of the park.

I was going to call my therapist, but I realized that she would have booked me for an appointment the following week. I needed someone to talk to right then and there. Then I called someone I knew from the treatment center who was suicidal as well as a huge success as an international business woman. I felt she would understand me.

I didn't need a counselor to check off the boxes of whether I was suicidal at that moment, going to hurt someone, and the list goes on. Who in their right mind would tell a shrink that they were con-templating suicide? We know what that will get you—a blue flashing light in your driveway with handcuffs escorting you to jail. I'd heard many horror stories from people who shared that the police was called on them. I didn't need the police. I needed someone who I felt got me and what I was experiencing and who could just listen to me and share with me how they managed the moments of deep depression.

But that didn't exist, so I ended up calling my son who was so comforting. But then I felt bad that I'd exposed him to my neurosis. I didn't want him to carry my burden.

I had come to realize that many people cannot handle my "weaknesses." Far too many people relied on me for their strength and encouragement, and when I didn't have on my cape, it threw them off. I often had to appear stronger than I was and in a positive mood because people needed that from me. But where do superheroes go when they need help? So this nonprofit was designed to help people having mental health challenges on life's journey. I was offering what I needed and was unable to get. Fortunately, I had learned to manage those moments a little better by stopping what I was doing, being still, becoming mindful, and rolling through the moment, knowing that it would pass if I didn't resist it. I gave myself permission to feel whatever I was feeling and to not beat myself up for the moments of anxiety, pressure, and so forth.

The simple truth was that I was depressed. And people often become depressed and suffer in silence, which exacerbates the situation, especially if they are career professionals. There was such a stigma associated with mental illness that many career professionals would not seek assistance out of fear of being labeled. In fact, it had become common knowledge for me that seeking help could be very disruptive in various parts of your life. So our nonprofit was to afford career professionals and veterans a venue to seek support, healing, and help without having to disclose to their insurance, employer, or others that they sought assistance.

Chapter 11

Lessons Learned
About the Disorder

Not cured but truly healed

I shared with you my career journey, leading with bipolar disorder. I want to share with you what has kept me balanced even during the many storms. I cannot say that I am cured, but I am truly healed. I don't kid myself into believing that I'll be able to stay off meds as a lifelong proposition, but for now my mental well-being is manageable. I've learned to distinguish between sadness and depression. Sadness is when you feel low because of an occurrence in life, while bipolar depression exists without the ability to attribute it to anything. Knowing the difference is significant for me because I can then consciously decide how to handle each and put them into perspective. One of the main reasons people are often devastated by mental illness is because of a lack of awareness, which leads to not getting diagnosed or proper treatment. I can certainly understand why. There is risk associated in getting diagnosed, but the consequences of not being diagnosed are far greater than anything that a diagnosis can cause.

What it is like to lead with bipolar disorder

For me, leading with untreated bipolar disorder was a duality. I often felt as if I were on a roller coaster ride being tossed side to side with little to no control over where my emotions would take me. Similar to a roller coaster, there were steep climbs and significant drops, and there was always the element of surprise as the car entered each new turn. At Universal Studios in Florida there is a roller coaster ride called Dueling Dragons. There are many twists and turns that cause you to grasp on to the handle and hold on for dear life while at other times you can raise your arms in the air and enjoy the ride. For the majority of my life, I have switched between grasping the iron bar of life to letting go and soaring to new heights. That is the beauty and curse of having bipolar disorder—the ever present dueling dragons. Specifically, the "dueling dragons" I experienced on a day-to-day basis were, on the negative side, denial, the need to self-medicate, paranoia, anger, depression, feeling out of control, resentment, and a sense of being overwhelmed. On the positive side, I was inspired by creativity, productive workaholism, a strong belief in myself, risk-taking, resilience, empathy, optimism, hope, and exhilaration.

As I reflect on my story, I realize that there are three big lessons that I have learned. First, I have bipolar disorder, and it will never go away. I have to accept this diagnosis, accept that bipolar disorder is a lifelong condition, and follow through on proper treatment. The quality of my leadership is fundamentally dependent on being on an effective treatment regimen, including medication when required. (In the upcoming part of this chapter, I describe the ten specific components of my regimen.)

Second, I need to know and accept myself for who I am. I cannot change the fact that I have bipolar disorder; I have to accept and honor that fact about me. I can, however, learn as much as possible about my bipolar disorder and how it affects me, and I can use that to grow as a person and as a leader.

Third, I've learned that forgiveness is paramount. I needed to forgive others and I needed to forgive myself. What makes forgiveness such a challenge is that it allows you to feel right about someone else being wrong. But whether right or wrong, bipolar disorder creates behaviors that can be and often are disruptive, and once I realized the impact and affect that I had on people, I was quite remorseful. I became paralyzed at one point because I would beat myself up based on the guilt and shame that accompanied clarity. But in order to move forward, I had to embrace forgiveness as a way of releasing myself and others from bondage.

I recently contacted the employee who attempted to sue me to ask forgiveness because she didn't deserve all that I dished out. I called her and surprised her. She was unable to speak with me at that time. This caused me to think that maybe my call did more harm than good. In a step program that I am inspired by, it states that you shouldn't contact someone for reconciling if it will cause more harm. My appearing from her past may have stirred up negative feelings. So I then texted her to share that insight. She called me and we talked. I explained my situation and asked for forgiveness. It was as much for me to heal as it was to help her heal.

Some people will ask me how important it is to be forgiven. In some cases, you may not be forgiven, which is fine because that is no longer your burden. Your only task is to extend a heartfelt genuine apology.

Accepting my diagnosis and following through on treatment

Reflecting on my journey, I realize that things could have been so much more harmonious and rewarding had I recognized and accepted that I did, in fact, have a mental illness earlier on in my career and life. However, we all have our own journeys and scripts, and my timing allowed me to find and save myself before I turned 50. The last couple of years have been a time of tumultuous change. I have come into my own by acknowledging my diagnosis, seeking professional help, and managing the disorder like any other medical condition that someone could be inflicted with as an aging adult.

The greatest difficulty of writing this book and my dissertation was to see in black and white the chaos and damage that I had caused. I have spent an inordinate amount of time and resources in making amends and repairing my landscape from the devastating storm, i.e., bipolar disorder.

Since accepting bipolar disorder, I have been diligent about therapy, taking my medicine when I need it, getting my rest, and practicing spirituality, all of which keeps me in the light. But never for a moment do I believe that I am cured. Bipolar disease is a lifelong sentence that I will have to live with, but if someone were to say that a pill could take it all away, I would decline that pill. I am thankful for all that I am and all that I have. I can, without reservation, say that the bipolar disorder has benefitted me greatly. I would not have started my company if I did not have thoughts of grandiosity, I would not have created award-winning workbooks and materials without the bipolar creativity, I would not have written two books that are huge successes around the world without bipolar speed of thought, and on and on. The list would be exhaustive, if I were to write about all of the perks associated with Bipolar II disorder! However, suicidal tendencies, violence, aggression, toxicity, and more are all byproducts of an untreated mental illness. These tendencies are much less of an issue now with the many mood balancing techniques I practice.

Recommendations

As a leader who has moved her company to a successful tier in the world of small business entrepreneurship, I feel that I can speak with a level of authority on how to lead a small business to success even while having bipolar disorder. I hope anyone who wants to manage their career with a mental illness will take to heart what I am writing. I look over the many years that I denied and ignored having bipolar disorder to my demise, but after I took responsibility for my medical condition, I was able to turn both my life and company around.

Here are the top 10 things that I recommend for people who struggle with mental illness:

1. Seek medical attention from a true psychiatrist

As a person with bipolar disorder, I suspected that something was wrong based on how I was feeling and the feedback from people within my inner circle. I believed that my actions and behaviors were just a "quirky" entrepreneurial spirit. However, when relationships were being destroyed, and I had suicidal thoughts and a host of other telltale indicators that something was not normal, I needed to seek professional medical attention from an actual psychiatrist. A general practitioner could diagnose, but there is more to treating bipolar disorder than a diagnosis. A person who suspects that something is wrong needs to know for certain what is going on inside her brain.

There are different types of bipolar disorders requiring different drugs and intervention(s). Then there are coupling disorders such as Post Traumatic Stress Disorder, impulsiveness, Attention Deficit Disorder, and panic attacks, to name a few. In fact, the list continues with a variety of disorders that may accompany a person's bipolar disorder. I would often utilize my primary physician to receive medication that treated some of the symptoms of the disease but it did not actually treat bipolar disorder itself nor other mental issues underlining my behavior. This proved to be disastrous. I should have been under the care of a psychiatrist who could prescribe the correct medicine and regulate my dosages. Anyone who understands the importance of expertise must seek medical attention from a psychiatrist even if you are leery and hesitant to know the truth. Receiving an accurate diagnosis is the foundation of a person's success in managing the disorder.

2. Accept and acknowledge that you have a mental illness

I could not embrace something that I was unwilling to accept. To live in denial of having a mental condition does not cause the condition to go away. It just prolongs the disruptive occurrences and deepens the moments of darkness. Yes, there are stigmas associated with mental illness, but placing my head in the sand did not change the reality.

For true mental health, a person with bipolar disorder must have (1) self-knowledge, (2) self-awareness, and (3) self-acceptance. The knowledge comes from being diagnosed; the awareness is recognizing how your disorder impacts you, and this can lead to acceptance. Anything short of this will place you in a vicious cycle of disruptive and destructive behaviors that you will be unable to accurately attribute to the real source. This inability to identify the source of these behaviors will then keep you locked in your current condition, which will only become magnified over time.

3. Stay on your medication

The biggest hurdle to recovery for me is not wanting to stay on my medication. This often creates an adverse effect, negatively impacting what the medication is designed to do. Getting on and off of medication creates more of a problem for me than either being on or completely off the medicine(s). Unfortunately, people, including me, complain that they do not like who they become as a result of the medicine. People often complain that they experience a dulling of senses, flatness in personality, feeling tuned down, and demotivated. But the Dr. Jekyll and Mr. Hyde effect is just as damaging as the personality I exhibit as a result of not taking my medication.

Research shows that patients often stop taking their medication: it is a textbook behavior. This is similar to a heart patient not taking her prescription medication. Eventually damage will occur and a heart attack or stroke ensues. Having a mental illness is no different than any other major health issue such as diabetes or heart problems. If I do not take my medication I am certain to have a relapse; it is just a matter of when and what ramifications will result.

At this very moment, I can honestly say that I am not on any medications and have not been medicated for nearly six months. I don't fool myself into believing that I'll never need meds again. I'm quite comfortable with taking a prescription medicine when needed. And I am prepared that such may happen next week, next month, or a year from now. I really don't know, but I accept that medicine is sometimes necessary. And all medicine doesn't have to be from a pharmacy. I believe that holistic health is a viable option to maintaining your mental health. I think that herbs, vitamins, and homeopathic medicine are valuable and effective. I suggest that you consult with a doctor who has a holistic practice for guidance.

4. Seek help from a therapist

It is a team effort: it takes a village to become and remain mentally balanced. A psychiatrist merely regulates my medication while a therapist supports me in achieving balance through discussion, disclosure, introspection, and counseling. This is something I cannot afford to decline as I lead my business. Leading and business ownership are difficult and arduous and, coupled with mental illness, the stakes are too high, with mountains that seem insurmountable if I do not seek professional help. I need someone who can guide me and provide insight to blind spots that exist in how I am managing my illness.

Keep in mind that therapists have specialties. It would be in your best interest to establish a relationship with someone who specializes in bipolar disorder and has an intimate knowledge of the condition to better serve you, especially when you are experiencing highs and lows. I went through a couple of therapists before I found a therapist who could support me and my idiosyncrasies. Be as diligent in securing a therapist's service as you are in hiring a CPA. Your mind is more important than your money.

5. Journal on a regular basis

A journal allows me to track my emotions, behaviors, and thoughts, and it serves as my higher self. In addition, it allows me to express my true thoughts and intimate feelings that I may be unable to share with anyone, including my therapist. I was able to recall years of behavior based on my extensive journaling. I write daily, if possible, and occasionally go back and read what I have written to see if there is a pattern of behaviors, thoughts, or feelings that will not serve me well.

The journal can help you identify problem areas that you can work on resolving. You can then share this information with your therapist or whomever is in your support circle to make sense of what is occurring. Reviewing your journal also allows you to see the positive growth that you will experience.

Journals help you to capture things in real time with honesty and candor. A journal is a gift to yourself. In fact, I have a journal with no other intention than it being read by my great-great-grandchildren. I want them to read my journal in the future and understand what it was like to live as a black woman in this time frame. What I would give to know my ancestors and what they experienced. When I write I'm very descriptive in detailing who I engage. For instance, I may mention my sons and I will give their full name and birth order. I may mention something about Google whereby I will explain what Google is because it may not be around in the future. I'm not writing to them or giving suggestions because what works today for me may not be relevant in the future. But I know that they should know who I am, what I am, and how I lived, which may help them to understand themselves and whatever may be passed down through my genes.

6. Create a support circle

I have gathered three to four people who will support me "unconditionally." This includes family members, a support group, friends, colleagues, and/or confidants who are strong enough to deal with my highs and lows. They are able to listen and accept when I am depressed without getting too wrapped up with my feelings. They must be able to shield themselves in order to support me. These are people whom I can talk to anytime and can be really honest about how I am feeling.

Take into consideration that there must be some boundaries set. Not everyone will be able to support you at this level, which is fine. I had to be strategic in whom I selected to create my support circle, understanding that they would be privy to information that I want to remain confidential. Also, bear in mind that many will have your highest interests at heart, but lack the empathy, compassion, or wherewithal to give you what you need, especially if you are in recovery. Often people, such as myself, with bipolar disorder have destroyed relationships, and upon rebuilding those relationships, they may unwittingly not understand what they have done, placing a strain on someone's ability to provide you with a supportive relationship. Attempt to select people who have not been adversely impacted by your actions or behaviors while depressed or manic. This may even mean establishing relationships with new and different people outside your existing network.

7. Forgive, forgive, and forgive again

One of the most difficult things I have experienced was feeling that people misunderstood or did not live up to my expectations, even if I was totally at fault in some situations. I have found, based on my research and discussions with many people with bipolar disorder, that they are often estranged from friends and family based on the disruptive behaviors that they have demonstrated or from being angry about one thing or another. To move forward, I had to learn to let go of past pain and forgive people for what they have actually done or for what I perceived they have done. Often people were merely reacting to my psychosis.

When a person with bipolar disorder feels an emotion, it is often deep and intense, even if misplaced, inappropriate, or imaginary. Therefore, I had to forgive others for things that I felt or thought that they did. This created a level of freedom and liberated me to rebuild and create new relationships. Also, I had to forgive myself. I could not continue to be consumed by the many bipolar mistakes that I had made, to be disappointed that I had a mental illness, or to be focused on a host of things that I regretted.

Learn to accept that you broke some eggs along the way and that you must forgive yourself. Forgiveness of self is greater than being forgiven by others or forgiving others, and it is much more difficult because you know exactly what you have done, felt, or thought. Give yourself permission to let go and to forgive for your own mental well-being.

8. Disclosure

There must be some truth-telling that you have with those who play a crucial role in your life. For me, it was more than just my family who was impacted by my bipolar disorder. I was with my employees more than anyone else in my life. My bipolar disorder impacted them daily, so it made sense that I would share what I was experiencing with them. Only you can determine who has been impacted by your disorder and will be subjected to your disorder in the future. However, once you have examined your relationships, it would behoove you to have a candid discussion with whomever to share with them who you are and what you are experiencing.

I was amazed that many people already sensed or believed that I had a mental condition of some sort. Now they are able to put a name and explanation to what they already suspected. You will find that this, too, is one of the most liberating exercises that will support you in your quest to forgive, because you will probably receive forgiveness from those whom you speak with about your condition. This is also an opportunity to seek support and understanding, especially in the workplace. There are risks associated with full disclosure, such as the stigma of a mental illness, judgment, and fear, but I can attest that what you will receive will far outweigh some of the negative reactions.

9. Pray and meditate regularly

I recommend these two action items because they helped me to stay grounded and balanced daily, and they are the source of my strength. If you do not practice a religion or spirituality, I implore you to find something greater than yourself to focus your thoughts on as a way of managing your emotions. This is merely one of a couple of things I do on a regular basis to keep my sanity.

Operating and owning a business are two of the most stressful activities that someone can pursue. I need to quiet my mind through mindfulness. If you are a leader with bipolar disorder you will have a full mind; however, by meditating you can achieve mindfulness. This means directing your thoughts to more positive outcomes when you begin to feel negative. It means managing your thoughts and not letting your thoughts and emotions manage you.

Just to be clear, praying is when you are speaking to God, and meditation is when you allow God to speak to you uninterrupted. Before I pray I call out words such as love, joy, hope, serenity, tranquility, balance, peace, etc. because words are very powerful. Then I pray, which then leads to meditating. When I meditate I become very still, and focus my attention and energy on being in the present and allowing things to slip from my mind. I have different meditations which include manifestation (bringing things into fruition), balancing (to harness peace and clarity), and seeking (allowing God to guide my intentions). I find that whenever I meditate I'm much calmer and at peace.

Also, I strongly encourage people to not only embrace having bipolar disorder, but to thank the Universe/God for such a gift. Even though at times it may seem like a curse, it is what it is and I am who I am. I have a cup that states *by the grace of God I am what I am* from 1 Corinthians 15:10. Every day during my prayer, I thank God for all that I have and all that I am. I cannot deny for a second that I am a successful leader and business owner because of *my* bipolar disorder, despite some of its disruptions!

10. Create a regimen

Bipolar disorder is synonymous with a duality of highs and lows, which can be disconcerting. I needed to have balance in my life to minimize disruptive incidents and destructive occurrences. This means going to bed at a more reasonable time than what I was accustomed to. I now go to bed by 10:00 pm without fail during the week unless I'm out and about. But ordinarily, I am at home, turning in around 10 pm. This ensures that I get the rest that I need to be mentally sharp the next day. Rest is vital to recovery and sustaining a positive outlook. I work more reasonable hours. As a person with bipolar disorder, I must self-regulate and pace myself to avoid becoming hypomanic or depressed. I created a work schedule for myself and I stick to it. Even with my new endeavor of building Indigo Insights, I do all that I can between 9 a.m. and 5 p.m., and basically turn it off thereafter unless I need to attend a function. I exercise for benefits ranging from endorphins to maintaining a healthy weight. I have a small frame, but I recognize that exercising is good for both physical and mental health. And I eat properly based on what my body calls for. The medications can cause my weight to fluctuate, so I create an eating schedule to maintain a healthy body weight and image.

In short, create a regimen to manage your life and mental stability. This will include sleep, eating, working, and exercising. A person with bipolar disorder may have other areas that they will need to manage in an effort to stay balanced. This can all be achieved through regimens.

Knowing and accepting myself for who I am

There was one philosophy that resonated with me during my matriculation through the Values-Driven Leadership Program. As I sat in class and read the various materials, I could not identify with many of the leadership theories that were taught because I inherently knew that my leadership practices were askew. But what spoke to me was authentic leadership. I had a deep yearning to be "authentic," but no matter how hard I tried, I couldn't seem to get there. I never knew what I was going to do from one day to the next, and I was constantly putting up false fronts all around myself to maintain a façade of being in control. I denied my bipolar disorder and actively tried to hide it from others. Because of my bipolar disorder and the way I dealt with it, I was the furthest thing from authentic.

Since I've gone through extensive treatment, things are noticeably better and my recovery is based on my personal techniques and practices. I have grown in self-knowledge and self-acceptance, and I believe this has helped me become a better person which has influenced every aspect of my life.

To truly be free, authentic, and mentally well, you must be self-aware. This means having self-knowledge, self-understanding, and self-acceptance that all intersect with one another:

1. Self-Knowledge

Self-Knowledge is recognizing and discerning the many traits and characteristics of oneself. It doesn't add value to what is considered a trait or characteristic. It merely identifies that such exists. For example, a person can identify what makes him tick and what ticks him off, and be able to see and tell others about his own personal values, beliefs and thoughts. That is the knowing that must be at the forefront of one's ability to be authentic. Self-awareness includes reflecting on your core values, identity, emotions, motives, and goals, and coming to grips with who you really are at the deepest level. Self-awareness cannot exist without self-knowledge, self-understanding, and self-acceptance; therefore, authenticity cannot exist without the quintessential components of the three aspects intersecting, thus creating true self-awareness.

2. Self-Understanding

Self-understanding is taking what you know to be a fact or even general truth regarding your knowledge about self and considering and comprehending from where that behavior, belief, etc. derives. Every aspect of our personality can be attributed to either DNA or an environment. This can lead to the whole debate of nurture versus nature. I believe that it is both, and the exploration of both will allow you to discover the hows and whys to life mysteries. This lends much to our being able to trace the root cause of such behavior and to bring meaning and clarity to our behaviors, be they good, bad, or indifferent. For example, once an individual is able to examine what makes him tick or ticks him/her off, s/he can then explore the conditions that caused such an impression. Whatever occurred, whether over time or through a brief encounter, caused him/her to adopt a particular behavior, value, or belief to either reinforce or guide that individual as a means to venture into the world or remain fixed in time. Again, one cannot be authentic without insight to where and why s/he drew from a certain well his/her values, beliefs, etc. that often drives those actions and behaviors, especially if such is based on a mental illness.

3. Self-Acceptance

Self-acceptance is the ability to examine both one's knowledge and understanding of self and to make a conscious decision to embrace and receive that truth as his/her truth. Self-acceptance is the lynchpin to all of this. A person must either accept or reject what s/he has come to know as a general truth about oneself (self-knowledge) and acknowledge from whence such knowledge comes (self-understanding). If someone is unable to accept the first two, then s/he is assuredly unable to have self-awareness, thus s/he cannot be authentic. This creates a disconnect and requires the individual to change. That change can then presumably cause the individual to not be authentic, thus creating a paradox. Self-acceptance does not mean to change what one feels is an ugly truth or inappropriate behavior. This is probably one of the most difficult things for a person with mental illness to embrace, which often leads to years without treatment.

You can fully accept things about yourself that you don't necessarily like. Self-acceptance is akin to saying, "This is who I am at this point in time, and while it may not be my ideal self, I'm not going to beat myself up over this fact." True growth is through self-acceptance, which allows you to see yourself more clearly and move deeper into your experiences. Self-acceptance paves the way to greater self-understanding—an essential ingredient for growth.

Now, I am truly authentic because I not only have self-awareness but a sense of self-acceptance. Rather than turning away from yourself (ignoring certain internal experiences), self-understanding allows you to move forward with greater self-knowledge and the tools necessary for change. The paradox of change is that you must learn to move toward and accept those things about yourself that you wish didn't exist (the things you want to change). Turning away will only keep these unfavorable parts of yourself energized, alive, and influencing your relationships.

I am now liberated to make a conscious decision about modifying my behavior. I cannot change me, but I can practice incorporating new ways and methods in behaving. I can learn from past experiences and understand why I am who I am and how to be an even better me. According to Tom G. Stevens, PhD, "We will *never get rid of all our inadequacies or negative subparts.* Getting rid of negative subparts is not our task. It is okay for those negative subparts to exist, but we must remove their power to control our lives. Our task is to strengthen the more functional parts of ourselves and learn ways of identifying, understanding, and coping with the more negative parts."

When people with a mental illness are willing to look inward, they become vulnerable and uncover the qualities that may impact their ability or inability to have healthy relationships. At this point, self-acceptance has to occur, which means looking inward and embracing all parts of oneself. When people look from within they take a first step of integrating a practical framework by becoming more self-aware, understanding how to self-regulate their impulses, and uncovering what drives them to achieve balance.

I contend that self-awareness is merely a step in the process to self-acceptance and that self-acceptance is what people must strive to acquire. People should be encouraged to embrace all aspects of themselves in an attempt to modify behaviors in an effort to be aligned with their core values and beliefs. According to Nassir Ghaemi in his book *A First-Rate Madness: Uncovering the Links Between Leadership and Mental Illness in Times of Crisis*, first and most important, mental illness doesn't mean that one is simply insane, out of touch with reality, psychotic. The most common mental disorders usually have nothing to do with thinking at all, but rather abnormal moods: depression and mania. This is important because people may benefit as leaders, not just directly from the qualities of mania or depression, but also indirectly from entering and leaving those mood states, from the alternation between being ill and being well. This is important to understand because you can learn to leverage and tap into your disorder when you are fully aware of who you are and what you are dealing with.

As a person who has led all of my life, I have pushed away followers, believing that I can never live up to their expectations of me because I know the insecure and vulnerable me who can be volatile. I have known that about myself but never understood why I could have a personality that was inviting and yet polarizing, accepting yet intolerant, loving yet angry, and gentle yet abrasive. I'm seen as two different people: the person who is loving and the person who is mean. I lived a life of duality before seeking treatment. But after removing the blinders and layers that covered my eyes and thoughts, I was able to piece together not just the whats to my behaviors, but the whys.

Over years of self-reflection, I was able to understand that from being abused emotionally and often physically as a child, I was angry and afraid to allow anyone to be close enough to see the scars and wounds from my life, in general. What may be invisible to the naked eye, I can see in plain view. And quite often I would dismiss or push away anyone who was able to penetrate my force field out of what I now know to be fear of intimacy. I never accepted the negative subparts of who I am. So I have made a practice of demonstrating my positive attributes and characteristics through my deeds. I give to so many causes; volunteer my time, tenth (10% tithe), and talents unselfishly; and personally create and fund a variety of scholarships. I even founded a nonprofit. I couldn't seem to give enough, but I didn't maintain relationships and my behavior in private was inconsistent with my deeds. Once realizing the whys, I was convinced that I needed to modify my behavior and heal my mind and spirit.

Francis de Sales tells us that we can't fight against our imperfections unless we face them. This involves the practice of the virtues of humility, patience, and gentleness that lead to self-knowledge and a high level of self-acceptance, as well as prayer and knowing how to direct our intention.

> Don't desire to be other than what you are, but desire to be thoroughly what you are . . . Believe me, this is the most important and the least understood point in the spiritual life. (To Mme Brulart, June 1607, AE, XIII, 291. English trans. in Letters of Spiritual Direction, 112)

Alexander Pocetto once said, "So 'I be me' is the greatest gift we can give to God and to each other." Seek to know as much about yourself as others do, and seek to understand that which you find in yourself, and then accept who you are with the ability not to change but rather rearrange. It is impossible to change who you are but reasonable to modify one's behavior to the situation and circumstance in which one finds him/herself. Nacastro says that self-acceptance leads to *self-intimacy.* Self-intimacy is the experience of feeling connected to all of yourself—the parts of yourself you naturally embrace as well as the parts you wish didn't exist. This connection allows you to feel grounded, giving you an emotional center that anchors your experiences. Such will lead to authenticity and healthy relationships.

I will share with you a quote that I believe embodies the essence of self-awareness and self-acceptance. Many of the negative attributes and characteristics that people with mental health challenges often hide or attempt to "change" are wounds being expressed through behaviors. Marion Woodman said, "At the very point of vulnerability . . . where the surrender takes place—that is where God enters. God comes through the wound." The wounds that I sought to hide are now open for God to enter so that I may become a better person who is healed and walking in the light.

As I began this book, writing about being normal, it should have become very clear that I wasn't normal at all. I have and have had an exceptionally wonderful life. It was filled with many tears but also joy and laughter. I have been blessed exceedingly, and I attribute much of who I am and both my successes and failures to bipolar disorder. However, I believe that I could have minimized the darker days had I known what I was dealing with and would have sought help many years ago. But I thought that I was normal.

I believe that many people with mental illnesses think that they are normal and that their unusual to bizarre behaviors and thoughts are commonplace. I was talking to my team about some of my behaviors and actions, and I honestly thought that everyone had similar occurrences. Initially, I asked myself what was the purpose of this book. I decided that I wanted to inform, inspire, influence, and educate. So here is where I feel the need to influence. I think it is clear that self-awareness is paramount. And that the more aware you are of your actions and thoughts, the more capable you will be in managing them more effectively. If you notice that you are obsessing over something or having thoughts that could harm you or others, you need to seek help. And if you know someone who has behaviors that would raise an eyebrow, it is incumbent upon you to say or do something.

Shame on the many friends and family members who recognize that something is wrong but refuse to address the issue out of fear that they will offend, or that the person is a grown-up and can take care of himself. I say to you that mental illness can be equated to bad breath. A person may have halitosis whereby everyone around him is offended, but he continues to talk as if nothing is wrong. In fact, he can be offered a mint and will refuse to take it, saying that he's fine. The same goes for mental illness. The person may believe that he is fine, but in fact he needs help.

People will ask me what you can say to someone in such a situation. The message doesn't have to be long or damning. Share with him your observation(s) and that you are concerned that he "may" need to speak with someone who can provide professional support. You can even ask a question such as, "Have you ever considered sharing your thoughts with a professional, such as a therapist or counselor, who can provide insight to how you are feeling or what you are thinking?" The toughest thing is just approaching the matter with nonjudgment, courage, and compassion, similar to offering someone with bad breath a mint. That is often a hint because we are very uncomfortable telling someone that their breath stinks or that they are turning your hair gray when they talk. But some people need more than a hint; they need a candid conversation that is grounded in compassion, love and acceptance.

It's a wrap

What may be taking you a few days to read has taken me months to write. Earlier, I wrote that I was not on any medication, but such has changed. I am once again on my medication, Abilify. I was sitting, meditating, when it occurred to me that I've been unable to focus, my thoughts are not "normal," I'm obsessing about several things, and I'm very agitated and irritable. But my greatest concern was that I had no filters. I've been speaking to people in a manner that I am even uncomfortable with. As I shared with you earlier, the lack of filters are apparent when someone is either manic or depressed, and that can be a calling card that you are experiencing an episode. I have become very in tune with my body and my mental well-being, and I realized that it was time to get back on my meds. I am self-aware, which I wrote about earlier, so I must take complete responsibility for my mental wellness.

There was no consulting anyone, conferring with people, or the gnashing of teeth. I just went to my medicine drawer and took a little pill that has a huge impact and regained control of my situation. I got off my meds for a very distinct reason and I always knew that returning to my meds was just a matter of time. I've accomplished what I set out to do, i.e., stop my company from bleeding out, write this book, and become ultra creative in directing my career. But I'm just drained from trying to keep it all together, to include my mental well-being. People with bipolar disorder often have a mind full of things, but instead you have to become mindful of things. I would

271

say that taking medication and then staying on one's meds is the biggest challenge to remaining whole and healthy, but it is about choices. We all make choices and I choose to be healed during my recovery and continued journey with Bipolar II disorder.

A strength-based approach

I often visit the internet to see a variety of resources that list famous people who have bipolar disorder. I would say that I am amazed but I am not. There are some incredible people with whom I share this disorder and I'm quite proud of these individuals and what they have accomplished. Here are just a few of my favorite famous people with bipolar disorder: Winston Churchill, Ted Turner, Abraham Lincoln, Patrick Kennedy, Robin Williams, and Heinz Prechter. They were often seen as people who were insightful to the extent that people didn't see what they had to share initially because it was so revolutionary. For instance, Winston Churchill warned of Germany's aggression and threat to the extent that he was publically ridiculed. Ted Turner believed that we were ready for a 24-hour news station when, at the time, we only had the six o'clock news and our flag playing on the television screen after a certain hour at night (who would watch that?). President Lincoln needs no introduction, Patrick Kennedy changed the conversation about mental health, Robin Williams was ingenious as he made us laugh out loud, sharing stories that also made us say "hmmm," and Heinz Prechter was a noted businessman who started a customized sunroof business. I'm sure he received stares when he suggested that we take a perfectly good car and cut a hole in the roof back in 1965. Unfortunately, Robin and Heinz committed suicide, which is an all too frequent telltale sign for people "suffering" with bipolar disorder.

Personally, I believe being bipolar is a unique gift that can be harnessed. Unfortunately, Americans, in general, focus on our weaknesses. For example, if a child were to come home with all As and Bs overall, but then there was a low C, the parent would zero in on that C and harp on and on about bringing up that grade. But what if we focused on the As and even Bs in an effort to strengthen that strength, rather than strengthening a weakness that may be a weakness for a variety of reasons? Maybe the C is in speech class, and the child is an introvert, but the A is in science. Maybe we've got it all wrong.

Why should someone with bipolar disorder work on being "normal" when the abnormal (all things being considered healthy and not dangerous) is a spark of genius that may come up with the cure for cancer or may invent another useful technology? If you look at any in-depth list of people with bipolar disorder, these people have contributed greatly to our world through the arts, sciences, math, etc. I want us to move in the direction of helping people with bipolar disorder work "the strengths" and minimize the weaknesses associated with bipolar disorder.

I truly hope that my sharing with you openly and with transparency helps you harness and balance bipolar disorder strengths. Then if you are a bystander, meaning family member or friend, I hope that you, too, can learn to leverage their strengths as opposed to seeing their weaknesses and attempting to address that. And if nothing else, maybe we will start to realize that every job and every environment is not suited for someone with bipolar disorder, which is not a bad thing but a reality. This merely means searching for a place and state where you are accepted, embraced, and valued for your differences and strengths.

Not romanticizing, but explaining

As I complete my thoughts and this book, I simply want to put it all on the line. Often people romanticize about the perks of bipolar disorder. There were times I longed for the incredible natural high. But I often felt as though I was being controlled by a cruel puppet master and had little to no power over what I would do and say when hypomanic. Being out of control would take the form of aggression and combativeness. I would cut people off when they were speaking to show my dismay or difference of opinion, I would require employees to work unreasonable hours because I was working those hours to accomplish unrealistic goals, and I would overpromise and over deliver, which was very taxing on the employees. Unfortunately, because I was the leader with no true peers, there was no one to reel me in when I went too far towards the edge. When I went out of control it was often scary for everyone involved, and even for me to see. This behavior created feelings of shame and guilt as I did things that made no sense and seemed illogical to me and others.

I was exhausted from living a whirlwind life, which led to many levels of resentment. I resented that I did not have the work/life balance that many of my employees enjoyed. I resented that I had to work twice as hard as everyone else and that there was no safety net in place for me, while my employees only had to work for their livelihood with a guaranteed check. Any entrepreneur knows that there is no safety net, and no one to provide for you if you fail, but because of my skewed thinking, that knowledge did not stop me from being resentful.

Redfield Jamison (1996) points out that this way of thinking is not uncommon for people with bipolar disorder. She argues that profound changes in mood, thinking, personality, and behavior can occur during all phases of manic-depressive illness. Even during normal states, many individuals with the illness, or those who have a cyclothymic temperament, will experience a striking fluctuation in the intensity of their perceptions and feelings. Resentment of others, along with paranoia concerning their intentions, often comes and goes in powerful waves.

My resentment came out during my bouts of depression and was a subconscious driver when I was angry. I can honestly say that I was also resentful that something was seriously wrong with me while others appeared normal. During my doctoral program, I would show up to class and could not understand why people were always so happy while I was either anxious or depressed. And if I was manic sitting in class, it was torture and I felt trapped, which made me resent being in school and not having the freedom that I was accustomed to having before becoming a student.

Burton (2009, p. 124) contends that "whilst people with mania are typically euphoric, optimistic, self-confident, and grandiose, they may also be irritable or tearful, with rapid and unexpected shifts from one extreme to another." Leading with bipolar disorder was like living a life of constant uncertainty. According to Fieve (2006, p. 25), "One cannot rely on the consistency of mood changes since bipolar illness often takes on a life of its own." There were no guarantees, and every day was different with no reliable way to predict what would happen. Therefore, I often felt overwhelmed by the many racing thoughts and impending feelings of doom and paranoia. Winning contracts was exciting, but when things were dire, such as losing a contract for reasons beyond my control, it could be a nightmare because everything rested on my shoulders. This would be very taxing because bipolar disorder magnified my feelings and perceptions, and I felt responsible for everyone and everything. Owning my own business gave me the luxury of being independent with unimaginable autonomy, which is essential when you have bipolar disorder, but it was also confining because I was responsible for the livelihood of my employees. That responsibility can weigh very heavily on any leader, but for someone who is bipolar and needs autonomy, it is particularly difficult.

My denial, self-medication, paranoia, anger, depression, feelings of being out of control, resentment, and feelings of being overwhelmed stifled the company's growth for 15 years. However, leading with bipolar disorder also had its positive attributes.

Redfield Jamison (1996), a noted authority on bipolar disorder, suggests that most people find the thought that a destructive, often psychotic, and frequently deadly disease such as bipolar disorder might be advantageous based on heightened imaginative powers, intensified emotional responses, and increased energy, but the relationship between mood disorders and artistic achievement or the link between madness and genius is well documented. Goodwin and Jamison (1990, p. 105) proposed that there is a particular link between creativity and bipolar disorder, since major depressive disorders appear to be particularly common among playwrights, novelist, biographers, and artists. They suggest that two aspects of thinking in particular are pronounced in both creativity and hypomanic thought: fluency, rapidity, and flexibility of thought on the one hand, and the ability to combine ideas or categories of thought in order to form new and original connections on the other.

Throughout my life, I have been creative, which has allowed me to develop and create new and innovative products and services. It's almost as if I am seeing things through a kaleidoscope. This creative vision is something I developed as a child; however, being bipolar suggests that I was born with an innate ability to be creative. My creativity began long before I created a student association as a teen and continues well past starting my own company as an adult. Creativity was the driving force that allowed me to build my business and create products that would separate me from the competition. Often clients secured our services because of the creative workbooks that I wrote, designed, and developed. My creativity was a game changer that allowed me to succeed in the marketplace and sell my original thoughts, materials, concepts, and products as commodities.

My bipolar disorder has also made me a quick thinker, and that fuels my creativity. Murray, Cunningham, and Price (2012) suggest that creativity and psychopathology share some common traits, such as a tendency to think out of the box, flights of ideas, speeding up thoughts, and heightened perceptions of visual, auditory, and somatic stimuli. It is not uncommon for me to resolve an issue before others even realize that there is one. For example, when I was hired to offer training as my first contract, I recommended much more than they wanted and created a buffet of services that led to a national award-winning mentoring program. While, initially, the client thought they needed only training, I was able to see further and create a broad range of workshops to full-scale national programs in diversity, leadership, management, and mentoring. This ability to think more quickly than others can be a blessing and a curse, as people are often confused or unable to connect the dots because my mind has taken a leap that others have yet to consider.

Redfield Jamison (1996) suggests that the increased energy that people with bipolar disorder experience includes expansiveness, risk-taking, and fluency of thought associated with hypomania and can result in being highly productive. I was productive with a dash of workaholism that provided me with the energy to work through the night and around the clock, producing quality work. I consistently performed at a high level and produced exceptional products. For example, I wrote an entire book in one week. The sales from this book range from one copy to 1,000 copies per order. I believe the book is thorough, thought-provoking, and an excellent resource. I attribute this success and productivity directly to bipolar disorder.

To deny a significant part of who you are creates an inner turmoil that must be resolved or it devours you. I opted to resolve this storm inside of me by working long unreasonable hours for years. I was putting in, on average, 12- to 14-hour days as a way to avoid dealing with my thoughts and feelings. If I stayed busy, I could ignore all symptoms and situations that would indicate that I was mentally ill.

A person in a manic phase typically experiences a sustained elated mood with a combination of the following features: increased activity, decreased need for sleep, inflated self-esteem, and grandiosity of thinking (Tse & Yeats, 2002). Because of the grandiosity that is inherent in bipolar disorder, I had a strong belief in self which allowed me to have the confidence to do things that others often could not or would not do. This gave me a sense of invincibility, which lent itself well to leading a company. I did not have people encouraging me as a rule of thumb, so I learned to be self-contained, which meant believing in myself.

I demonstrated my belief in myself when I went to college, even after being told that I was not college material. I continued acquiring degrees even though my family tried to discourage me out of fear that it would cause too much stress. When I was unable to get my old job back, I started my company with no promise of business. I did not have any potential clients, but I had me and my knowledge, skills, and abilities. These assets made a difference in many organizations, which strengthened my belief in myself. Ironically, what often came across as a strong belief in self was actually grandiose thinking and an inflated self-esteem; however, the end result was that I saw myself as capable and powerful enough to do whatever I set out to do. I found great success in this outlook and disposition as a gift of being bipolar. In every curse is a blessing; in every storm is a rainbow.

According to Redfield Jamison (1996), many of the changes in mood, thinking, and perception that indicate mania—restlessness, exhilaration, expansiveness, irritability, grandiosity, quickened and more finely tuned senses, intensity of emotional feelings, divergent thoughts, and rapidity of associational process—are highly characteristic of being a risk taker. I have always been a risk taker, which has allowed me to see and seize opportunities that were obscure. I took the risk of starting an association in high school, I took the risk of joining the Marine Corps upon high school graduation, and then made an ongoing string of major, but risky, decisions throughout my life and career. I took risks that won the company substantial contracts that any ordinary or "normal" person would see as impossible and beyond their ability and range. These risks allowed us to make the Inc. 500 list two years in a row after 15 years of business. Nearly everything that I have accomplished could be attributed to being a risk taker.

It is important to note that not all risk-taking is positive. Risk taking was a double-edged sword for me. It motivated me to do things that others would not, such as going door-to-door to sell my products in a federal building. It also caused me to rush into contracts with people who lacked integrity, push the envelope too far with some clients, and make unwise financial decisions. I believe the positive far outweighed the negative risks that I have taken.

Luthans (2002, p. 702) defines resilience as "the dependable capacity to rebound or bounce back from adversity, conflict, and failure or even positive events, progress, and increased responsibility." It is a personal characteristic of the individual or a set of traits encompassing general sturdiness, resourcefulness, and flexible functioning in the face of challenges (Luthar, Cicetti, & Becker, 2000). Sutcliffe and Vogus (2003) suggest that resilience does not simply emerge in response to specific interruptions or jolts, but rather develops over time from continually handling risks, stresses, and strains. Resilience is the ability to withstand negative occurrences over the long haul in the face of repeated setbacks and positive but potentially overwhelming events. Ghaemi (2011) suggests that mental illnesses, such as bipolar disorder, can have a particularly strong effect on promoting resilience in people because such an illness is recurrent by nature. The episodes go away, but they always come back. People with bipolar disorder know that they will go through episodes again and again, so they learn to develop coping styles, ways to recognize the episodes when they begin, or to help control them, which leads to resilience.

As a leader with bipolar disorder, I have been tested by adversity over and again and have demonstrated adaptive psychological responses. My illness created a level of resilience that kept me moving forward when everything was saying to stop or turn around. Throughout my life, I have had many triumphs, such as acceptance by a journalism instructor while pursuing my Associate of Arts Degree, and a highly successful career as CEO, speaker, and author. I have also had disappointments, such as mistreatment by my parents, sexual harassment and racism while in the Marine Corps, failed marriages, the many terminations. And the list goes on, but none of these have deterred me from moving forward. At times, I did become depressed or sad about situations, but I would eventually and, oftentimes, quickly recover. I did not allow myself to wallow in despair, and I believe that is what saved my life and prevented me from committing suicide over these many years.

I believe that the resilience associated with my bipolar disorder has helped me succeed as a leader because of my inherent optimism. In turn, optimism and positive emotions promote adaptive coping and openness to social support and are associated with greater flexibility of thinking and exploration and a broadened focus of attention (Frederickson, 2003). Other psychosocial characteristics linked to resilience include having a sense of purpose in life, a high moral compass, spirituality, religion, and the ability to find meaning in the midst of trauma (Pargament et al., 1998, 2005), all of which have helped me survive and thrive.

Lastly, it was exhilarating being manic. Bipolar II's hypomania can generally make a person feel vivacious and exhilarated (Fieve, 2006,

p. 24). It was as if I was watching the world through Technicolor lenses while others were still seeing things in black and white. The ups and downs of business development were a rush and a welcome part of owning a business because it tapped into the bipolar nature of things. The ride was worth taking.

Fieve (2006, pp. 11–12) describes bipolar disorder as "a complex genetic disorder characterized by unusual mood swings between major depression and extreme elation, accompanied by disturbances in thinking, distortions of perception, and impaired social functioning." There were days when I moved at a rabbit's pace, accomplishing many things at once with an ongoing burst of energy with no end in sight. I would find myself speeding through the city at night to simply push my car to top speed. I did the same during the day with myself in the office. I would push to see how fast I could go because I was experiencing a euphoric feeling that cannot be succinctly or adequately described. In short, I felt on top of the world and simply "great," as if I were invincible.

For me, leading with bipolar disorder was like riding the Dueling Dragons roller coaster, as I discussed earlier. Every day there were ups and downs and twists and turns, and I was never sure where they would lead or where they would end up. While my life was inspired by creativity, productive workaholism, belief in myself, risk-taking, resilience, empathy, optimism, hope, and exhilaration it was also weighed down by denial, self-medication, paranoia, anger, depression, feeling out of control, resentment, and a sense of being overwhelmed. It was both exhilarating and exhausting. But similar to any ride, you will experience some dark moments, but if you hold on you'll be in the light. You just gotta hold on!

Lessons Learned About the Disorder

If while reading this book you felt as if I were speaking to you because you have experienced some of these feelings or situations, I am confident that you will now have the courage to seek help because you are compelled to embrace your total self and live life versus participating in a slow death. I hope that you've been inspired to change. As Dr. Wayne Dyer would say, "When you change how you see things, the things you see will change." And for you who are either a friend, colleague, or family member, be encouraged. Know that you have taken a huge step just by reading this book. You are a supporter, but a supporter of what? Support wellness by encouraging whoever you believe will benefit from help to seek professional help. And remember that it's not you nor is it about you. Their disappearing acts, bizarre behaviors, and other things are similar to having a cat. They will often need time alone to heal. And understand that you'll need time to heal and recover as well. Being in a relationship with someone who has bipolar disorder can be taxing because you were or are on the ride with them. So give yourself permission to take time out, too, to regroup and recalibrate. In short, know that it will all work out and that you should adopt my regimen as your own until you have your own in place.

This has been a cathartic experience for me, and it would be wonderful if my sharing my journey from the darkness into the light will cause you to be more compassionate with yourself and others, and that you will become a voice to change the conversation about mental illness to mental wellness.

Photos

Indigo's basement which housed her new business, in 1995

Indigo's reception area at her office, in 2010

Indigo's Mugshot for DeKalb County Jail, in December 2012

Indigo photo op at *Inc. Magazine's* Gala, in 2012

Indigo with her longtime employees Lisa Rozzelle and Tammy Davis

Indigo's photo taken at Graduation for PhD, in May 2014

Indigo at a book signing on her two books *Playing by the Unwritten Rules*

Indigo speaking at a conference on her book(s) *Playing by the Unwritten Rules*

Article in the *Atlanta Journal Constitution* that depicts Indigo's success as a business woman, in 2012

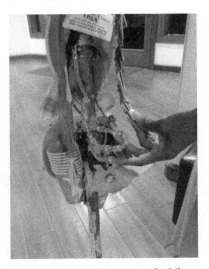

An *Inc.* article that detailed the changes Indigo made in her company, 2012

The spirit stick Indigo received while at Sierra Tucson, in 2013

Resources

American Academy of Child and Adolescent Psychiatry
202-966-7300
www.aacap.org

American Counseling Association
800-347-6647
www.counseling.org

American Foundation for Suicide Prevention
888-333-2377
www.afsp.org

American Psychiatric Association
888-357-7924
www.psych.org

American Psychological Association®
800-374-2721
www.apa.org

American Psychotherapy Association
417-823-0173
www.americanpsychotherapy.com

National Alliance on Mental Illness (NAMI)
(800) 950-NAMI
www.nami.org

National Institute of Mental Health (NIMH)
866-615-6464
www.nimh.nih.gov

References

American Psychiatric Association (2013). *Diagnostic and Statistical Manual of Mental Disorders* (5th ed). Desk Reference to the Diagnostic Criteria from DSM-5 Washington, DC

Burton, N. (2009). *The Meaning of Madness*. Oxford, England: Acheron Press.

Fieve, R. (2006). *Bipolar II*. New York, NY: Rodale Books.

Fieve, R. (2006). *Bipolar Breakthrough*. New York, NY: Rodale Books

Frederickson, B. (2003) "Positive emotions and upward spirals in organization." In K. Cameron, J. Dutton, & R. Quinn (Eds.), *Positive Organizational Scholarship: Foundations of a New Discipline* (p. 163–175). San Francisco, CA: Berrett-Koehler.

Ghaemi, N. (2011). *A First-Rate Madness: Uncovering the Links Between Leadership and Mental Illness*. New York, NY: Penguin Books.

Hornbacher, M. (2009). *Madness: A Bipolar Life*. New York, NY: Mariner Books.

Luthans, F. (2002). "The need for and meaning of positive organizational behavior." *Journal of Organizational Behavior*, 23, 695–706.

Luthar, S., Cicchetti, D., & Becker, B. (2000). "The construct of resilience: A critical evaluation and guidelines for future work." *Child Development*, 71(3), 543–562.

Murray, E., Cunningham, M. & Price, B. (2012). "The role of psychotic disorders in religious history considered." *Journal of Neuropsychiatry and Clinical Neuroscience*, 24(4), 410–26.

National Institute of Mental Health (2014). "Bipolar disorder." Retrieved from http://www.nimh.nih.gov/health/topics/bipolar-disorder/index.shtml

National Institute of Mental Health (2008). "Bipolar disorder." Retrieved from http://www.nimh.nih.gov/health/publications/bipolar-disorder-in-adults/index.shtml

Nicastro, R. (2009). "How a lack of self-acceptance can hurt your relation-ship." Retrieved April.

Pargament, K., Smith, B., Koenig, H., & Perez, L. (1998). "Patterns of positive and negative religious coping with major life stressors." *Journal for the Scientific Study of Religion*, 37, 711–725.

Redfield Jamison, K. (1996). *Touched with Fire: Manic-Depressive Illness and the Artistic Temperament*. New York, NY: Simon and Schuster.

Substance Abuse and Mental Health Services Administration Center for Mental Health Services. http://www.samhsa.gov/, (12/2/2014).

Sutcliffe, K. & Vogus, T. (2003). "Organizing for resilience." In Carver, C. & Scheier, M. (Eds.), *Positive Organizational Scholarship* (pp. 94-113). San Francisco, CA: Berrett-Koehler.

Tse, S. & Yeats, M. (2002). "What helps people with bipolar affective disorder succeed in employment: a grounded theory approach?" *School of Occupational Therapy*, Otago Polytechnic, Dunedin, New Zealand: OS Press, Work 19 (47–62).

CPSIA information can be obtained
at www.ICGtesting.com
Printed in the USA
BVHW081143050720
582986BV00001B/72